DOCUMENTS OF SOCIAL HISTORY
Editor: Anthony Adams

A SOCIAL HISTORY OF TRADITIONAL SONG

Reginald Nettel

A SOCIAL HISTORY
of
TRADITIONAL SONG

AUGUSTUS M. KELLEY · PUBLISHERS
NEW YORK 1969

Published in the United States by

Augustus M. Kelley · Publishers

New York, New York 10001
© 1969 Reginal Nettel
First published in 1954 under the title *Sing a Song of England*
SBN 678.07506.9
Library of Congress Catalogue Card No. *70-93274*
Printed in Great Britain by Redwood Press, Trowbridge, Wiltshire

SING A SONG OF

England

A SOCIAL HISTORY OF
TRADITIONAL
SONG

by

Reginald Nettel

PHOENIX HOUSE LTD
LONDON

Printed in Great Britain by
The Aldine Press at Letchworth for
Phoenix House Ltd, 38 William IV Street,
Charing Cross, W.C.2
First published 1954

Contents

The Long Song Seller. Mayhew's *London Labour and the London Poor*.

Foreword

I SPENT THE FIRST ten years of my life mainly in a small town in the midlands, where the chimes in the tower of the parish church played *The Blue Bells of Scotland* and *The Bailiff's Daughter of Islington* as I went past on my way from school. I knew the name of the first of these tunes but not that of the second, which I was not taught officially. Times have changed; I now know *The Bailiff's Daughter of Islington* to be a variant of the tune of *The Seeds of Love* and *The Sprig of Thyme*—one of the loveliest creations of the mind of man—yet I do not blame my teachers for leaving me ignorant of this in my boyhood, for they were characteristic of their period. In half a century I have seen our English folk-songs come into their own. More than this, if I turn a switch I may hear one of them coming to me in all the trappings of a modern orchestral work or sung by a singer who has served his time in a dance band, so wide is the appeal of folk-songs at the present day. How long this situation will remain I cannot tell, but I believe it to be a healthy sign that we are more favourably disposed towards our heritage of English song than we have been in the past.

Yet all is not satisfactory—indeed can never be so. This transformation has been brought about by people who loved these tunes for their own sake, as I love Bach's *Kunst der Fuge* or Mozart's *Jupiter* symphony, and some of them will be very annoyed when they read this book and see the songs mixed up with the non-musical facts of history. Can I not let sleeping dogs lie? Must I remind my readers that once the English treated the Jews with all the tricks lately revived in Germany, and, moreover, believed a pack of lies as fully as the Nazis? Reach for your daggers if you must, but the ballad of *Little Sir Hugh* will remain; you do the cause of musical history no good by ignoring the words of songs, and words carry a meaning not to be found in the shape of a melody. It is natural for us to like a song for its singability, and many songs are popular for no other reason, but the best of all songs are those wherein the singer reveals something of his inner self which in the process of expression ceases to be commonplace.

This we all know to be true of songs by great musicians, but the

9

same holds good for songs of humbler origin: it is largely snobbery
which makes us claim that expensively-produced music is more
sincere than that which comes for nothing. A look through some of
the stories of great operas should teach us to be careful. Think what
Steele said of the plots of Handel's operas, and even worse—have
a look at some nineteenth-century ones. Donizetti's *Linda di
Chamouni* has a story not very far removed from that of the rude
Victorian ballad, *She was poor, but she was Honest*. Think, then, of
the impudence of the socially superior people who spent so much
time improving the musical taste of the working classes in the nineteenth century! They had the effect sometimes of making men
ashamed of a heritage which was not all bad, and the reaction has
had to come. Between the appearance of this book originally in 1954
and today (1969) this reaction has come, and it has come principally
from the United States, where their definition of folksong has always
been different from the European conception.

Admittedly the Americans seem to have been a long time
establishing their own types of song, but in folksong at any rate this
was beneficial, for they carried on a culture which the English
were tending to distort—the culture of the old English puritans;
such men as John Bunyan. Consider this early spiritual from the
camp meetings in the U.S.A. It was brought to England in 1806 by
Lorenzo Dow, called 'Crazy' Dow, a fiery preacher from the
American frontier:

> Come all ye wand'ring pilgrims dear
>   That are to Canaan bound,
> Take courage and fight valiantly,
>   Obey the trumpet's sound;
> Our Captain has before us gone,
>   He's God's eternal Son;
> Then pilgrims dear, pray don't you fear,
>   But let us follow on.
>
> Thro' a dark, howling wilderness,
>   Where chilling winds do roar;
> A land of drought, of pits and snares,
>   To Canaan's peaceful shore.
> But Jesus Christ will with us go
>   And lead us on the way;

Should enemies examine us
  He'll teach us what to say.
APOLLYON:
Good morning, brother traveller,
  Pray tell me, what's your name?
And where it is you're travelling to?
  Also from whence you came?
PILGRIM:
My name it is the Pilgrim bold;
  To Canaan I am bound;
I'm from the howling wilderness
  And the enchanted ground.
APOLLYON:
Pray, what is that upon your head
  Which shines so clear and bright?
Also the covering of your breast
  So dazzling to my sight?
What kind of shoes are those you wear,
  On which you boldly stand?
Likewise the shining instrument
  You bear in your right hand?
PILGRIM:
'Tis glorious Hope upon my head,
  And on my breast my shield;
With this bright sword I mean to fight
  Until I win the field.
My feet are shod with Gospel Peace,
  On which I boldly stand;
And I'm resolved to fight till death
  To win fair Canaan's land.
APOLLYON:
You'd better stay with me, young man,
  And give your journey o'er;
Your Captain now is out of sight,
  His face you'll see no more.
Apollyon, sir, I am by name;
  This land belongs to me;
And for thy arms and pilgrim's dress
  I'll give it all to thee.

PILGRIM:

"Oh no," replied the Pilgrim bold,
"Your offering I disdain!"
A glittering crown of righteousness
I shortly shall obtain.
Oh, if I only faithful prove
To my great Lord's commands,
I jointly shall be heir with him
To Canaan's richest lands.

As well as the tune used in America, there are tunes to this spiritual preserved in Cornwall and the Isle of Man. The American and English folk cultures in 1806 were not separated—they could blend. Look, too, at the verses. The style is that of the old English Mummers' Play, and Pilgrim himself a transference of the character of St George to that of Bunyan's puritan hero. You will find the Mummers' Play referred to in chapter two of this present book, pages 49 to 51, and glance also at the ballad of *Robin Hood and the Pedlar* on pages 20 to 22, where you will find a situation very similar to the encounter of Pilgrim and Apollyon, with a similar style of versification. We are in fact in the presence of the universal folk-hero who never dies.

Where are such religious songs in the English hymnbooks? They are not there; nor are they in the American ones. You may argue that they are not hymnology but folksong, but that is cheating, for the conception of folksong did not arise until the end of the nine-teenth century, when most of the hymnbooks had been written. George Pullen Jackson, in chapter twenty-one of his *White Spirituals in the Southern Uplands* examines the nature of this abandonment of the old songs and concludes that many people may have wanted to retain them, but that the reformers of church music who had the compiling of the hymnbooks used their authority as experts to make a clearance. So it was in England too. I am not totally averse to the change, since it gave the English northern coun-ties and the Welsh their fine technique in choral singing, but the untrained singer fell into contempt.

In the United States however there was another element, absent from the British scene; this was the presence of another race—the negroes. When we speak of spirituals today we associate these songs entirely with the negroes, simply because it is the negro versions of the spirituals which have captured the imagination of the modern musical world. They gave their own turn to the style—freer in rhythm and more unrestrained in expression. They kept open another line of development which at length came to be admired among the whites. But there had been a change: the white spirituals had been heroic, in the Bunyan tradition, while the negros meditated on the hope of escape from slavery into a new life beyond the grave.

Deep river—my home is over Jordan.
Deep river—I want to cross over into camp ground.

The folk-hero in the negro idiom passed over to the work-songs and the songs of protest. Only later did he come to be related to a religious urge for practical reform, such as was advocated by Martin Luther King. All along there is evidence that the theory of J. J. Rousseau is not entirely wrong; there is a culture among simple men equally as valuable as that of the educated classes, and in some ways it may be superior. But the English folksong collectors went a bit too far with their theory, and shut their eyes to what they did not want to see. It was there nevertheless. The working classes are no more angelic than the successful. That, certainly, is one of the lessons of the modern scene.

Early in the twentieth century, essays written by working-class students in adult educational organisations were shown to university dons and undergraduates. In these it was noted that in spite of their writers' difficulty in setting down what they wanted to say, the matter was of academic interest because it expressed points of view overlooked up to that time by orthodox teachers. This study has had its effect on the teaching of sociology, but few of those who pioneered these studies came away with much greater respect for the working man. He was in fact very backward in some of his ways. The noble peasant or the noble artisan is no more innocent than the noble savage. He did exist, however, and in his peculiar culture he carried the seeds of a human understanding which leaves him poor indeed if it is thrown out of gear. Now, by the process of educational reform, his sons are becoming intellectuals and putting the apparatus into reverse. They do not share their fathers' crude ideals. They will voluntarily give their blood to a hospital but disdain their fathers' pride in having shed it for their country. They scoff with Marx at the parson's dope, but not at the use of hallucinatory drugs. They sneer at Catholic pilgrimages to holy shrines but make long journeys to sit at the feet of Eastern holy men. Some of us have outgrown the small child's delight in shouting in caves or under bridges, but spend considerable sums of money on electronic equipment to amplify our mating cries to the verge of stupor.

Many pour money into the coffers of pop-stars as, aforetime, worshippers poured it into shrines to the Virgin, but the pop-star is neither the god of their idolatry nor their intercessor; he is their medicine-man—their interpreter of the earliest god of all—the god carved in the chalk at Cerne Abbas, with his swinging club and enormous genitals. The pop-singer is the modern priest, divinely intoxicated with sound, wine, sex and dope.

Between the pop scene and the cult of 'big' music today stands the folksinger. The minstrel boy of the educational centres, strumming his guitar in the Burl Ives manner, and knowledgably familiar with Brendan Behan's language. He sings with an American accent the old English songs described in this book, and he adds a few of his own in the self-same idiom. He is at his best in hatred—when he sings of white men's belligerency, of Colonialism, of the Pill or of blood-sports, but he has nothing new. Here, for example, is John Gay in 1729 on the last of these themes—blood-sports:

> The sportsmen keep hawks and their quarry they gain;
> So the woodcock, the partridge, the pheasant is slain.
> What care and expense for their hounds are employed!
> Thus the fox and the hare and the stag are destroyed.
> The spaniel they cherish—whose flattering way
> Can as well as his master cringe, fawn and betray.
> Thus staunch politicians—look all the world round—
> Love the men who can serve as hawk, spaniel or hound.

In the same play by Gay (*Polly*) you will find British colonialism under attack in just the same way as today. This is traditional song not only in its subjects but in its essence.

Traditional songs are for the most part subjective, and therefore tell us of the feelings of people as they were and are, be the ballad singer affluent, as he is today, or in the direst poverty, as he was when Henry Mayhew noted him down on the streets of London in 1851, in *London Labour and the London Poor*.

The themes of the [mediaeval] minstrels were wars, and victories, and revolutions; so of the modern man of street ballads. If the minstrel celebrated with harp and voice the unhorsings, the broken bones, the deaths, the blood, and all the glory and circumstance of a tournament—so does the ballad-singer, with voice and fiddle, glorify the feelings, the broken bones, the blood, the deaths, and all the glory and circumstance of a prize-fight. The minstrel did not scoff at the madness which prevailed in the lists, nor does the ballad-singer at the brutality which prevails in the ring. . . . In the bestowal of flattery or even of praise the modern minstrel is far less liberal than his prototype; but the laudation was, in the old days, very often paid for by the person whom it was sung to honour. . . . Were the same measure applied to the ballad-singer and writer of today, there can be no reason to doubt that it would be attended with the same result. In his satire the modern has somewhat of an advantage over his predecessor. . . . The ancient professors of street minstrelsy unquestionably played and sang satirical lays, depending for their remuneration on the liberality of their out-of-door audience; so it is precisely with the modern. The minstrel played both singly and with his fellows; the ballad-singer works both alone and with his 'mates' or his 'school'.

Now he calls himself a folksinger and works with his 'group', his largesse more than a mediaeval knight's ransom. He knows nothing about Henry Mayhew and his definition of folksong is wider than the strict limits drawn by Cecil Sharp; but he is in the tradition. When you come to the end of this book, turn back to this foreword and, as in the content of the folksongs themselves, you will find that the end is in the beginning.

My thanks are due to many people for assistance and advice in writing this book, chief among them W. E. Tate of Leeds University and E. D. Mackerness of Nottingham University, who have read right through it, one for accuracy of historical facts and the other for the relationship to literature and music. E. J. Nicol read the first five chapters with special reference to folk-dances, A. L. Lloyd read the section on sea shanties and industrial songs, Frederick Keel the chapter on the early work of the Folk Song Society, Frank Howes the final chapter. I am grateful to Col. G. Jellico for advice about army songs, Margaret Dean-Smith for sending me a useful bibliography at the outset of my task, Walter H. Chapman for information about the Padstow ceremony, and Sara Jackson,

Librarian of the English Folk Dance and Song Society, for un-grudging help in the course of collecting material and assistance in finding owners of copyright.

To the English Folk Dance and Song Society I am also indebted for permission to quote the Malchair tune in Chapter VII and all the songs from their Journals collected by Lucy Broadwood, to Miss Maud Karpeles and Messrs Novello & Co. for songs from Cecil Sharp's collection, Miss A. G. Gilchrist, O.B.E., for songs she has herself collected, to Messrs J. Curwen & Sons for *Strawberry Fair*, Mrs Margaret H. P. Parrington for Ivor Gatty's version of *The Derby Ram*, Iolo A. Williams for words of *The Royal Oak*, Clive Carey for *John Riley*, A. L. Lloyd and Messrs Lawrence & Wishart for *The Gresford Disaster*, and Moore Orr for advice on gramophone records.

For permission to quote copyright passages I am indebted to: Mrs W. H. Davies and Jonathan Cape Ltd for *The Autobiography of a Super Tramp;* Messrs Gerald Duckworth & Co Ltd for *Folksongs of the Upper Thames* and *Round About the Upper Thames* by Alfred Williams; Miss D. E. Collins and Methuen & Co. Ltd for *The Ballad of the White Horse* and *The Secret People* from *Collected Poems of G. K. Chesterton*; Mrs George Bambridge for *Song of the Banjo* by Rudyard Kipling; Miss Maud Karpeles for *English Folksong—Some Conclusions*, by Cecil Sharp.

Every effort has been made to trace the owners of copyright in songs and extracts from writings quoted. Should any material have been included inadvertently without the permission of the owner of the copyright, acknowledgment will be made in future editions.

R.N. 1969

I. Pagan Introduction

Before the gods that made the gods
Had seen their sunrise pass,
The White Horse of the White Horse Vale
Was cut out of the grass.

G. K. CHESTERTON

I

'MOST OF YOU have probably travelled down the Great Western
Railway as far as Swindon. Those of you who did so with their eyes
open, have been aware, soon after leaving the Didcot station, of a
fine range of chalk hills running parallel with the railway on the
left-hand side as you go down, and distant some two or three miles,
more or less, from the line. The highest point in the range is the
White Horse Hill, which you come in front of just before you stop
at Shrivenham station.'

That passage is from the first chapter of *Tom Brown's Schooldays*,
describing the England its author remembered in his youth, about a
hundred years ago,[1] yet in many respects it is true today. Indeed,
the only statement which 'dates' the passage I have quoted is the
reference to the railway company, which is now nationalized. This
is the scene which gave typical Englishmen like the Browns a
philosophy as well as a living. This is England.

'If you love English scenery and have a few hours to spare, you
can't do better, the next time you pass, than stop at the Faringdon
Road or Shrivenham station, and make your way to that highest
point. And those who care for the vague old stories that haunt
country-sides all about England, will not, if they are wise, be
content with only a few hours' stay; for, glorious as the view is, the
neighbourhood is yet more interesting for its relics of bygone times.
I only know two English neighbourhoods thoroughly, and in each,
within a circle of five miles, there is enough of interest and beauty to

[1] Thomas Hughes (1822–96).

17

last any reasonable man his life. I believe this to be the case almost throughout the country, but each has a special attraction. . . .'

Times were changing when the author wrote, but even before 'the confounded Great Western' carried away Alfred's Hill to make an embankment some of the old customs were in decline. But when were they not? It is, and always has been, part of the creed of the Browns to lament the decline of old times; yet, like the Browns themselves, the old ways have a habit of persisting into an age which, by all the rules, should have outgrown them. There on the hill is the old White Horse, which the country folk still believe was cut by King Alfred's men to celebrate a great victory over the Danes, but which an archaeologist will tell you belongs to the early Iron Age; cut in the chalk it may have been at that time, but the divine horse was old even in those days; it may be descended from the divine horse of Crete and Scythia, and even prior to them—the emblem of the fertility god which men have worshipped apparently from the time they became men. If ever there was a creed outworn in these days, surely this is it? But are we right in so assuming? The farmers of the Vale may now use tractors and chemical fertilizers, but fertility must go on whatever methods are used. All that has happened is that some men may think they have found in their own skill and knowledge of chemistry a substitute for the hand of God which guided their forefathers.

But even so, it will be urged, the faith of our forefathers had entirely superseded the primitive faith which might have been responsible for the choice of a white horse to be cut on the downs. (There is no certainty on the matter, and the White Horse Hill itself was not the centre of their religion.) Why then, did Thomas Hughes's locals clean the figure of the horse with such zest,[1] and why do we depute the Office of Works to do so?

We are, for all our modern ways, men in the presence of an eternal mystery. There above the White Horse, on the very tip of the downs, stands an ancient fortification far older than the horse itself, and of dimensions which would make a strenuous job for us in this bulldozer age, yet it was made—when? Two thousand years before Christ would be a modest guess, by men who had only stone implements and needed protection for themselves and their cattle. That perhaps would be the beginning of it, and the road which lies beside the encampment—the Ridgeway—leads over the downs

[1] Cf. Thomas Hughes, *The Scouring of the White Horse,* 1858.

from the East Midlands, where lived the fair-haired 'Peterborough Folk' who hunted and fished, and traded with the swarthy New Stone Age men of the South of England, who came about 2500 B.C. from the Continent—originally from the Mediterranean basin. About 1900 B.C. came another race we call the Beaker Folk, because of their distinctive pottery, who were more adaptable than the New Stone Age men, and understood how to make tools and weapons of bronze, and who buried their dead in round barrows instead of in long barrows as the earlier men had done. Back and forth they moved along the Ridgeway, these prehistoric men, and to this day their handiwork inspires respect. The Ridgeway itself and the fortified hill we can understand, and compliment them on having done so workmanlike a job, but the mystery behind their art is more fascinating still, for their best work was done for what may appear to us as the most impractical reasons. For example, the women of the Bronze Age made pots good enough for family use, but the pottery made for the dead is far superior in craftsmanship. The dead were treated to luxuries they had not enjoyed in life. The fortifications are remarkable, but the great stone circle on Avebury Hill, to which the Ridgeway leads, is prodigious; and again it serves no practical purpose from our modern point of view, being a laboriously constructed scheme to accommodate their religious observances. (Stonehenge is more imposing though not really so large as Avebury.) The mounds in which the dead of the Stone and Bronze Age folk are buried remain, as do the cromlechs dotted about the country, but the habitations of the living folk are gone. Their religious life was more important to them than their practical life, it would appear; sacrifices to the gods would always mean renunciation of treasured possessions which could be ill afforded—such is the very nature of sacrifice.

'A bird in the hand', we say, 'is worth two in the bush', by which we perpetuate a selfish doctrine that tangible things are real, while imagined things are often no more than illusions. Primitive man was somewhat more realistic than this; he built his earthworks on the hills, and surmounted them with a stockade which would keep off wild beasts from his family and his cattle, but against greater dangers these things were powerless. The greatest danger of all would be the failure of the crop; then animals, men, and all would perish. The crop depended on the climate, which was a very real thing to him— a thing to be appeased, to be encouraged. How could the sun be made beneficent except by example? How could the living things which died every autumn be expected to revive the following spring in a world where they were not wanted? They must be encouraged. By showing approval these living things might be multiplied; the elaborate plan of stone circles at Avebury was a place where the ritual could be carried out; the White Horse cut in the turf of the hill at Uffington is said to be a representation of the vital god which gave fertility to the earth just as a fine bull gave fertility to the herd, or a fine specimen of manhood to the tribe. It is said also to have become a tribal emblem, and certainly appears on Celtic coins.

But now we have gone far from Tom Brown, from Dr Arnold's muscular Christianity at Rugby School and the good old days the Browns enjoyed at home in the Vale of White Horse. But have we? Read further on in *Tom Brown's Schooldays*.

'Here at any rate lived and stopped at home, Squire Brown, J.P. for the County of Berks, in a village near the foot of the White Horse range. And here he dealt out justice and mercy in a rough way, and begat sons and daughters, and hunted the fox, and grumbled at the badness of the roads and the times. And his wife dealt out stockings, and calico shirts, and smock frocks, and comforting drinks to the old folks with the "rheumatiz", and good counsel to all, and kept the coal and clothes clubs going, for yule tide, when the bands of mummers came round, dressed out in ribbons and coloured paper caps; and stamped round the Squire's kitchen, repeating in true sing-song vernacular the legend of St George and his fight, and the ten-pound Doctor, who plays his part at healing the Saint—a relic I believe of the old middle-age mysteries. It was the first dramatic representation which greeted the eyes of little Tom, who was brought down into the kitchen by his nurse to witness it, at the mature age of three years.'

> In comes I, old Father Christmas,
> Welcome in or welcome not,
> Sometimes cold and sometimes hot,
> I hope Father Christmas will never be forgot.

The actors were dressed in paper costumes, with long strips hanging down over their faces so that their features could not be recognized. After Father Christmas enters St George, with much swinging of his wooden sword and boastful swagger; he fights a knight from 'Turkeyland' in the 'most dreadful battle that ever was known' until the latter falls, killed by a vicious thrust from the 'blade' of the Christian knight.

Now the villain is dead you might think that the play is over, but if so you have underestimated the rural mind. Life is brief, but the folk tradition goes on interminably; how can you have a play if the villain is removed in the first five minutes? In comes a doctor to bring the knight to life with several ludicrous remedies:

> Give him a bucket of dry ashes to eat,
> Groom him down with a besom stick,
> Give him a yard and a half of pump-water to drink.

for which advice he suggests a fee of fifty guineas but adds that he will take ten pounds. He is not one of those quack doctors 'going about from house to house telling you more lies in one half-hour than what you can find true in seven years', but nevertheless

> I can cure the itchy pitchy,
> Palsy and the gout;
> Pains within or pains without;
> A broken leg or a broken arm,
> Or a broken limb of any sort.
> I cured old Mother Roundabout—

and as many others as you may find on a newspaper advertisement for a penny laxative. There follows a great deal of comical hocus-pocus and the Turkish knight is revived; it may not be sense, but it is funny. At last enters an old woman (actually a man like all the other actors)

> In comes I, old Betsy Bub;
> On my shoulder I carry my tub,
> And in my hand a dripping-pan.
> Don't you think I'm a jolly old man?

Why a character who announces herself as Betsy Bub should be regarded as a jolly old man is not for the audience to ask. The whole thing may have meant something once, but now all is comical confusion. Berkshire is perhaps more confused than most places, for generally they make sen:se out of Betsy Bub easily enough:

> In comes I, Beelzebub,
> On my shoulder I carry my club,
> And in my hand a dripping-pan,
> And I think myself a jolly old man.

If you should doubt the Browns' belief that this is a relic of mediaeval drama, look about in old churches for pictures or carvings of Beelzebub; in time you will find one with a club, or frying some poor soul in a pan held over the eternal fire; but the figure is older than this. He was not always a devil: that was what Christianity made of him. Long before the time of Christ he was a god above all other gods; his club and his dripping-pan were magic symbols; stylized representations of the male and female genital organs, revered because on their functioning depended the continuance of life. Betsy Bub is a man-woman—a hermaphroditic character, older than the Beelzebub of the midland folk-drama—not sure of 'her' sex because all sex is here portrayed.

We are indeed not present at a piece of nonsense, but at a poor descendant of a drama of the gods. The theme originally was around the facts of life. Fertility was essential, but not at one time only; every year it must be renewed; every year nature died, to be revived in the spring of the next year. This revival in primitive civilizations was the function of a select body of men, among whom the medicineman was both respected and feared. In the play he had become a quack doctor.

If the folk of Berkshire know this today, however, it is because learned men have told them. Berkshire legends were in Tom Brown's day vaguely deemed to be survivals of early Christian lore mixed with popular history and accepted as local evidence of a hereditary heroism. (The 'myth and ritual' theory expounded today is largely speculation but cannot be easily refuted.) To the rustics, with little or no school-learning, such legends were the means by which they discovered and fostered among themselves a love of their country, as did Job Cork, a shepherd of Uffington with some pretensions to poetry.[1]

[1] Not folk-song as usually defined; even though it is the work of a shepherd and incorporates the belief of the folk, it is an individual's poem.

Ah, zur, I can remember well
The stories the old folk do tell—
Upon this hill which here is zeen,
Many a battle there have been.

If it be true as I heerd zay,
King Gaarge did here the dragon zlay,
And down below on yonder hill,
They buried he, as I've heerd tell.

Saint George has become King George; Job Cork indeed would
receive short shrift at an examination in history; but to judge the
verses thus is merely pedantic; Job Cork tells us what the folk wish
to think, not what the textbooks can prove. Folk-song too is a
record of rural beliefs, their transformation, resuscitation, and
preservation; in it we must look not for dry exactitude but for the
mystery of life itself and the dreams of man. Admiration of the place
is not enough, as we can tell from another local poem.

In rural ville is seldom seen
A better inn, it's neat and clean.
Here's on the table London fish,
As fresh and good as heart could wish;
And here's the best of Berkshire bacon,
With sundry joints and fattened capon.
And we believe, in White Horse Vale,
There's scarce a better, purer ale;
And those who choose, when here they dine,
Will meet with rich and generous wine.

A palate will not make a poet, nor will a university education, if
we are to trust this verse by Dr Rose, once curate of Baulking
chapelry in the Uffington parish. It is a verse of a man and of a day,
and that is all you can say of it. The folk-song *John Barleycorn* is for
eternity.

There came three men out of the west
And fought for victory;
And they have made a solemn vow
John Barleycorn must die.

There were three men came out of the West, Their for-tunes for to try, And
these three men made a so-lemn vow, John Bar-ley-corn must die. They
plough'd, they sow'd, they har-row'd him in, Throw'd clots up—on his head, And
these three men made a so-lemn vow. John Bar-ley-corn was dead.

> They ploughed him in the earth so deep,
> With clots upon his head;
> Then these three men they did conclude
> John Barleycorn was dead.

Like the knight from Turkeyland in the Mummers' Play. But
whoever knew a ballad stop at two verses? Back he comes to life,
without even a ten-pound doctor.

> There he lay sleeping in the ground
> Till rain from the sky did fall;
> Then Barleycorn sprang a green blade,
> And proved liars of them all.

> There he remained till Midsummer,
> And looked both pale and wan;
> Then Barleycorn grew a long beard,
> Much like unto a man.

> They hirèd men with scythes so sharp,
> To cut him off at knee;
> See how they served poor Barleycorn!
> They served him bitterly.

They hirèd men with forks and rakes
    To pierce him through the heart;
But the carter served him worse than that,
    For he bound him to a cart.

And then they brought him to a barn,
    A prisoner to endure;
And soon they fetched him out again
    And laid him on the floor.

They hirèd men with crabtree sticks,
    To beat him, flesh from bones;
But a miller served him worse than that,
    For he ground him 'tween two stones.

They flung him in a cistern deep,
    And drowned him in water clear;
But the brewer served him worse than that,
    For he brewed him into beer.

Yet still he was alive and master of them all.

Oh, Barleycorn is the best grain
    That ever was sown on land;
It will do more than any other grain
    By the turning of your hand.

It will turn a boy into a man,
    And a man into an ass.
It will change your gold into silver,
    And your silver into brass.

It will make the huntsman hunt the fox
    That never wound his horn;
It will bring the tinker to the stocks,
    That people him may scorn.

Put white wine in a bottle,
    And cider in a can;
John Barleycorn in a brown bowl
    Will prove the strongest man.

John Barleycorn is creator, destroyer, alchemist, and friend. This is the Corn Spirit in a brown mug, and soon he will be in you. He will give you life, for he is the essence of life. Do all you can to kill him and again he will revive. He is not for a day but for all time. In reverence of him they cut the White Horse on the hill and the virile figure in the chalk at Cerne Abbas; for his worship they toiled to make the stone circles on the uplands; they buried their dead with gifts which would be useful when the dead awakened; they danced the dance of life and death, or rather death and life, for that is what they wished. To this day they make a Corn Dolly from the last sheaf gathered at the harvest, and hang it in the house until next year. And all these things they did, not perfunctorily, but with formalized behaviour which raised their deeds above the common. They elevated the natural to the supernatural; started with skill, added faith, and ended with art.

II

'There's nothing like the old country-side for me,' wrote Hughes, 'and no music like the twang of the real old Saxon tongue, as one gets it fresh from the veritable chaw in the White Horse Vale: and I say with "Gaarge Ridler" the old West-country yeoman,

> Throo aall the waarld awld Gaarge would bwoast,
> Commend me to a merry owld England mwoast:
> While vools gwoes pratin' vur and nigh,
> We stwops at whum, my dog and I.'

Hughes quoted this verse, as is evident from his accompaniment, to emphasize his belief that there was, at any rate in his time, no place like home. Scholars, however, prefer another interpretation. It seems that the song was originally Caroline loyalist, dating from 1657, and its inner meaning was known only to members of a secret society planning to aid the restoration of Charles II. They stayed at home in England, planning in dangerous times, while others talked loudly from a safe distance across the Channel. The dog referred to was a symbol of the faithful adherent of the Royalist cause who nosed out those in despair, gave them courage, and similarly sought out likely recruits to the society. Such hidden meanings are of the greatest interest to lovers of the old songs who have antiquarian leanings, but thousands of Gloucestershire [1] folk have sung that song without any knowledge that it had any meaning other than the plain meaning Hughes sees in it.

So it must always be. We are not all scholarly men. Either we sing a song because it has a good tune or because it appeals to an ideal conception of life. *John Barleycorn* is a drinking-song, and a good one; so far as the singers are concerned it has for centuries been nothing else. As for folk-dancing—it is a pleasant recreation, in some cases requiring considerable practice, and a skill of which the dancers become naturally proud. In the case of the traditional teams there is also in evidence a collecting-box. It was held of old that the drunk were divinely inspired. This is one of several reasons why the folk-dancer drinks all the liquor offered to him. He certainly does not dance mainly in order to obtain free beer, or money to buy it. Dancing and drinking both had in them something of the adoration of the gods. To this day we say not that liquor is 'in a man', but that he is 'in liquor'. When he pledges in it we think of him not as depressed, but as elevated. Anyone inclined to the base and uncharitable (and unhistorical) thought that folk-dancers perform mainly for beer and coppers should look further into history, where he will find that in some places local charities were kept going from funds collected by traditional dancers. It takes all sorts to make a world—anthropologists, antiquaries, trained musicians, folk-singers and dancers, people who like a good tune and those who can't tell *God save the weasel* from *Pop goes the Queen*; if folk-songs and dances are to be considered in relation to social history we must take the English as we find them, look at them in the round, which is the way we see all objects except when we interpose some gadget between our eyes and the view. Specialization will intensify our knowledge of some aspect of the problem; various specialists will show us different close-up views; we must, however, in the end stand back and see the whole in relation to its surroundings. To do this is the object of this book.

Specialization can be dangerous, especially when it comes to interpreting symbols. Any Freudian will tell you about phallic symbols, and any Marxist about the relationship of music to social history; the trouble is that so few of them will step outside their theoretical boundaries. One result of this is that they like to prove

[1] It is a Gloucestershire song; see Chapter V, p. 108, for details.

that observant, thinking people believe as they themselves do; those who don't they dub eccentric or worse. A new type of specialist in music, however, is the musicologist, who applies scientific methods to musical problems, including musical history. Though his task would seem as forbidding as his title, the comparative musicologist has of late years done much to elucidate the early history of music. This he does by careful recording of music made by primitive tribes, and comparing these with music found in our Western civilization. 'Why does man sing?' he asks. 'Is it not easier to make a straightforward statement in speech? Is it not more natural to do so?'

The answer seems to be that when singing, one is not trying to be natural, but supra-natural. The indeterminate rise and fall of the speaking voice is made in song to adopt a formal pattern requiring the use of notes in a determined system.[1] The voice, moreover, is differently used; the head is thrown back and the sound is uttered in prolonged spells which employ mouth-shapes and nasal resonance not considered in normal speech. It is 'unnatural' in so far as it is not commonplace; the desire of the singer is for something out of the common—something superior to his ordinary mode of expression. It may have a practical value in that a sung sound will carry further than a sharp short series of sounds, but this feeling of the supra-natural action is clearly the very thing required to inspire himself with courage, praise his own or his tribe's heroism, or to offer in sacrifice to the supernatural. Song and singers are in a mysterious way 'superior'.

Dancing, too, is a superior accomplishment. It elevates the soul through the influence of rhythmic action. Rhythm gives life to tired muscles, makes possible a display of athletic prowess which will prove infectious to the tribe, leads to imitation, and by inculcating the imitation of desirable behaviour unifies the action of the tribe. A hunters' dance will stimulate men to hunt, and the storehouse will be filled. It is done by the leader, or medicine-man, symbolizing the animal to be hunted, then leading his followers into the action of attacking that animal. A war-dance must inspire courage, hatred of the enemy, and control the plan and moment of attack. It is done by the imitation of symbols in sequence. At the moment of doing it the warriors are divinely inspired, according to their concept of

[1] We are not concerned here with which came first, speech or song, but only with the qualities of song.

divinity. Music and dance, then, were clearly supernatural to primitive men, but nevertheless they were practical behaviour, since without the help of the gods the tribe would fail, or fall into decline through lack of sustenance or regenerative power.

These things can be observed today and compared with similar rites described in history. In time some of us have outgrown our old conceptions, and no doubt think them childish and unreal—even sinful. In our case the strongest attack on pagan beliefs came through Christianity. Christianity effected a transformation of thought without which our civilization would have been impossible to achieve. Why, then, all this pother about pagan influences in folk-song and dance? Are we still concerned with stamping them out?

Far from it. We are concerned to preserve them. Their evil has been removed, though we may still feel the power of the old beliefs if we go to the right places. If by any chance you should be at Padstow on May Day you will see the main square decorated with green garlands, all swinging from the houses to a flower-bedecked pole in the middle of the square. This is their Maypole. Then at eleven in the morning you should go round the corner to where

> All that company rum
> Will out of the Golden Lion come,
> A pirate beating the Brenton Drum
> That from Waterloo did come.

But though the drum came from Waterloo, the custom is far older.

> Unite and unite, and let us all unite,
> For summer is a-come unto day,
> And whither we are going we will all unite,
> In the merry morning of May.

The tune I will not print, because if I did so I should deceive you. It does not sound as you would play it, but is sung with an emotional fervour in which the actual notes are subservient to a semi-hypnotic effect. The tune is sung on the appearance of a strange figure—a man bearing a structure on his shoulders like a circular collar some four feet in diameter, stiffened with a wooden hoop, from the circumference of which hangs a skirt made of the same canvas as the collar, the whole liberally smeared with tar. On his head is a fearsome mask looking rather like that of an African medicine-man, with a conical (fool's) cap. Before him dances the 'teaser' or 'clubman' with a 'club' in his hand, shaped not a bit like a cudgel but like a fire-bellows held by the nozzle. To the accompaniment of the song and a band of accordions the hobby-horse—for that is what the strange monster is, as anyone can tell from the small horse's head and tail fastened to the canvas hoop—capers, swirls, throws up his wide skirts fore and aft, and if the onlookers are not quick he will smear their clothes with tar. If he succeeds in engulfing some young woman within his skirt she is lucky, and may expect to marry before a year has elapsed. Children are frightened by the savage appearance of the hobby-horse, but he is not dangerous, and never was; soon they will learn to make their own hobby-horses. Once the horse (always called the Old 'Oss) was able to chase people up the steep streets, but that was in the good old days; now the event is so popular that his crew of Doom Bar Pirates have to make way for him.[1]

All is merry.

> With a merry ring adieu the merry spring,
>   (For summer is a-come unto day)
> How happy is the little bird that merrily doth sing
>   In the merry morning of May.

> The young men of Padstow might if they would
>   (For summer is a-come unto day)
> They might have built a ship and gilded her with gold,
>   In the merry morning of May.

> The maidens of Padstow might if they would,
>   (For summer is a-come unto day)
> They might have made a garland with the white rose and
>   the red
>   In the merry morning of May.

---

[1] The Doom Bar is a sandbank outside the harbour. The 'pirates' are a recent addition to the 'Obby 'Oss ceremony, looking very much as though they come from Gilbert and Sullivan's Penzance.

Arise up Mr —— and reach me your hand,
    (For summer is a-come unto day)
And you shall have a lively lass with a thousand pounds
    in hand,
    In the merry morning of May.

Arise up Miss Padstow, all in your cloak of silk,
    (For summer is a-come unto day)
And all your body under as white as any milk,
    In the merry morning of May.

All this is understandable, but now comes a change. The tune grows wilder, then drops into a dirge.

Where is St George? Where is he O?
He is out in his long-boat all on the salt sea O.
Up flies the kite and down falls the lark O,
Aunt Ursula Birdwood she had an old ewe
And she died in her own park O.

The 'Obby 'Oss collapses on the ground. The 'clubman' pets him—strokes the diminutive wooden head with his club; then suddenly the 'Oss springs to life again. He has died and been revived. The tune returns to its former vigour.

With the merry spring adieu the merry ring,
    (For summer is a-come unto day).
How happy is the little bird that merrily doth sing,
    In the merry morning of May.

Now fare you well and we bid you all good cheer,
    (For summer is a-come unto day),
We call no more unto your house before another year,
    In the merry morning of May.

Meanwhile the young women of Padstow have been out in the fields and woodlands to collect fresh flowers and branches, bearing which they join the throng.

Where are the maidens that here now should sing?
(For summer is a-come unto day),
They are in the meadows the flowers gathering,
In the merry morning of May.

It all goes to your head like wine.[1]
At Minehead in Somerset the hobby-horse again is a complete disguise for its wearer, and is a fearsome apparition; the body has taken on some of the shape of a boat, but the ornamentation is animal. This horse does not go through the life and death ritual, but merely walks through the town on May Day, calling on certain houses where the custom is encouraged. Then there are the 'hooden' horses still to be seen in certain parts of England—Kent, Hampshire, Dorset, Wiltshire, Cornwall, and Somerset; this type of hobby-horse has the head or skull of a horse stuck on the end of a pole, below which hangs a draping completely covering the man holding the pole. In Derbyshire and parts of Yorkshire the Old Hoss becomes a sheep, or Old Tup. The head may be an actual sheep's head obtained from a butcher, a pair of ram's horns, or a wooden head with wonderful eyes made with the glass marbles found in mineral-water bottles, nailed to the head with black tacks which make them look like a comic version of a film star's eyelashes.

The Old Tup moves round the assembled company, smelling out 'malefactors'. 'Who loves ——?' (a local character none too quick-witted). 'Who wet her bed last Christmas?' The Old Tup sniffs round and settles on the 'culprit'. Beneath the innocent custom lies an old belief that the community is suffering from the unconfessed crimes of its members. The community must be purified, the air cleansed; sacrifice is needed—someone must be chosen as a scape-goat, to expiate the sins of all. In Derbyshire and south-west Yorkshire the scapegoat is the Derby Ram. At Castleton the characters associated with the song were 1. The Old Tup. 2. The Butcher. 3. Boy with basin. 4. Little Devil-doubt. 5. Clown. 6. Collector. At Braithwell there is no Little Devil-doubt or Clown, but there is an Old Woman, and a Farmer who leads in the Old Tup. Several variants of the song have been collected; one of which, from Staveley, runs as follows.

---

[1] Those who take part in the ceremony today are children or descendants of former mayors of Padstow, who take great pride in the tradition.

As I was going to Derby
　　All on a market day,
I met the finest tup, sir,
　　That ever was fed upon hay.
　　　　Fay-a-lay, laddigo lay.

This tup was fat behind, sir,
　　This tup was fat before,
This tup was nine feet high, sir,
　　If not a little more.
　　　　Fay-a-lay, etc.

The horns that grew on this tup's head
　　They were so mighty high,
That every time it shook its head
　　They rattled against the sky,
　　　　Fay-a-lay, etc.

1st Actor: Is there a butcher in this town?
2nd Actor: Our Bob's a blacksmith.
1st Actor: I don't want a blacksmith; I want a butcher.
3rd Actor: Well, here I am. I'm a butcher. Where d' you want him
　　　　sticking—in t' eard or in t' arse?
1st Actor: In t' eard, o' course.
3rd Actor: Well, I'll stick 'im in t' arse then.

　He does so, thereupon the Old Tup squeals and falls down. Then
the butcher sticks him in the head. The song is renewed.

The butcher that killed this tup, sir,
　　Was in danger of his life;
He was up to his knees in blood, sir,
　　And prayed for a longer life.
　　　　Fay-a-lay, etc.

And all the men of Derby
　　Came begging for his eyes,
To make themselves some footballs of,[1]
　　For they were football size.
　　　　Fay-a-lay, etc.

[1] Neither the football Tom Brown played at Rugby nor the sort we pay to see, but
the traditional football played in some towns (e.g. Ashbourne) at Shrove-tide, where
all the town is the area of play and as many as will may join in.

And all the women of Derby
  Came begging for his ears,
To make their leather aprons of
  To last them forty years.
    Fay-a-lay, etc.

And all the ringers of Derby
  Came begging for its tail,
To ring St George's passing bell
  From the top of Derby jail.

The object of the performance is no more than the collection of
money;

And now my song is ended;
  I have no more to say;
Please give us all a Christmas-box
  And we will go away.

This is the tune they use at Staveley:

As I was going to Der-by Up-on a mar-ket day, I saw the fi-nest

tup, sir, that e-ver was fed on hay. Fay-a-lay lad-di-go lay.

The Old Tup does not come to life again. He is a sacrificial
emblem; by his death the tribe was cleansed; so he was regarded not
with contempt but with veneration; everything about him was made
superlative, and this led to a spate of glorified lying. The lies persist
for their absurdity when the pagan belief is no more, and *The Derby
Ram* is a comic song.

The man that owned this ram, sir
  Was counted very rich,
But the man that sung this song sir,
  Is a lying son of a bitch.

The scapegoat in the Old Testament was not killed, but after a ritual celebration was turned out into the desert. Similarly in Greek drama King Oedipus is blinded and driven from the city, an outlaw who has sinned against the strictest laws of the tribe with patricide and incest. Freud has shown how these ideas have persisted in tribal law.[1] It must not be assumed that the guilty ones cursed the society which outlawed them: they themselves believed in the necessity of expiation. Two variants of the ballad of *Edward* may be quoted to illustrate this. The Scottish one is terrible, telling as it does of a man who murdered his father at the instigation of his mother.

'Why does your brand sae drop wi' blude,
  Edward, Edward?
Why does your brand sae drop wi' blude,
  And why sae sad gang ye, O?'
'O I hae killed my hawk sae gude,
  Mither, mither;
O I hae killed my hawk sae good,
  And I had nae mair but he, O.'

'Your hawk's blude was never sae red,
  Edward, Edward;
Your hawk's blude was never sae red,
  My dear son, I tell thee, O.'
'Oh I hae killed my red-roan steed,
  Mither, mither;
O I hae killed my red-roan steed,
  That erst was so fair and free, O.'

'Your steed was auld, and ye hae got mair,
  Edward, Edward;
Your steed was auld, and ye hae got mair;
  Some other dule ye dree, O.'
'O I hae killed my father dear,
  Mither, mither;
O I hae killed my father dear,
  Alas, and wae is me, O.'

---

[1] Sigmund Freud, *Totem and Taboo*, 1918.

'And whatten penance will ye dree for that,
    Edward, Edward?
Whatten penance will ye dree for that?
    My dear son, now tell me, O.'
'I'll set my feet in yonder boat,
    Mither, mither;
I'll set my feet in yonder boat,
    And I'll fare o'er the sea, O.'

The outlawry is self-inflicted. He will leave his home, let it fall into ruin, and leave his wife and children to beggary; never will he see them more. As for his mother:

'And what will ye leave to your ain mither dear,
    Edward, Edward?
And what will ye leave to your ain mither dear,
    My dear son, now tell me, O?'
'The curse of hell frae me sall ye bear,
    Mither, mither;
The curse of hell frae me sall ye bear:
    Sic counsels ye gave to me, O!'

In another version of this song, which Cecil Sharp found preserved in Kentucky, the crime is the murder of a brother-in-law for the apparently trivial offence of a dispute about a bush. It may mean a dispute about a neighbour's landmark, the cutting down of which would be unlawful; we cannot tell from the song, but the outlawry is again self-inflicted. *

What has come this blood on your shirt sleeve? O dear love tell me This is the blood of the old grey horse that ploughed the field for me, me, me, That ploughed the field for me.

* Incest is not ruled out. The 'bush' may refer to the female sex organ.

'What has come this blood on your shirt sleeve?
  O dear love tell me.'
'This is the blood of the old grey horse
  That ploughed the field for me, me, me,
  That ploughed the field for me.'

'What has come this blood on your shirt sleeve?
  O dear love, tell me.'
'This is the blood of the old greyhound
  That traced that fox for me, me, me,
  That traced that fox for me.'

The reply states that the blood looks too pale for that of a grey-hound, and the question is repeated—'What has come this blood on your shirt sleeve?'

'It is the blood of my brother-in-law
  That went away with me, me, me,
  That went away with me.'

'And it's what did you fall out about?
  O dear love, tell me.'
'About a little bit of bush
  That soon would have made a tree, tree, tree,
  That soon would have made a tree.'

'And it's what will you do now, my love?
  O dear love, tell me.'
'I'll set my feet in yanders ship,
  And I'll sail across the sea, sea, sea,
  And I'll sail across the sea.'

'And it's when will you come back, my love?
  O dear love, tell me.'
'When the sun sets into yanders sycamore tree,
  And it's that will never be, be, be,
  And it's that will never be.'

The pathos is intense, but the tragedy is in the singer's own conviction of his guilt. Fate can strike no harder blow. The individual conscience has come into conflict with tribal laws which cannot be questioned.

But though man's conscience will outgrow the cruder beliefs, the ritual may go on of its own volition. The club of the Padstow clubman is not merely a heavy stick, but an article shaped something like a table-tennis racket—a refinement possibly of the mummers' dripping-pan. His 'horse' wears a pointed hood (like a fool's cap). That most respectable of heraldic animals, the unicorn,[1] has a single conical horn, which anthropologists tell us is a phallic symbol. It is further found wherever magic is depicted—as in astrologers and witches; in the Court Fool and the Fool who appears among English Sword and Morris dancers. The sword itself is a symbol: seen at Bampton, Oxfordshire, when the Morris dancers are out, its relationship to the fertility cult can hardly be in doubt, for with the dancers is a man with a cake, baked in an iron cake-tin through which a sword has been driven, the handle underneath and the point standing up above the cake. This sword is decorated with flowers. The cake-bearer carries a collecting-box, but he does not beg; he will ask you if you care to taste the cake. If you are wise you will put something in the box and take a bit of the cake to eat. Then, if the corn-spirit does not enter into you it can only be because there is no corn-spirit, which, surely, is absurd.

This sword is not used in the dance; it is a true sword. The Bampton Morris dancers will be dealt with later in this book; here we are concerned with the north-country sword-dance and its relation to the folk-play and the various pagan symbols so far described. There exists a written version of this play hailing from Revesby in Lincolnshire, dating from 1779. The cast consists of six sword-dancers and their father the Fool. The Fool is not an idiot, but the wise man of the cast. There are also a Hobby-horse and a Dragon, with no speaking parts, and a Man-woman named Cicely. The eldest of the six dancers, sons of the Fool, is named Pickle Herring, and is a rival with his own father for the affections of Cicely. The sons plan to kill their father. He, warned of this approaching disaster, says that he is not prepared to die, but that when he does it will be for the public good. The sons dance round him with their swords, ending by inter-locking these in a star-shaped pattern called the 'Lock'.[2] At the end of the figure they hand the Lock to the Fool, who looks at it, says

---

[1] Traditionally associated with purity. Its horn is a sovereign remedy against poison. The creature gores its hunters but is mild and amiable when sought by a virgin.

[2] Other names for the Lock are 'Rose', 'Nut', and 'Glass'.

it is a fine looking-glass, and throws it on the ground and stamps on it. He is not ready yet. Again they dance, again end by forming the Lock, and place it round his head, threatening to cut it off. The Fool now plays for time by saying that he has not made his will. Making the will can delay the end quite a long time, but eventually the dances come to their last. It seems a pity, but it has to be. There is no malice in it; the Fool explains that they are only children, and the sons do it because they must to inherit his estate. With the Lock round his neck the Fool stands; his sons, taking each his own sword by the handle, withdraws it, breaking up the Lock. The Fool falls dead.

But not for long. Soon he comes to life again, and the rest of the play is taken up with the wooing of Cicely by Fool and Pickle Herring. During this the Fool grows younger and Pickle Herring grows older.

Here is the life and death ritual in essence. The Lock symbolizes the sun, upon which fertility depends. This play and dance, called the Plough Play, are derived from the original ritual, whereas the Mummers' Play seen by the author of *Tom Brown's Schooldays* in the White Horse Vale is a perversion, having been subjected to literary influences, dating certainly from Johnson's *Seven Champions of Christendom* (c. 1597), which was in turn influenced by *Bevis of Hampton* and *Sir Guy of Warwick*.[1] Artificial as the White Horse on the hill may seem today, the stones of Stonehenge and Avebury, the Hobby-horses, Old Hosses, Tups, and sword-dances, they were once a matter of life and death. Blood may indeed have flowed where now a comic figure prances. Sex was not a sinful practice but a sacred duty.

[1] Anglo-Danish legends with a bearing on early Arthurian legends.

II. The Green Man

What shall he have that kill'd the deer?
His leather skin and horns to wear.
Then sing him home.

AS YOU LIKE IT, IV. ii.

I

ABBOTS BROMLEY is in Staffordshire, lying within the ancient forest of Needwood. It is a pretty place, with good trees, half-timbered architecture, at least one inn for which I can vouch, and a handsome church dedicated to St Nicholas. Go there at any time and your journey will be well rewarded. While in the church observe the curious collection of reindeer horns hanging on the wall, and remember if you will that St Nicholas is the same as Santa Claus, who goes about the world on Christmas Eve with a reindeer sledge. Go there preferably, however, on the Monday succeeding the first Sunday following the 4th of September—which is the day on which they now begin Wakes week [1] at Abbots Bromley—and you will see a sight quite unique, whatever your belief in Santa Claus may be.

Down the street comes a procession of men in single file bearing those very horns they keep normally in the church. Three of the horns are painted white, the remaining three dark brown; [2] they are fixed to wooden blocks shaped somewhat like an animal's head, with a short stick protruding where its neck would be. The short stick forms the handle by which the head and horns are held breast-high, the main branches of the horns (which are heavy) resting for further support on the shoulders of the men.

Down the street they come, following their leader—the three white, then the three dark heads. The leader will occasionally go into a winding or serpentine motion, which is followed by the remainder; then he sweeps round towards the middle of the file, and

---

[1] Actually the date of a fair granted by Henry I. The Wakes properly should be held on St Nicholas's day, 6th December.
[2] Previously dark blue, and, earlier still, red.

40

breaks through it in front of the leader of the dark heads, thus cutting the line in two—lights and darks; the leader of the dark heads turns off into another circle, followed by his men; then the two circles—light and dark—straighten out opposite each other so that they now form two opposed lines of dancers. Their ancient ritual is about to begin.

The six men with horns are the most spectacular characters in this picturesque group, but there are also in attendance a Fool, a man dressed in skirts and carrying two emblems, one a club and the other shaped like a small ladle or large tobacco pipe (called 'the pipe'), a Hobby-horse, a boy with toy bow and arrow, and, for good measure, a boy with a triangle to help the rhythm of the tune played by the man with a concertina. The boy with the bow and arrow dances opposite the hobby-horse in the lines. Forward they move towards each other, with a strange loping gait, the horns apparently about to clash. As they come close together the boy with the bow shoots at the hobby-horse. They retire. Then forward again, only to retire a second time. After several of these movements the dancers pass through the opposite line, each man passing his opponent to the left and proceeding beyond, where the dancers turn about, ready to repeat the dance from the other side of the road.

The dance completed, the leader moves away down the street and the others tail on behind, until the place is reached where they decide to go again through the ritual. They will go on all day, making a round of the streets in the town, and the outlying houses and farms, and any farmer who is not visited will wonder what he has done to incur such bad luck. Their costumes are modern inventions supposed to be olde Englyshe, with flat hats, sleeveless coats over red or blue-sleeved shirts according to which side they represent, knee-breeches with oak-leaf pattern, and green stockings. This dress dates from 1904, and is altered from a previous one designed in 1887, based on costumes depicted in an edition of Shakespeare's *Henry IV*, Part I, published in 1778, and in turn derived from the design of a painted window now at Minsterly but formerly at Betley in Staffordshire. What the Abbots Bromley dancers wore before 1887 is a matter of conjecture, but there is verbal evidence that they wore their own clothes with bits of red or blue material attached.

The man-woman is called Maid Marian. This ought to give us the origin of the dance, but it does not. In fact it is misleading. Mention

Maid Marian to any schoolboy and he will recall that she was loved by Robin Hood, who in turn was a gallant outlaw in the reign of the wicked King John. Robin Hood robbed the rich to give to the poor, shot the king's deer, and had his head broken by a giant called Little John. Nor are schoolboys any more gullible than their elders, who have attributed Robin Hood and his merry men to a certain phase of witchcraft. Others will even say that Robin Hood himself was an outlawed Earl of Huntingdon. Actually the Abbots Bromley characters go back earlier than their names. The hobby-horse and the man-woman we know, Robin Hood is timeless; in Ireland he is Rory o' the Hills, in modern America they have Jesse James, who fought the wicked railroad-makers, and in Australia they have the outlaw Jack Dougan, 'the Wild Colonial Boy'. *

The Abbots Bromley dance and its characters summarize everything in English folk-dance, but in an individual way. The hobby-horse is of the type slung from the wearer's shoulders, making him a draped horse below the waist and rider above, but the wooden animal-heads with their short handles, by which the six dancers carry the antlers, are derived from the 'Old Tup' kind of head with the pole cut short. The six dancers—three opposite three—may have the same origins as Morris dancers, but these are not all. In spite of the Robin Hood characters the dance cannot be pinned down to any historic event or period; it is just fanciful. How long it has gone on we do not know; it has been claimed that before the Dissolution of the Monasteries it was performed each Sunday in front of the church, a collection taken, and the proceeds given to the Abbot for charity.[2] (In 1222 the Abbot of Burton-on-Trent founded Abbots Bromley as a tiny borough having, with the king's consent, the liberties enjoyed by the men of Lichfield.) Certainly Dr Plot, who published his *Natural History of Staffordshire* in 1686, saw the horns and hobby-horse in the town hall (where they were then kept) and states that the dance was performed at Christmas, New Year, and Twelfth Day, the proceeds, after paying for a feast of cakes and ale, going to pay for repairs to the church and for the relief of the poor. However pagan this dance may have been in origin, the Church accepted it. Only during the Commonwealth does it seem to have been discontinued. To Dr Plot, however, the six reindeer horns were supplementary, the principal character being the

* And, of course, Ned Kelly.
[2] F. W. Hackwood, *Staffordshire Curiosities and Antiques*, 1905.

hobby-horse, 'a person that carried the image of a horse between his legs made of thin boards, and in his hand a bow and arrow, which passing through a hole in the bow and stopping upon a sholder it had in it, made a snapping noise as he drew it to and fro in time to the musick'. Dr Plot did not see the dance performed, but he was told 'they danced the hays and other country dances'.

To dance the hey you follow your leader, who winds in a serpentine manner through a line of dancers coming in the opposite direction. Dr Plot's reference to the hey was, then, to the manner in which the leader cut through the line of dancers in the preliminary serpentine movement. It is a very ancient dance-figure, though not so old as a chain-dance, which is what happens when we link hands and move sideways or round in a ring. There was an old name for this behaviour—it was called a 'carol', and the music for it was often sung by the dancers. The name has remained with the music but not with the dance. Any number may join in—men and women. It is a community dance.

The practice of linking hands and following in line—or following even without linking hands—is so natural that one has no need to seek explanations. By imitation of the leader it becomes a dance. Two lines of dancers linking hands in couples make a procession, which may have a certain dignity not enjoyed in the hey; two lines of dancers opposite can advance and retire, and from this practice primitive war-dances may have started, but the action has been applied to any custom which it suits.

Of the processional dances, that performed on the second Saturday in May at Helston in Cornwall is one of the most famous. It is truly traditional and may be a survival of a spring ceremony of purification; at one time the dancers carried sprigs of May blossom and green broom, with which they dusted objects in the houses through which they passed—a sort of ceremonial spring-cleaning. The procession winds in and out through the houses—in at the front door of one house and out at the back, on to the back door of the next house and out at the front.

All the community may take part in the dance if they wish, but in practice this would be inconvenient. There are three 'runs' nowadays; one is led by the mayor, another is for the children, and yet another for the general public. In days gone by the townsfolk made a great deal of the custom, in a more vigorous way. The day was ushered in by gangs of lads with song and percussion. They struck anything which would make a hollow noise—drums, kettles, pots. They would seek out the diligent, and anyone found at work would be seized, set astride a pole, and thereon carried shoulder-high to the river. He was not thrown in, but was ordered to jump across the river at a wide space. If he was foolish enough to attempt this he would get a wetting, but he could avoid the jump if he compounded with his tormentors with a payment towards their fund for buying beer. At nine o'clock this diversion would give place to another, when the rascals all went to the grammar-school and demanded a holiday for the boys. This was granted. Then the custom was to collect money contributions from houses in the town; next to go out into the country to gather flowers and oak-leaves. With these in their caps the revellers would dance through the town to the sound of a fiddle, going in and out of houses, and woe to any householder who tried to stop them. The dance by the select party of respectable Helstonians would take place later, when the lords of misrule had had their fling.

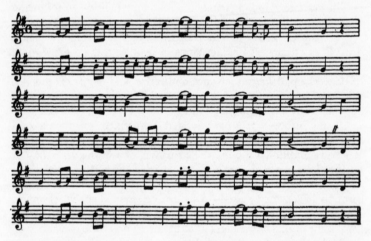

During the present century the Helston ceremony has been purged of its horseplay. The day is an official holiday, and the gathering of green boughs and singing in the streets takes place in the Hal-an-Tow ceremony (the words of the song are given on page 55) distinct from the processional dance. This leads us to a further observation, for while a processional dance is admirable in the streets, May dances in the woods were often (though apparently not at Helston) round dances.

One can dance a round dance at any time—crowds do it spontaneously on Mafeking and Coronation nights—but May and Midsummer are the times when the folk made a speciality of it. Then they danced round a bush, a tree, later a Maypole; to left, to right, forward to the votive object and retire, as now they do in *Sellenger's Round*.

The May bush round which the traditional dance takes place is a happy symbol; it flowers and smells fragrantly. Old pictures of dancers, however, sometimes show a man carrying a green bush on a pole, in attendance on the dancers but not necessarily the centre of their dance. The green bush is earlier than the blossom. The first sign of awaking life is the green shoot, as we know from what happened to the irrepressible John Barleycorn. 'Mister Green' survives as a nickname for a barman. The very word 'bar' used in this sense is alleged to derive from 'bower'[1]—the green arbour set beside the place where local festivities were carried on. If the dancers moved from place to place they took their bower with them. At Castleton in Derbyshire the bower (here called 'garland') is made to fit over a man seated on horseback, completely hiding him, but with a space left through which a beer-mug may be conveyed to the mouth. Underneath the garland he is dressed in a costume of the time of Charles II, and the ceremony takes place on 29th May (Oak Apple Day). He is attended by a 'Queen'—a veiled man-woman—and by the dancers—now, alas, little girls who are fitly rewarded with lemonade—and after the festivities the garland is hoisted to the top of the church tower. 'Good wine', we all know,

[1] Bar, Low Lat. *Barra* (perhaps Celtic origin). Bower, A.S. *búr*.

'needs no bush.' The bower or bush was the first tavern sign. This custom goes back well before the time of Charles II.

Divine inebriation! Partaking of the spirit of the corn god that we may be enlivened! The character dressed in green leaves who in various places accompanied the dancers was called 'Jack-in-the-Green'. Another name was 'Robin-in-the-Wood', or simply 'the Green Man'. Not merely may he be seen on an inn sign; there are many carvings of the Green Man to be found in our churches—not necessarily hidden away under misericords or in dark corners, but on pews and roof-bosses, where all can see them. The little girls who drink windy waters at Castleton Garland Festival are the delight, no doubt, of sentimental onlookers, but the Victorian age which substituted these for the virile attendants on the Green Man did something which even the allegedly dour Puritans of the Commonwealth could not wholly do.

But even the Victorians could not kill Robin Hood. For Robin Hood is probably descended from the Green Man, or Robin-in-the-Wood. He has ceased to be a supernatural being but has taken on a popular historical significance. He is a folk-hero.

II

It may be that the common people have bad judgment in their choice of heroes. Apart from William of Normandy, who was the greatest conqueror of our land? Julius Caesar, surely; and he wrote a book about it which well-educated schoolboys are forced to read. But where is Julius Caesar in popular history—or William the Conqueror for that matter—apart from the convenience of their dates? True, the author of *Tom Brown's Schooldays*, who had read his Caesar, attributed the camp on White Horse Hill to the Romans, and the Ridgeway too, but the country folk stuck to St George and Alfred the Great for their history. Apart from these there was King Arthur and his knights—higher in the literary hierarchy than the story of Alfred and the cakes—but where are they in the history books?

William divided up the country among his followers; most of the Saxon thanes were dispossessed, and many of the free tenants were degraded into the unfree classes—villein, bordar, cottar; below these were the serfs. Castles were built to hold the native people in subjection, and these had to be paid for. Labour had to be provided, and food for the retainers who manned the castles.

Those who till the soil have never been in any doubt as to where the money must be found. We may still see inn signs called 'The Five Alls', depicting the King ('I rule all'), a Bishop ('I pray for all'), a Soldier ('I fight for all'), a Judge ('I judge all'), and finally a Farmer ('I pay for all'). From the productive resources of the land the whole community has to be kept. The ploughman knows it too.

> Come all you jolly ploughmen of courage stout and bold,
> That labour in the winter in stormy winds and cold;
> To cloathe your fields with plenty, your farmyards to renew,
> To crown them with contentment, behold the painful plough.

All tradesmen looked down on the ploughman, but if he had failed none could have survived. The Norman conquerors not only looked down on peace-loving men, but greatly increased the number of non-productive workers. Moreover, they were fond of hunting. This indeed was the source of grievance which gave new impetus to the legendary spirit of the woods—the Green Man.

William I passed strict laws to protect the greater beasts of the forest—the deer and the wild boar. Large tracts of country where these animals lived were made subject to special forest laws, which not only forbade anyone to kill the king's beasts without his authority, but forbade cutting down trees or in other ways interfering with the lairs of the animals. This from the farmer's point of view was foolish, for the great beasts had to be kept down and clearings in the forests enlarged in order to bring more land under cultivation. Moreover, though men had long passed the state of civilization in which they lived by hunting, the beasts were nevertheless a welcome addition to the larders of those who happened to live in areas where they abounded. Nobody thought it wrong to kill a wild boar or a deer, or to improve or extend his land at the expense of the moor or forest; so the forest laws created statutory crimes, and criminals who had no sense of their guilt. To make matters worse, only districts in the scheduled forests were subject to this law; if a deer got out of the forest into a non-scheduled area it could be taken and killed. Worst of all, the laws were arbitrary, made by the king for his own convenience, and not derived from the customs of the land. The Englishman was devilishly conservative; this sort of thing galled him.

Foresters had to be appointed to police the forests. Verderers' courts, additional to the other courts of law, were set up, and men from the forest areas had to sit in them. The foresters were most unpopular; their purpose was resented, their work obstructed; they had to be brutal in the performance of their duty, and all classes of forest dwellers were affected. 'If any one doe offer force to a Verderer, if he be a freeman, hee shall lose his freedom, and all that he hath. And if he be a villein, he shall lose his right hand.' The punishment in each case was to deprive the offender of his means of making a living. It is easy to guess what happened; the man became a beggar or a criminal. Then, 'if such an offender doe offend soe againe, he shall lose his life'.

Escape, and he was an outlaw, but he lived. Such an outlaw was very different from the self-outlawed sufferer in the ballad of *Edward,* however, because he had no sense of guilt. He had a sense of being a victim of injustice. The hatred of the king's servants grew in intensity. They for their part made matters worse by establishing a simple form of graft. For a consideration, permission to cut timber might be granted; meeting places were appointed where the annual payments were to be made; here certain of the foresters set up their bower, and sold 'scot ale' to those who had to attend. It was bad enough to have to pay the king for clearing your own land, without having to drink his health (or avoid doing so) in ale sold at a handsome profit by his collectors. Those who had to pay these dues were men with some property; it must not be thought that only the idle and dissolute hated the foresters: 'I'd rather go to my plough than serve in such an office', said a Northamptonshire gentleman in 1251.

So there grew up a legend about men who had done no crime, but who went in fear of their lives; outlaws living in the depths of the forest, secure because they were better foresters than the king's men; better bowmen; friends of the poor and of their country; haters of tyranny. Chief of them was Robin Hood, said to be an outlawed nobleman; but with him were Little John the giant, Friar Tuck the hedge-priest (with his fair share of worldly failings, but not a wicked man), Allan-a-Dale the minstrel, and Will Scarlet the honest English yeoman. They were an idealized community; a Merry England in miniature. Centuries after their time ballads were

sung at every fair telling of their goodness and their prowess,[1] and
all these ballads told attractive stories of characters such as men
wanted to be. Therein lay their appeal. Their structure was simple
and easily memorable.

There chanced to be a ped-lar bold, A ped-lar bold he chanced to be. He
put his pack all on his back, And so mer-ri-ly trud-géd o'er the lea.

'O pedlar, pedlar, what's in thy pack?
    Come speedily and tell to me.'
'I've several suits of the gay green silks,
    And silken bowstrings by two or three.'

'If you have several suits of the gay green silk,
    And silken bowstrings two or three,
Then, by my body,' cries Little John,
    'One half your pack shall belong to me.'

'O nay, O nay,' said the pedlar bold,
    'O nay, O nay, that never can be,
For there's never a man from fair Nottingham,
    Can take one half my pack from me.'

Then the pedlar he pulled off his pack,
    And put it a little below his knee,
Saying: 'If you do move me one perch from this,
    My pack and I shall gang with thee.'

Then Little John he drew his sword,
    The pedlar by his pack did stand,
They fought until they both did sweat,
    Till he cried: 'Pedlar, pray hold thy hand.'

[1] The Robin Hood ballads date from the fifteenth century onwards. *Robin Hood
and the Monks* and *Robyn and Gandelyn* are perhaps the earliest.

Then Robin Hood he was standing by,
　　And he did laugh most heartily,
Saying: 'I could find a man of smaller scale
　　Could thrash the pedlar and also thee.'

'Go you try, master,' says Little John,
　　'Go you try, master, most speedily,
For by my body,' says Little John,
　　'I am sure this night you will know me.'

Then Robin Hood he drew his sword,
　　And the pedlar by his pack did stand;
They fought till the blood in streams did flow,
　　Till he cried: 'Pedlar, pray hold your hand.'

'O pedlar, pedlar, what is thy name?
　　Come speedily and tell to me.'
'Come, my name I ne'er will tell,
　　Till both your names you have told to me.'

'The one of us is bold Robin Hood,
　　And the other Little John so free.'
'Now,' says the pedlar, 'it lays to my good will,
　　Whether my name I choose to tell thee.

'I am Gamble Gold[1] of the grey green woods,
　　And travelled far beyond the sea,
For killing a man in my father's land,
　　And from my country was forced to flee.'

'If you are Gamble Gold of the grey green woods,
　　And travelled far beyond the sea,
You are my father's own sister's son,
　　What nearer cousins can we be?'

They sheathed their swords, with friendly words,
　　So merrily they did agree,
They went to a tavern and there they dined,
　　And cracked bottles so merrily.

　　　　　[1] Possibly a corruption of 'Gandelyn.'

A ballad should always relate a story; it should also be impersonal, and have a simple metre which forms a structure for lines easily remembered. There is much repetition of the dialogue phrases in the above ballad, making for ease in improvisation. Given the form and the substance of the narrative, a minstrel could make up his song to please his audience, just as a good comedian today reacts to the laughter across the footlights. A ballad has something more than its plot, however, it has an appeal to the imagination of the hearers. The ballad of *Robin Hood and the Pedlar* is in its bare bones merely a story of an attempt at highway robbery by two men against one, but the fight is fought fairly, according to the rules, and the losers take a sporting view of their defeat. Then the winner takes a sporting view of his opponents and tells them who he is.[1] He is a murderer—an outlaw—but he is a relative, and one in a similar plight to the others, so all are friends. The narrative is idealized in such a way as to elevate the characters above their circumstances. The effect is to build up morale in the simple hearer; he associates himself with the hero and dreams ennobling dreams. It is fiction; but fiction, allied to circumstance, can be a constructive process.

There is at the back of the Robin Hood legend a common acceptance of what is right and wrong, even though this may officially be condemned. Such an ethical feeling has always been strong among the English. There is a nursery song, very simple in its form, which embodies a belief going back to the dawn of human history, but every verse shows the folk thinking in communal terms.

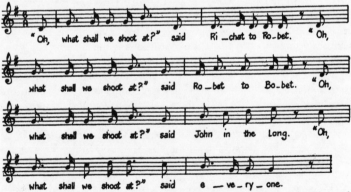

[1] This was a great concession to an enemy. A man's name was proper to him, and might be used by a malicious person to operate an evil spell.

Oh, what shall we shoot at? said Richat to Robet.
Oh, what shall we shoot at? said Robet to Bobet.
Oh, what shall we shoot at? said John in the Long.
Oh, what shall we shoot at? said everyone.

We'll shoot at the wren; said Richat to Robet.
We'll shoot at the wren; said Robet to Bobet.
We'll shoot at the wren; said John in the Long.
We'll shoot at the wren; said everyone.

The apparently useless custom of hunting the wren went on until the end of the nineteenth century, when Sir James G. Frazer saw it celebrated in the Isle of Man. He relates the origin of the custom to his general theme in *The Golden Bough*. The wren is the king of birds; whoever kills a wren or disturbs its nest will incur bad luck; but because it is so full of power—so virtuous—it is especially valuable as a sacrificial offering. 'The worshipful animal is killed with special solemnity once a year; and before or immediately after death he is promenaded from door to door, that each of his worshippers may receive a portion of the divine virtues that are supposed to emanate from the dead or dying god.' The wren was therefore caught on Christmas Eve by all the servants of the house going out in a body. Once caught, the little bird was fastened on the end of a pole, with wings outstretched, and carried in procession to each house.

There are many versions of the song of *Richat and Robet,* and an old Oxfordshire shepherd when singing it would stamp violently when he sang 'everyone'; he declared that it was a defiant song. Certainly there was an element of Saturnalia in the custom, for while they had the wren in their possession the killers behaved as they pleased, even to their masters.[1] It is not unthinkable that at some time in history the king of birds may have acted as a ritual substitute for the king himself. (More than one specialist has thought so.) The song itself, however, reveals no more than a mystic importance attached to the little creature, and a feeling that his body will revive all the town. The version given here is one sung in the Vale of the White Horse.

---

[1] The custom pertains to the behaviour of a 'Lord of Misrule'. Such characters were universal: the Court had its Jester, choir boys the Boy Bishop, Oxford University its *Terrae Filius*, etc.

After the first two verses (already given) the dialogue proceeds:

How shall we carry it home? said Richat to Robet, etc.

We'll hire three men; etc.

How shall we cook it? etc.

We'll hire six cooks; etc.

How shall we eat it? etc.

We'll invite all the town; said Richat to Robet.
We'll invite all the town; said Robet to Bobet.
We'll invite all the town; said John in the Long.
We'll invite all the town; said everyone.

The scraps for the poor; said Richat to Robet.
The scraps for the poor; said Robet to Bobet.
The scraps for the poor; said John in the Long.
The scraps for the poor; said everyone.

The importance of the smallest bird known in Britain is shown by the number needed to cook it, and the number it will feed!

Defiance and self-help are bound up together in a custom going back to time immemorial. The song of *Richat and Robet* has been differently interpreted by various scholars, and may even have meant different things at different times. So old is the song that all is a matter of speculation. A ballad, however, is a different matter, for it tells a story. Stories of Robin Hood are many, and in all of them the character persists; the legend is not entirely anti-clerical or anti-royalist. Richard I is honoured in the legend—a real Lionheart and a fair dealer—while King John is a bad king in every way. The English yeoman is shown as a worthy man. The legends, in fact, are opposed to all tyranny and all hypocrisy, but not to Church and State. How far are they true to history?

They are not true in cold facts, but in warm ones. A ballad must use imagination; it appeals to the wishful part of man. Until the end of the reign of Henry II (1154–89) forest laws were extended, but Richard I (1189–99) wanted money for foreign adventuring, which he got partly by granting rights of disafforestation. Of course he was popular in the greenwood! King John stayed at home and hunted. He was strongly opposed to disafforestation. We must not leave the matter here, however; everyone held strong views about forest rights. When Queen Eleanor was crowned in 1236 the Earl of Arundel could not serve as her butler because he had been excommunicated by the Archbishop of Canterbury. It happened that when this high prelate, Edmund Rich, was hunting on the Earl's estates in Sussex the Earl's men seized the Archbishop's greyhounds! Kings and Bishops had as much to do with the Robin Hood tradition as the yeomanry. Nature too, played a part. The Black Death of 1348–9 depleted the population and raised the importance of the yeoman; gunpowder blasted the bogy of chivalry. The descendants of those men who shot the king's deer and saw in Robin Hood an ideal to which they would attain, were invaluable at Crécy and Agincourt, yet were they any the better off for their prowess?

It is not in the Robin Hood tradition to ask. The English longbow was itself soon to give place to the musket, but the ballads of Robin Hood went on. Perhaps the English have been lax in their choice of heroes; perhaps they have been a little mad, scatterbrained, cruel, but they have been loyal to their inheritance. In the Revesby folk-play (mentioned in Chapter I) the father tells the audience with pride that all his sons have been through Coxcomb College. By this we assume that he means they have been initiated into the facts of life, and chosen to play the roles of perpetuators of fertility. In our churches the Green Man is represented as a face peering through a mass of foliage; he has a satyr-like expression (like Puck or Robin Goodfellow). The Revesby mummers talk of cock's combs, the Court jester had such an ornament on his cap; in the Abbots Bromley dance they carry real horns—magnificent horns of reindeer, which never lived in their forest, but were obtained from afar—horns of which to be proud.[1] Think, then, of Shakespeare's merry fellows in the imaginary Forest of Arden, how they sing:

[1] The Danes brought reindeer horns to Britain but there is no proof that the Abbots Bromley horns came from this source. A second set of horns (elk) is said to have been lost.

Take thou no scorn to wear the horn—
It was a crest e'er thou wast born;
   Thy father's father wore,
   And thy father bore it.
The horn, the horn, the lusty horn
Is not a thing to laugh to scorn.

The horns, like the mythical forest, are timeless. Robin Hood may appear in a folk-song at any period, and in any place. Even at Helston; but why not? It is May.

Robin Hood and Little John
   They both are gone to the fair O,
And we will to the merry greenwood
   To see what they do there O;
And for to chase O, to chase the buck and doe,
With hal-an-tow, jolly rumble O, to chase the buck and doe.

Chorus:

And we were up as soon as the day
   For to fetch the Summer home O;
The Summer and the May,
   Now the Winter is a-gone O.

You cannot tie these songs down to any period, for they may pick up ideas to add to their store as a squirrel picks up nuts.

Where are those Spaniards
   That make so great a boast O?
Why, they shall eat the grey goose feathers,
   And we will eat the roast O.
In every land O, the land where'er we go,
With a hal-an-tow, jolly rumble O, the land where'er we go.

And we were up as soon as the day
   To fetch the Summer home O,
The Summer and the May,
   Now the Winter is a-gone O.

The enemy was not now the British monarch but the foreigner who threatened us with his Armada, but the spirit is the same; the English 'won't be beat'.

> God bless Aunt Mary Moses
> And all her power and might O,
> And send us peace in Merry England,
> Send peace by day and night O.
> To Merry England O, both now and ever mo',
> With a hal-an-tow, jolly rumble O, both now and ever mo'.

Who was Aunt Mary Moses? Alas, she is to be seen no more, but in years that are past she was the man-woman of the Helston dance.

III. The Christian Revolution

##

Nowell sing we, both all and some,
Now Rex pacificus *is ycome.*

THE CHRISTIANS were a singing community from the first. They sang at the Last Supper; St Paul also implored Christians to be filled with the Spirit, 'speaking to yourselves in psalms, and hymns, and spiritual songs, and making melody in your heart to the Lord'. They sang whatever music was suitable for their devotions, which means that they were at first dependent mainly on Hebrew songs in praise of God, and even on Jewish temple ritual. There still exists in the Mass a passage taken over from the Jewish rite; we know it as the *sursum corda*; in the English of the Communion Service it is expressed thus:

Priest: Lift up your hearts.
People: We lift them up unto the Lord.
Priest: Let us give thanks unto our Lord God.
People: It is meet and right so to do.

Man is influenced by all sorts of ideas impinging on his current way of life. Few of these are received into the conscious stream of man's convictions, but those which are, and which remain, are the best suited for the purpose men seek. Of all the philosophy of the East but little has found permanent expression. The last paragraph of the Gospel according to St John tells us:

And there are also many other things which Jesus did, the which, if they should be written every one, I suppose that even the world itself could not contain the books that should be written. Amen.

St John was but echoing a thought much older than his time; a thought which many writers before and after him have noted. Possibly they took it from each other. The Talmud says:

If all the seas were ink, and all rushes pens, and the whole Heaven parchment and all sons of men writers, they should not be enough to describe the depth of the mind of the Lord.

While in the Koran it is written:

And were the trees that are in the earth pens, and the sea ink with seven more seas to swell its tide, the words of God would not be spent.

In the simple mind the profundity is lacking, but the images used in these quotations are reflected in a children's rhyme.[1]

> If all the world were paper,
> And all the seas were ink,
> And all the trees were bread and cheese
> What would we have to drink?

No irreverence is intended, for nothing holy is suggested. The simple mind will wander away from a prescribed path unless it is constantly redirected. That is one of the problems of the Church.

From about the third century A.D. holy men seeking seclusion from the world began to associate themselves in monastic orders, devoting their lives to the constant praise of God. In the holy office, which was their daily worship, the psalms were sung right through once a week. The music was plainsong and the style of performance antiphonal—that is, the monks were divided into two parties, each singing alternate lines of the psalm. This was in the Hebrew tradition, and even in Jewish folk tradition, for we can read in the Bible how the women of Israel lined the street on David's return from battle, answering each other in song, one side singing 'Saul hath slain his thousands', and the other answering 'David his ten thousands'. Plainsong served admirably for the service of God— an eternal flow of praise sublimating in melody the common speech of men, but of a seemly simplicity. When unseemly elements were introduced by clever musicians (and this was one of the Church's problems) discipline had to be evoked to purify the tradition. St Ambrose and St Gregory are the two most famous names in the ordering of Christian church music, but it must not be thought, as some treatises have suggested, that they created the musical system known as the ecclesiastical modes. Their task was to sort out the relevant from the irrelevant among the music being used in the Church, to decide what was to be preserved, and to classify the system advocated. The so-called ecclesiastical modes were the way

[1] Cf. Opie, *The Oxford Dictionary of Nursery Rhymes*, 1951.

music was made generally at the time, secular as well as sacred. To St Ambrose, however, we owe the introduction of the Syrian preference for offering praise in the form of metrical sung verses. The singing of hymns with versified texts became very popular.

> Veni, creator Spiritus,
> mentes tuorum visita,
> imple superna gratia
> quae tu creasti pectora.

This hymn is one of the oldest in the Christian Church, going back prior to the tenth century, but still most fitting for celebrations of dedication to God, whether of priests or kings. It has a perfect tune.

Plainsong notation shows the curve of the melody—the uplifting of the spirit as the line ascends. The first phrase of the tune rises from the bottom space of the stave to the third line up; the second phrase drops from there, but only to climb again; it settles to the pitch of the third line at the beginning of phrase three, and this phrase turns round this tonal centre; in the last phrase it falls again to the tonal centre on the bottom space from which it started. If you cannot read the notation your eyes will nevertheless see the shape of the tune; if you hear it sung your ears will concentrate on the uplift from the lower tonal centre to the higher one; the spiritual elevation as the melody curves now over, now under, this upper centre; and the feeling is of repose as the melody declines at the end to the lower centre. If you can sing it you will feel the spiritual elevation even more naturally. All folk-song demonstrates this feeling for tonal centres, with the emotional uprush to the higher level and the fall or cadence to the final. It is an instinctive process; the clergy did not invent it, but, as they were the scholars of the Middle Ages, it fell to them to analyse the principles of music and to provide a means of writing down what was required. The upper tonal centre they called the Dominant, the final centre the Final. It is as simple as that; the Dominant is the dominant or prevailing centre of spiritual elevation, and the Final actually suggests finality—repose—a satisfactory completion of the tune. They put into academic language what every peasant with a musical ear knew instinctively. On this matter the scholars and the illiterate were not opposed.

It was Gregory the Great who sent Augustine and his forty monks to Christianize southern England in A.D. 597. They were by no means the first Christian missionaries, but musically they are of importance to us. They concentrated their efforts on King Ethelbert, won him over, and the kingdom became Christian. Such is the story; but did anyone ever change his belief in religion in response to a royal decree? The common people would not understand Christianity as a result of the king's conversion, and in fact pagan and Christian ideas would go on until understanding was achieved; fertility rites would still go on, and divine inebriation. (Try to persuade a farmer against the prime necessity of fertility and the result would be contempt, even today.) The Church did not deny the facts but condemned the pagan ritual. The process of education towards the acceptance of the Christian life began, and it began from the only point possible—the point where pagan and Christian thought met. One of these is supposed to be preserved in the *Dilly Song*, of which even the name is a mystery—it comes from Cornwall and is thought to be of Celtic origin. The song is responsorial; a soloist sings the first line and the company answer with the refrain; a second soloist sings the third line and the first soloist completes the verse.

> I'll sing you one O.
> *Green grow the rushes O.*
> What is your one O?
> One is one and all alone
> And ever more shall be so.

Every boy who goes to Eton learns this song, and is told that it was once used as a means of teaching the Creed. God is God and all alone and will be for ever. There is mystery about the symbols in the song; the riddle has to be unravelled, and that makes it attractive to learn. The song goes on:

> I'll sing you two O.
> *Green grow the rushes O.*
> What are your two O?
>> Two, two, the lily-white boys,
>> Clothèd all in green O.
>> One is one and all alone
>> And evermore shall be so.

The song is cumulative. With each verse another riddle is added to the list. Altogether there are twelve. The last verse of all therefore will run:

> I'll sing you twelve O.
> *Green grow the rushes O.*
> What are your twelve O?
>> Twelve for the twelve apostles,
>> Eleven for the eleven who went to heaven,
>> Ten for the ten commandments,
>> Nine for the nine bright shiners,
>> Eight for the eight bold rangers,
>> Seven for the seven stars in the sky,
>> Six for the six proud walkers,
>> Five for the symbol at your door,
>> Four for the Gospel makers,
>> Three for the rivals,
>> Two, two, the lily-white boys,
>> Clothèd all in green O,
>> One is one and all alone
>> And evermore shall be so.

The mystic symbols can be explained in this way. The two lily-white boys are Christ and John the Baptist; three rivals are the Magi; the four Gospel makers are obviously the Evangelists; six proud walkers are those who bore the water-pots at the feast of Cana; eight rangers can be the archangels; nine bright shiners for the orders of angels or the nine joys of Mary; ten commandments; twelve apostles, eleven of whom went to heaven, for Judas turned traitor. All these symbols cannot be related to the Christian creed as it is affirmed in the Mass, but they are mostly associated with Christian belief in its wider aspect. Some of the symbols, however, do not fit into Christian lore, or only fit with a squeeze. 'Five for the symbol at your door' may be Hebraic, the symbol being the one-line pentagon which the Children of Israel marked over their doors when the plagues ravaged the land of Egypt. It can be a symbol of the true God, but it is not Christian. The five wounds of Christ is a more likely interpretation. The seven stars in the sky are the Great Bear, or the Planets, which again can only be drawn into Christian teaching from afar. The evidence points to a traditional song of great antiquity being transformed to Christian purpose; it did not stop at the version we have given—the history of this one song would provide material for a book. For the present we will leave it with the thought that all the lore contained therein derives from the Mediterranean basin.

The Fathers of the Church had need of symbols for another purpose in the early days of Christianity. Then there was need for telling friend from foe without revealing too much. The secret password can be employed at such times. 'Follow me,' said Jesus, 'and I will make you fishers of men.' So the fish became in the early Christian Church a symbol of a Christian, to be used for ornamental designs wherever these were appropriate. It was a learned symbol, the explanation being that the Greek ἰχθύς was an acrostic for Ἰησους Χριστὸς Θέου Ὑίος Σωτήρ (Jesus Christ, Son of God, Saviour).[1] In this case the symbol and the love of song and romance combine to produce a work of great beauty which, judging from its wide distribution, must also have been extremely popular. The version here given was taken down in 1914 by Lucy Broadwood from the singing of Mrs Joiner of Chiswell Green, Hertfordshire.

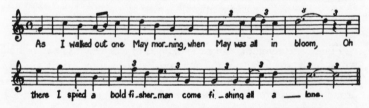

As I walked out one May mor_ning, when May was all in bloom, Oh there I spied a bold fi_sher_man come fi_shing all a ___ lone.

[1] For simpler minds baptism by water and the word would explain the symbol: 'We are born in water like the fish,' said Tertullian.

As I walked out one May morning,
  When May was all in bloom,
Oh there I spied a bold fisherman,
  Come fishing all alone.

I said to this bold fisherman,
  'How come you fishing here?'
'I'm fishing for your own sweet sake
  All down the river clear.'

He drove his boat towards the side,
  Which was his full intent,
Then he laid hold of her lily-white hand
  And down the stream they went.

Then he pulled off his morning gown
  And threw it over the sea,
And there she spied three robes of gold
  All hanging down his knee.

Sometimes the three robes are three chains of gold. Gold, any-way, is a symbol of integrity. The river, the sea, the royal fisherman, the three robes of glory (or vestures of light), are all mystic symbols used continually by the early Church. From this point in the story the attitude of the singer changes; there comes instant recognition and adoration, humility and a free pardon leading to the mystical union of the bride and bridegroom in the House of the Father. Profane songs of love-matches do not follow this train of thought, which further suggests the religious origin of the folk-song.[1]

Then on her bended knees she fell:
  'Pray, sir, pardon me
For calling you a fisherman
  And a rover down the sea.'

'Rise up, rise up, my pretty fair maid,
  Don't mention that to me,
For not one word that you have spoke
  Has the least offended me.

[1] See *Journal of the Folk Song Society*, vol. v, pp. 132–3; and Frank Howes, *Man, Mind, and Music*, 1948, pp. 35–9.

'Then we'll go to my father's hall,
And married we shall be,
And you shall have your fisherman
To row you on the sea.'

Then they went to his father's house,
And married now they be;
And now she's got her fisherman
To row her down the sea.

The attraction of the song is in its wish-fulfilment, it is in the tradition of many songs wherein the young woman in love yearns for a perfect, or at any rate socially superior, lover. Thus it is preserved in the folk mind intact, though its inner meaning was forgotten by the singer.

It must always be kept in mind that if a song is attractive in itself it will be sung, whatever its meaning may have been at some time in the past. The meaning may be forgotten but the singer tends to preserve the song merely for his own pleasure. Music especially—which has no meaning apart from the words with which it is associated—is conservative. There are preserved many tunes in pentatonic and modal forms; tunes which skilled musicians at some time in history might have altered had they had their way. The folk however, have been great preservers of ancient thought. The theme of the bleeding knight and the Holy Grail has been treated by innumerable poets, artists, and of course by Wagner in *Parsifal,* but there is a folk-song extant which may go back to the very origin of the legend, before Christianity reinterpreted the characters which had served the Druids or the worshippers of the bloody cult of Mithraism. We know it as *Down in the Forest.*

Down in the fo-rest there stands a hall, (The bells of Pa-ra-dise I heard them ring) Is co-vered all o-ver with pur-ple so tall, (And I love my Lord Je-sus a-bove a-ny-thing.)

Down in the forest there stands a hall,
(The bells of Paradise, I heard them ring)
Is covered all over with purple and pall
(And I love my Lord Jesus above anything).

In that high hall there stands a bed,
(The bells of Paradise, I heard them ring)
Is covered all over with scarlet and red
(And I love my Lord Jesus above anything).

All in that bed there lies a knight,
(The bells of Paradise, I heard them ring)
Whose wounds they do bleed with main and with might
(And I love my Lord Jesus above anything).

And under that bed there runs a flood,
(The bells of Paradise I heard them ring)
The one half runs water, the other runs blood,
(And I love my Lord Jesus above anything).

And at the bed's foot there lies a hound,
(The bells of Paradise, I heard them ring)
A-licking the blood as it daily runs down
(And I love my Lord Jesus above anything).

All at the bed's head there flowers a thorn,
(The bells of Paradise I heard them ring)
Which never so blossomed since Jesus was born
(And I love my Lord Jesus above anything).

Robin Hood, it will be recalled, was treacherously bled to death, but this only means that a very much older belief was transferred to his image. The most sacred spot in England is Glastonbury, where, long before the coming of St Augustine, British monks had established a monastery. Their traditions were from the north and from Ireland—basically Celtic. To Glastonbury it was said that Joseph of Arimathea brought the chalice in which the blood of Christ on the cross had been collected. At Glastonbury he built round this chalice, or Holy Grail, a frail hut to which pilgrims came in veneration. Today the visitor may see the ruins of the great Abbey which arose on that site, and the Holy Thorn which still flowers on the old day of Christmas. This is a cutting perpetuating the life of the original one. Historians may deny the truth of the story of Joseph of Arimathea coming to Glastonbury, and botanists can explain the flowering of the thorn at Christmas (which is no mystery at all when you know its species), but the faith of men for centuries was centred on that spot. In the song we have quoted the hound is Joseph of Arimathea and the thorn is that which we still know. The bleeding knight is Jesus. Glastonbury is rich in Celtic legend and Celtic relics. Near by is King Arthur's Causeway and his capital at Camelot; Celtic valour blended with the true Faith; troubadours carried the legends in song and story, and when chivalry had itself become legendary they came back to us in the romantic language of Malory's *Morte d'Arthur*. These were not the legends of the folk alone, but of all classes of men. The musical skill of the troubadours was directed to the ruling class, but it was fundamentally the music of folk and of church too, before the development of ecclesiastical polyphony (which is the interweaving of many different strands of melody into a composite whole). Norman troubadours had their carols and their ballads, and they took their themes one from the other. Here is one of the earliest ballads:

> Ore oez un bel chancon
> Des Jues de Nichole, qui pas trèison
> Firent la cruel occision
> De un enfant que Huchon out non.

> En Nichole, la rich citié,
> Dreit en Dernestal, l'enfant fui née
> De Peitevin le Ju fu emblé
> A la gule de aust, en un vespri.

The language is Anglo-Norman, but the thought is like any other ballad. Translated it might go:

> You shall hear a good song if you listen to me,
> Of the Jews of Lincoln, who treacherously
> Did plot and practise their villainy,
> And slew the child Hugo upon a tree.

In the city of Lincoln, rich and gay,
He was born in the Dernestal, all men say;
Now Peitevin the Jew has stolen away
The innocent babe at the close of day.

This is the beginning of one version of a story which embraces an essential part of English history in the thirteenth century. It has survived in folk-song and in English literature; Chaucer refers to it in *The Prioress's Tale* and Marlowe in *The Jew of Malta*. Crown, Church, and people were all involved in the events surrounding the death of a boy named Hugh; his age was about nine years, the date, 1255.

'Little Sir Hugh', or St Hugh, was the son of a Lincoln woman named Beatrice, and about the end of June (or possibly the end of August) in that year, he was found dead at the bottom of a well at the house of a Jew named Copin. Neighbours asserted that the boy carried the marks of crucifixion.

It was widely believed that Jews had a custom of crucifying a Christian child on Good Friday. Soon the news had spread that Copin the Jew had enticed the boy into his house to play, and that little Hugh was then tortured and finally crucified by Jews under the rule of a Rabbi called Peytinin the Great. Lincoln was a place renowned for its Jewish financiers in the early Middle Ages; Aaron of Lincoln in the twelfth century was one of the richest men in the country, whose debtors were spread everywhere. The stone house believed to be that used by the Lincoln Jews for a synagogue may still be seen on Steep Hill in that city. The Jews were the bankers of the time; they came into the country after the Norman Conquest and provided the capital needed for the consolidation of that conquest. They were useful to the State, but, being non-Christian, were anathema to the Church. So their position in England was precarious. They lived in districts still perpetuated by the name 'Jewry' or 'Old Jewry', doing the necessary work which Christians were at that time forbidden to do. It was against the doctrine of the Church for Christians to engage in usury. The Jews' rates of interest were high and their treatment of debtors ruthless, but certainly no worse than the treatment they received from Englishmen not in their power.[1] They were hated; they exploited the

[1] And by those indebted to them also. Many Jews' houses were looted in order to destroy documents.

English, and the English exploited them. Not content with borrowing money under contract from the Jews, the Crown repeatedly forced them to grant huge sums towards State expenditure until, in 1290, their vast resources being completely mulcted, they were driven from the country by Edward I.

The Church was always hostile. In 1144 a Christian boy of twelve was found dead in Thorpe Wood near Norwich. The story told by his mother was that a man called at their home and offered a situation for her son William in the kitchen of the archdeacon of Norwich. The mother allowed him to be taken away, but an aunt of the boy, suspicious, ordered her daughter to follow the man and the boy in order to see where he was taken. The girl said that he was taken to a Jew's house. Next, the boy was found dead. The Jews were accused of having committed a ritual murder. Such was the credulity of the people that the corpse of William was soon said to be working miracles. This was an excellent thing for the Church. William ultimately became a saint; his body was translated four times, on each occasion to a place of higher honour, until it lay at last in a chapel in the cathedral church, on the north side of the High Altar. This was the prototype of many such events; it was perhaps easy for a widow, when she lost her son by a violent death, to seek revenge upon the heathen. In later years the crime would have been attributed to witchcraft; in the twelfth and thirteenth centuries the Jews[1] were held responsible.

St Hugh of Lincoln was such a case. His death was made a reason for a pogrom. Many Jews were arrested, some executed, many tortured, and the whole Jewish community forced to pay an enormous sum to obtain the release of their compatriots from prison. The king and the Church profited; Hugh was made a saint and his bones an object of veneration, his mother basked in his reflected glory, and the populace had a scapegoat in the Jews which satisfied their blood-lust and raised them in the approval of Church and State. What better subject for a ballad?

> It rains, it rains, in merry Lincoln,
>   It rains both great and small,
> When all the boys came out to play,
>   To play and toss the ball.

[1] From the Christian point of view much the same. Both were heretical.

It rains, it rains in merry Lincoln, It rains both great and small. When all the boys come out to play, To play and toss the ball

They play, they toss the ball so high,
 They toss the ball so low,
The toss it over the Jews' garden,
 Where all the fine Jews go.

The first that came out was a Jew's daughter,
 Was dressèd all in green;
'Come in, come in, my little Sir Hugh
 To have your ball again.'

'I cannot come there, I will not come there,
 Without my playmates all,
For I know full well from my mother dear
 'Twill cause my blood to fall.'

The first she offered him was a fig,
 The next a finer thing;
The third was a cherry as red as blood,
 Which tolled the young thing in.

She sat him up in a gilty chair;
 She gave him sugar sweet;
She laid him out on a dresser board,
 And stabbed him like a sheep.

One hour and the school was over;
 His mother came out to call,
With a little rod under her apron
 To beat her son withal.

'Go home, go home, my heavy mother—
 Prepare a winding sheet;
And if my father should ask of me,
 You tell him I'm fast asleep.

My head is heavy, I cannot get up,
The well is cold and deep;
Besides, a penknife sticks in my heart,
So out I cannot creep.' [1]

All accounts blame the Jews, yet the legal evidence is flimsy and very largely hearsay. One party said that Copin enticed the boy Hugh into his house to play. (The ballads prefer to say that he was invited into a house by a Jew's daughter to reclaim his ball.) The Jews tortured him for ten days, feeding him meanwhile to keep up his strength; then he was crucified. Another account says much the opposite. According to this he was almost starved for twenty-six days while the Jews sent word to their brethren in other parts of the country to come to the ritual. This account says that on the twenty-sixth of August he was tried before a man acting the part of Pilate, was scourged, crowned with thorns, and crucified in mockery of Christ. There was evidence of a gathering of Jews at Lincoln at that time, but this was explained by the Jews as a gathering to celebrate a wedding. This it may well have been. The Jew Copin was tortured until he gave the names of those present, and an account of the crimes they committed on the boy. On his evidence the king's officers acted.

Years ago we should have said this story told of barbarous times, but now it has a modern ring, if we choose to omit the element of Christianity. All in all, we may doubt at times if materialist development has done anything to refine the popular mind. Are we, for all our scientific aids, able to provide finer architecture than the men of the thirteenth century? Can we provide better tunes than theirs? These things were done in response to ideals and beliefs, and mediaeval art bears evidence that such things were not held in contempt. The scales of justice were tipped against the prisoner, and his predicament was often a matter of diversion. It was a cruel age, yet one with a keen sense of humour. Their sense of fun peeps out from many a corner of our ancient churches, some of it even indecent, but while they were close to a belief which glorified fertility and ritual sacrifices, we profess to have left such things behind.

The Church encouraged a high standard of music, such as we

[1] Collected and arranged by Cecil J. Sharp; by permission of Novello & Co. Ltd.

cannot achieve today except by imitation, but to them it was a living tradition. They had taken it in part from an older faith and attributed their psalms to David. David danced before the Ark of the Lord, but this was conveniently forgotten when instructing the plain man, for dancing before a sacred object might put ideas into his head which the Church would have great difficulty in explaining.

Dancing was denounced by leaders of the Church, but this did not stop the populace from dancing; the dance went on as a secular accomplishment over which the Church had no control. On May-nights, Midsummer-nights, and at Christmas, the dancers had their fling, and their delights, as we have seen, never got right away from the pagan rituals which once they had served. The Church was wise in education, but always in a dilemma. The people loved mimicry, dressing up, and play-acting; the clergy took advantage of this to teach the Bible story. They acted in the churches. Then the revelry seemed inappropriate for such a place and the miracle-plays were given in the churchyard; at length they moved into the streets, and the craftsmen's guilds vied with each other in presentation of the various plays. Whitsuntide was a favourite time for such things. The performances took place on wheeled platforms called 'pageants', which were drawn through the town in succession. By remaining in one place the folk could see each play in turn, and in between could while away the time by singing carols on the subject of the play.

In the Coventry play of *The Nativity*, the lines were halting but the carols were superb. Herod raged, the angel came, Joseph and Mary set out with the Holy Child for Egypt, and women sang to their babes before the soldiers came to cut them down.

Herod (raging madly):
>   Out villain wretches, hereupon you I cry
>   My will utterly, look that it be wrought,
>   Or upon a gallows both you shall die,
>   By Mahound, most mightiest, that me dear hath bought!

1st Soldier:
>   Now, cruel Herod, sith we shall do this deed,
>   Your will needfully in this must be wrought.
>   All the children of that age, die they must need,
>   Now with all my might they shall be upsought.

2nd Soldier:

> And I will swear here upon your bright sword,
> All the children that I find, slain they shall be;
> That make many a mother to weep, and be full sore afeard,
> In our armour bright, when they us see.

Herod: Now you have sworn, forth that ye go,
> And my work that ye will both day and night,
> And then will I fain trip like a doe;
> But when they be dead, I warn you, bring them before my
>   sight.

.   .   .   .   .   .

Angel: Mary and Joseph, to you I say,
> Sweet word from the Father I bring you full right;
> Out of Bethlehem into Egypt forth go ye the way,
> And with you take the king, full of might,
> For dread of Herod's rede.

Joseph: Arise up, Mary, hastily and soon!
> Our Lord's will needs must be done,
> Like as the angel bade.

Mary: Meekly, Joseph, mine own spouse,
> Toward that country let us repair,
> In Egypt—some token of a house—
> God grant us grace safe to come there.

Exeunt Joseph and Mary. Enter women with babes. They sing.

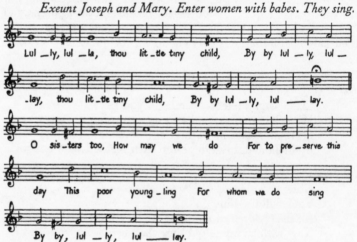

Lul—ly, lul—la, thou lit—tle tiny child, By by lul—ly, lul—lay, thou lit—tle tiny child, By by lul—ly, lul——lay.

O sis—ters too, How may we do For to pre—serve this day This poor young—ling For whom we do sing

By by, lul—ly, lul——lay.

This is a true carol of the period, composed of uniform stanzas and a burden. This burden, a distinct unit, starts the carol and is repeated after each verse.

This was the situation in the fifteenth century, when the word 'carol' had lost its association with the dance; their styles of costume we may see today in many a church window—angels dressed in feathered tights and with bare hands and feet (always men). The music was vastly different from plainsong. It was music on a sacred theme but not for ritual purposes. Music for the church ritual must be suitable purely for that use; plainsong has never been surpassed for its purpose, as musicians today are willing to admit; it makes use of voices in unison, the whole of the musical feeling being conveyed in the turn of the melody. During the fourteenth and fifteenth centuries, however, church musicians devoted their efforts to the development of many voices singing together their different melodies; this was the art of polyphony. Some of the world's greatest music has taken this style, which, once developed, was to revolutionize men's attitude towards the art of music.

Polyphony did not come entirely out of the schools, however; there was the practice of descant, which in thirteenth-century England meant adding an improvised melody above a well-known melody as the latter was being sung. Written examples of this remain from the end of the century, but unwritten ones may have been known earlier. In Wales the practice of penillion singing still persists, in which a harpist plays a common tune and a singer invents a tune to go with it. Mediaeval musicians practised 'organum', which was the running of a tune at different levels (a fourth, fifth, or octave apart) described in detail in any good history of music. This was a precursor of singing in many parts; it had its origin in folk music in the Mediterranean basin, and was contemporary with another folk fashion of singing in parallel thirds, practised by the Northern races, including the Celts. These usages were combined and applied to Church music round about the time when Chaucer was enriching English poetry with his humanistic verse; they were the work of scholars whose whole lives could be devoted to the development of their art.

It is then but natural that these musicians should discover ways of manipulating music which went beyond the knowledge of common men. The Masses of these composers were for trained singers to sing; a break took place between them and the common minstrels

* c

and simple folk, which some have interpreted as a kind of class war; it did divide people according to their educational opportunities, but the spiritual welfare of the people was never actually imperilled by music which was in any case only possible in monasteries or cathedrals or collegiate churches where trained choirs were to be found. The parish churches sang plainsong. There were the friars, from 1221, moving between ecclesiastical establishments and people, and important in the founding of universities; they, the common minstrels, the parish priests, clerks, and trained musicians must all have had a hand in the making of carols.

The carols come to us from the fifteenth century, a heritage from the time when the Bible was attracting attention and its story came to men as so much other information came, by word of mouth through ballads, plays, and carols. Of all these the carols are most distinctive; they satisfied intelligent men as well as idlers; if we think of them as Christmas hymns that is our misfortune, for they were not necessarily hymns, not necessarily for Christmas, and were not necessarily biblical. The *Boar's Head Carol,* still sung with its traditional ceremony at Queen's College, Oxford is secular, with a little Latin worked in to please the merry scholars.

Caput apri defero,
Reddens laudes Domino.

The boar's head in hand bear I,
Bedecked with bays and rosemary;
I pray you, my masters, be merry,
　Quot estis in convivio:

Caput apri defero,
Reddens laudes Domino.

The boar's head, as I understand,
Is the rarest dish in all this land,
Which thus bedecked with a gay garland,
　Let us *servire cantico.*

Caput apri defero
Reddens laudes Domino.

Our steward hath provided this,
In honour of the King of bliss,
Which on this day to be servèd is,
    In Reginensi atrio:

        Caput apri defero,
        Reddens laudes Domino.

At this point we may conveniently refer to the *Dilly Song* given earlier in this chapter. There are many versions of it. That given relies on the unexplained riddle for its attraction, but the one which follows—a carol version of the same theme—is self-explanatory; yet imagination still colours the exposition of the faith, the twelve riddles being considered as the twelve numerals on a dial. That is its name, *The New Dial.*

> *In those twelve days let us be glad,*
> *For God of his power hath all things made.*
> What are they that are but one?
> *What are they that are but one?*
> One God, one Baptism, and one Faith,
> One Truth there is, the scripture saith.
>
> What are they that are but two?
> Two Testaments, the old and new,
> We do acknowledge to be true.
>
> What are they that are but three?
> Three Persons are in Trinity,
> Which make one God in unity.
>
> What are they that are but four?
> Four sweet Evangelists there are,
> Christ's birth, life, death, which do declare.
>
> What are they that are but five?
> Five senses, like five kings, maintain
> In every man a several reign.
>
> What are they that are but six?
> Six days to labour is not wrong,
> For God himself did work so long.

What are they that are but seven?
Seven liberal arts hath God sent down,
With divine skill man's soul to crown.

What are they that are but eight?
Eight beatitudes are there given;
Use them right and go to heaven.

What are they that are but nine?
Nine Muses, like the heavens' nine spheres,
With sacred tunes entice our ears.

What are they that are but ten?
Ten statutes God to Moses gave,
Which, kept or broke, do spill or save.

What are they that are but eleven?
Eleven thousand virgins did partake.[1]
And suffered death for Jesus' sake.

What are they that are but twelve?
Twelve are attending on God's Son;
Twelve make our Creed. The Dial's done.

---

[1] There really were eleven virgins—not 11,000. Written in Roman numerals,
XI.M.V., intended as an abbreviation of eleven martyr-virgins, was read as XI millia
(11,000) virgins; so the carol has got 10,989 virgins too many.

IV. The Food of Love

##

Play on;
Give me excess of it.

TWELFTH NIGHT, I. i.

IN ALL THE MUSIC we have considered so far, one thought has been paramount; it was not primarily valued for itself alone, but was made to serve some purpose: primitive ritual in the dance, story-telling in the ballads, Christian teaching in the riddle of the *Dilly Song*, and race-hatred in the ballad of *Little Sir Hugh*. If we follow our theme into the Court we shall find music used there for ceremonial purposes, with trumpets decorated with heraldic banners, and the general effect both loud and bright. Music here was secondary to the grandeur of the spectacle, whereas in church it was secondary to the ritual. This is not special pleading for a convenient theory, however obnoxious it may seem to the modern musical specialist, but a simple statement of history. The conception of music as justified for itself alone is a modern theory, being presented today with great fervour by professionals who like to have their own way, but it is not proved true to the exclusion of older beliefs. Shakespeare was certain of the effects of music on his playhouse audiences: he never used it amiss, and in his speeches says of music what all men thought at that time. When Bassanio goes to choose which of the caskets contains Portia's picture, she cannot tell him what she thinks; but Shakespeare adds music to the scene, and Portia's thoughts on music beautify and elucidate the emotional situation.

Portia: Let music sound while he doth make his choice;
Then, if he lose, he makes a swan-like end,
Fading in music: that the comparison
May stand more proper, my eye shall be the stream
And watery death-bed for him. He may win;
And what is music then? Then music is
Even as the flourish when true subjects bow

77

> To a new-crowned monarch; such it is
> As are those dulcet sounds in break of day
> That creep into the dreaming bridegroom's ear
> And summon him to marriage.[1]

Soon comes the music, as Bassanio makes his choice. For the audience it is a moment of suspense. The song tells of fancy, which to Shakespeare and his audience is here the fantastic or the cunningly contrived. (A *Fancy* was *inter alia* the English name for a *Fantasia* in music)—so—

> Tell me where is fancy bred,
> Or in the heart or in the head?
> How begot, how nourished?
>   Reply, reply.
> It is engender'd in the eyes,
> With gazing fed; and fancy dies
> In the cradle where it lies.
>   Let us all ring fancy's knell;
>   I'll begin it, Ding, dong, bell.

And Bassanio's choice is affected by the thought that external show is not all. 'So may the outward shows be least themselves,' he says; 'the world is still deceived with ornament.'

So is it with folk-song. Beautiful as these may be in form, there lies within the best of them something personal to the heart of man or woman which is too deep for logic; it will not reveal itself by artifice alone, but depends on human hopes and disappointments—feelings which all can reciprocate; music and verbal imagery come into the song to elevate it above the commonplace, as Portia thought to dignify the possible failure of Bassanio with the image of the swan which sings as it dies. The song, however, is supplementary—the human emotion is the basis of the art. So it is with this folk-song.

> In my garden grew plenty of thyme,
> It would flourish by night and by day;
>   O'er the wall came a lad,
>   He took all that I had,
>   And stole my thyme away.

[1] *The Merchant of Venice*, Act III, Sc. ii.

Artifice is there in all conscience, with a pun on the ideas of thyme the herb and time for duration, but the pun for some reason is not vulgar, though the theme is common enough—the loss of virginity, by implication, even though the act is not mentioned. As in *Hamlet* Laertes said of Ophelia's song, 'This nothing's more than matter'. *Hamlet* is an excellent play for those who would know more about folk-songs.

'There's rosemary, that's for remembrance; pray you, love, remember; and there is pansies, that's for thoughts. . . . There's fennel for you, and columbines; there's rue for you: and here's some for me; we may call it herb-grace o' Sundays. O! you must wear your rue with a difference. There's a daisy; I would give you some violets, but they withered all when my father died.' [1]

For the violet is a frail flower, fragrant, but passing too soon; so Ophelia thinks of her father. It is all expressed by the symbolism of flowers, which an Elizabethan audience would understand. The puns are images which bind together two different thoughts into a common bond. Rue is a bitter herb used in medicine, so the verb 'to rue' implies bitterness in repentance. 'Sinner's rue' can be a description of the plant, or a moral statement if the apostrophe were left out (and the apostrophe is only for the eye). When Shakespeare made Ophelia mad he simplified her mind; took away the trained lady and left the natural young woman who has suffered from a fate she did not choose. The flower symbols he used were effective partly by reason of their simplicity; and the fact that they were to be found in so many folk-songs would also tend to suggest the basic humanity of his theme.

> With June is the red rose in bud,
> But that was no flower for me;
> I plucked the bud and it pricked me to blood,
> And I gazed on the willow tree.

The rose stands for passionate, mature love, but it carries a thorn which will wound; and what is left then? Lifelong disappointment which is symbolized by the willow. Now we can feel with Desdemona in *Othello*. The song she sings in her distress is remodelled from one familiar to Shakespeare's audiences; it is not a folk-song, but consider nevertheless its poetry.

[1] *Hamlet*, Act IV, Sc. v.

A poor soul sat sighing by a sycamore tree—
  Sing willow, willow, willow—
With hand in his bosom, and head upon his knee—
  Sing willow, willow, willow;
O willow, willow, willow shall be my garland—
  Sing all a green willow—
  Willow, willow, willow—
Aye me, the green willow shall be my garland.

He sighed in his singing and made a great moan,
                    Sing willow, etc.
I am dead to all pleasure, my true love she is gone,
                    Sing willow, etc.

By cutting out the repeated refrain we can concentrate on the story, such as it is.

The mute bird sat by him was made tame by his moans;
The true tears fell from him would have melted the stones.

Come all you forsaken, and mourn here with me,
Who speaks of a false love, mine's falser than she.

Let love no more boast her in palace or bower,
It buds but it blasteth, e'er it be a flower.

Thou fair and more false, I die with thy wound;
Thou hast lost the truest lover that goes upon ground.

Let nobody chide her, her scorns I approve;
She was born to be false, and I to die for love.

Take this for my farewell and latest adieu;
Write this on my tomb, that in love I was true.

Shakespeare has to change the sex of the song-character to apply to Desdemona, but he does something else—he selects.

The poor soul sat sighing by a sycamore tree,
  Sing all a green willow;

Her hand on her bosom, her head on her knee;
    Sing willow, willow, willow;
The fresh streams ran by her, and murmur'd her moans;
    Sing willow, willow, willow;
Her salt tears fell from her and softened the stones;
    Sing willow, willow, willow.[1]

Shakespeare has avoided the sentimentality of the original, where the moaning lover really sighs not for his beloved but for himself. Such songs of melancholy were a fashion at the time, but Shakespeare had to strengthen the character to fit into the tragic mould in which Desdemona was to be cast. We expect such strength of character from a mind as rich as Shakespeare's, but the question may well be asked, have we any right to expect it from simpler minds? Perhaps not, but what about this?

'Twas early in the Springtime of the year,
    When the sun did begin to shine;
Oh I had three branches, all for to choose but one,
    And the first I chose was thyme.

Thyme, thyme, it is a precious thing—
    It's a root that the sun shines on;
And time it will bring everything to an end—
    And so our time goes on.

And while that I had my thyme all for my own,
    It did flourish by night and day,
Till who came along but a jolly sailor lad,
    And stole my thyme away.

And now my thyme is perished for me,
    And I never shall plant it more;
Since into the place where my thyme did use to spring
    Is grown a running rue.

Rue, rue, it is a running root,
    And it runs all too fast for me;
I'll dig up the bed where thyme of old was laid
    And plant there a brave oak tree.

[1] *Othello*, Act IV, Sc. iii.

Stand up, oh stand up, my jolly oak!
    Stand you up, for you shall not die!
For I'll be so true to the one I love so dear
    As the stars shine bright in the sky.

The sentiments speak for themselves. True courage is cast into a beautiful mould. But let us not leave folk-song thus, for it may be an exception; let us go on to its companion song, different in its ending, but equally staunch.

I sowed the seeds of love;
I sowed them in the spring;
I gathèred up in the morning so soon
While small birds did sweetly sing.

My garden is well planted
With flowers everywhere,
But I had not the liberty to choose for myself
Of the flowers that I loved dear.

My gardener he stood by,
I asked him to choose for me;

He chose me the violet, the lily and the pink,
But these I refused all three.

The violet I did not like,
Because it fades so soon;
The lily and the pink I did overthink,[1]
And I vowed I would stay till June.

For in June there's a red rosebud,
And that's the flower for me,
So I pulled and I plucked at the red rosebud
Till I gainèd the willow tree.

For the willow tree will twist,
And the willow tree will twine;
I wish I was in a young man's arms
That once had this heart of mine.

After the words, the tunes. Here are eight out of the innumerable
variants known.

[1] 'Overthink' = reject.

All eight versions of this tune given have been selected from the larger list quoted by A. H. Fox Strangways in Chapter VI of his book *The Music of Hindustan*. He has taken them from the much more comprehensive number which have appeared in the *English Folk Song Society's Journal*. Fox Strangways there uses them to illustrate the nature of modal music, and the reader who desires to know the way in which Eastern and Western minds think in terms of music should read this book.

Variation of melody is a factor of the greatest importance in all folk-song, so much so that Cecil Sharp, who did more actual field-work in this than anybody in England, said that variation of the tune was so natural to folk-singers that they were not aware they did it. The reason is that the singer thought of the tune as a vehicle to carry the words, which were the essence of the song. Again we must try to adapt ourselves to a difference of opinion between folk-singers and educated music-lovers, for the poems of folk-songs are in educated opinion the weaker partner, as inferior to the tunes as the plumage of a hen bird is to that of its mate. The tune would vary from verse to verse in order to fit the words or adapt itself to the emotional stress; it came from the heart rather than from the head.

Nevertheless there are styles of singing dictated by mental qualities which will inflict themselves on a song; Cecil Sharp heard a group of singers joining in the chorus of *Brennan on the Moor,* but all singing their own variations of the tune without apparently knowing that these made (to Sharp's ears) 'cacophony . . . which grew worse rather than better as the song proceeded'.[1] There is a name for this behaviour which has only lately found its way into musical treatises—heterophony.[2]

In the variants quoted I have arranged the eight versions according to what I feel to be their singers' show of spirit, No. 8 being a lively effort with dash in its later-middle section, but I do not insist that I am right in this arrangement. No. 6 in particular (a hypodorian version in twelve-eight time) may strike some readers as the proper version to come at the end. In any case we must free ourselves from the notion that folk-song is a process of musical evolution inevitably developing to a single pinnacle of perfection. In my opinion the most satisfactory version quoted here is No. 5,

---

[1] Cecil Sharp, *English Folksong—Some Conclusions*, 1907, p. 19.

[2] The eight variants of *The Seeds of Love* as quoted do not represent heterophonic style. They are of varying length and in different keys.

with its magnificent octave leap on the dominant. The last four tunes are of ten bars instead of eight; in these versions the last line is repeated—the mind of the singer meditates on the theme.

These are true folk-songs, but because we have compared them with Shakespeare's songs we must not restrict them to the folk-singers of his period. They are meditative songs, and meditation takes time. In turning over the song in one's mind changes come to be made in its structure and message; this is the basis of the evolutionary theory as applied to folk-song. Modern psychologists tell us that we forget a thing because we do not wish to remember it; if this is true it may well be that among those folk-singers whose minds are more refined than the average, the crude lines of a song slip the memory, and others have to be substituted to fill the gap. Such a theory would account for these meditative or dream-songs being of such high quality, but we must allow time for this process to work—probably centuries. The singer producing a song out of his own head immediately would probably produce something very crude unless he were a man with a good cultural background.[1] That cultural background need not be literary, nor the result of scholastic conditioning, but may be a folk-culture existing in sound and taught orally by singer to singer. Such culture will always exist and its adherents will often think it better than the art of the trained mind, but this is by no means trustworthy opinion. We have compared examples of folk-song with the thought of Shakespeare in order to show how some folk-songs will stand the comparison, but Shakespeare knew as well as anyone that the folk also produced some dreadful rubbish.

He is not antagonistic to his working-class characters except when they are bad men, but he knows their limitations as poets. After all, Shakespeare and his fellow playwrights had got away from the halting lines of the miracle plays which the balladeers were still using. This is the style of the honest mechanics in *A Midsummernight's Dream*.[2]

Peter Quince: Well, we will have such a prologue; and it shall be written in eight and six.

Bottom: No, make it two more; let it be written in eight and eight.

[1] This can be proved from comparisons in ballads. Many ballads were topical and had only an immediate appeal.
[2] Act III, Sc. i.

A line of eight feet followed by a line of six feet is the sort of thing Bottom sang later in the scene.

> The ousel cock, so black of hue,
>   With orange-tawny bill,
> The throstle with his note so true,
>   The wren with little quill.

Titania: What angel wakes me from my flowery bed?

Bottom: The finch, the sparrow, and the lark,
         The plain-song cuckoo gray,
     Whose note full many a man doth mark
     And dares not answer nay.

As for eight and eight, *As You Like It* [1] contains a good deal of parody of style—fashionable and folk—including this.

Touchstone: I'll rhyme you so eight years together, dinners and suppers and sleeping-hours excepted: it is the right butter-woman's rank to market.
Rosalind: Out, fool!
Touchstone: For a taste:
     If a hart do lack a hind,
     Let him seek out Rosalind.
     If the cat will after kind,
     So be sure will Rosalind.
     Winter garments must be lined,
     So must slender Rosalind.
     They that reap must sheaf and bind,
     Then to cart with Rosalind.
     Sweetest nut hath sourest rind,
     Such a nut is Rosalind.
     He that sweetest rose will find
     Must find love's prick and Rosalind.
This is the very false gallop of verses: why do you infect yourself with them?
Rosalind: Peace, you dull fool! I found them on a tree.
Touchstone: Truly, the tree yields bad fruit.

[1] Act III, Sc. ii.

Public playhouses in Shakespeare's London were disreputable places. Ladies would be masked when they attended. Shakespeare himself wrote of the temptation to use bawdy jests to tickle the ears of the 'groundlings' in the theatre pit,[1] but it is not in the great plays that we should look for smut. This was the lure of the afterplay, which came on when the main drama had finished. The afterplay was called a 'jig', and was a ballad, sung and danced, sometimes with dialogue inserted. The jigs were the comedians' opportunities —bawdy, satirical, even libellous. They played down to the public, and not merely the cheap public in the pit, but the educated public in the galleries and on the stage. Often these people had had a hand in the affair, to make fools of their political enemies; the mob always responds to such slush. Among the comedians was Will Kemp, who created the part of Dogberry in *Much Ado about Nothing*; Will Kemp has been credited with a jig called *Rowland*, followed by *Rowland's Godson*, about 1590. The fact that Kemp played in these does not prove he wrote them. *Attowell's Jig*, about five years later, used four tunes, *Walsingham*, *The Jewish Dance*, *Bugle Boe*, and *Go from my Window*. These are folk-songs, and good ones. In 1595 Will Kemp took part in a jig called *Singing Simpkin*, which had a vogue fit to make Gilbert and Sullivan gasp. It ran intermittently for a century on the Continent and in England. The attraction of rough humour and catchy tunes is no new thing.

Something must be said about the influence of these jigs on continental taste. They spread across the Low Countries and into Germany, where they proved popular, and stimulated the German form of comic opera with spoken dialogue called *Singspiel*. When you see Mozart's *Magic Flute*, think of the Elizabethan afterpieces they forbore to teach you when you were at school, then you will understand better the greatness of Mozart, though this opera itself has no English influences unless they be in Freemasonry.

The Third Parte of Kemp's Jig (*Singing Simpkin*) may be taken as a sample of the popular style in Shakespeare's theatre. There are four characters: Simpkin, a clown; Bluster, a 'roarer', or bully; an Old Man; and his wife who is cuckolding him. Let us take a short extract from the middle of the jig, when the dramatic action is brisk. The old husband is away, and Simpkin has been making love to the old man's wife. They have been interrupted by a knock on the door, and, thinking that this denotes the return of the husband, the

[1] *Hamlet:* 'He's for a jig, or a tale of bawdry, or he sleeps.'

wife has concealed Simpkin in a large chest. She opens the door, but the visitor is not her husband but Bluster, come also to make love.

Bluster: Where is the foole thy husband?
            Say, whither is he gone?
Wife: The Wittall is a-hunting,
Bluster: Then we two are alone.
            But should he come and find me here,
                What might the cuckold think?
            Perhaps he'd call the neighbours in—
Simpkin: And beat you till you stink.
Bluster: Yet in the bloody war full oft
                My courage I did try.
Wife: I know you have killed many a man—
Simpkin: You lie, you slut, you lie.
Bluster: I never came before a foe,
                By night nor yet by day,
            But that I stoutly roused myself—
Simpkin: And nimbly ran away.
Bluster: Within this chest I'll hide myself,
                If it chance he should come.
Wife: O no, my love, that cannot be,
Simpkin: I have bespoke the room.
Wife: I have a place behind here,
                Which yet is known to no man.
Simpkin: She has a place before, too,
                But that is all too common.
                            There is a knock at the door.
Old Man: Wife, wherefore is the door thus barred?
                What mean you, pray, by this?
Wife: Alas, it is my husband!
Simpkin: I laugh now till I piss.
Bluster: Open the chest, I'll into it,
                My life else it may cost.
Wife: Alas, I cannot open it.
Simpkin: I believe the key is lost.

This is a situation similar to many which have been staged in comic opera. In fact, the persons of an elderly man with a young wife or lover being outwitted by the lady, the crafty young yokel, and the

boastful coward are stock characters in *opéra buffa, opéra comique,*
and *singspiel,* to say nothing of English comic opera. To extricate
the lover from his predicament without revealing to the husband the
wife's infidelity is a task calling for as much ingenuity as the solution
of 'who did the murder' in a modern thriller. The rule was that the
extrication must come as a result of the types of behaviour to be
expected from the characters employed. The wife in *Singing
Simpkin* plays off the three men accordingly. Bluster is commanded
to draw his sword, and with a great shout rush from the house as
though in pursuit of an enemy. The husband accepts the explanation
when, later, Simpkin is discovered. Simpkin pretends he has come to
buy cider. The husband, aided by his wife, cheats Simpkin of half a
crown, and the latter is driven from the house with blows. Thus
marital harmony is preserved and the rascals get out of the house
without their full intentions being revealed. The husband is
deceived, the lovers escape, and the wife preserves her mastery of
the situation by reason of a quick wit.

Comedians thrive on self-advertisement, and Will Kemp was no
exception. Among his best publicity campaigns was the publication
of *Kemp's Nine Daies Wonder, Performed in a Daunce from London
to Norwich* undertaken in 1600. An illustration shows Kemp dancing
alone to the music of a man playing on the pipe and tabor (the latter
being a small drum and the former a long whistle on which the
whole scale can be played with the breath and three fingers of one
hand). Kemp is dressed in a flowered costume with bells about his
calves and flowing wide ribbons (or napkins) from his arms. The
costume, and the step he is making, can still be seen in some parts
of England, particularly in the Cotswolds. Certainly the custom of
dancing the Morris dances has gone on in an unbroken tradition
at Bampton in Oxfordshire each Whit Monday for four hundred
years. Headington Quarry, near Oxford, is another village where the
tradition has been preserved. There is also a distinctive Derbyshire
Morris, and in Lancashire it takes on another style, but fundamentally these dances all derive from the Spring Festival. They are
the successors of the ritual dance of the young men who awakened
the year to life; their waving handkerchiefs and gay ribbons give
their dance an airy 'lift', and their jingling stamp would waken any
spirit from its grave.

Kemp used the dance for advertisement because of its great popularity in the reign of the first Elizabeth. He did not have to do all his

own advertising however; once given a start others did it for him; indeed he picked up from a common catch-phrase which Shakespeare quotes in *Love's Labour's Lost* and *Hamlet*—'The hobby-horse is forgot'. Kemp, in his *Nine Daies Wonder*, quotes it thus: 'But I had the heaviest way that ever mad Morrice dancer trod'.

> With hey and ho, through thick and thin,
> The hobby-horse quite forgotten,
> I followed as I did begin,
> Although the way were rotten.

Which is no better as poetry than it ought to be. But Thomas Weelkes the madrigalist was an artist of another stamp, and you will find this in his *Ayeres or Phantasticke Spirites*, of 1608: [1]

Since Robin Hood, Maid Marian, and Little John are gone-a,
The hobby-horse was quite forgot when Kemp did dance alone-a.

Which Weelkes set to the tune of *Nobody's Jig*, a variant of the *Helston Furry* tune.

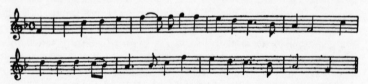

Weelkes then switches to triple time for a new musical quotation to the words

> He did labour after the tabor,
> For to dance then into France.

The tune being known as *Watkins' Ale*.

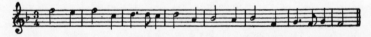

The Watkins celebrated in this tune was 'Mother Watkins', which will serve as a reminder that the brewing of ale was once a domestic duty. It is in the canzonets and ballets of the Elizabethan

[1] Cf. John Horton, 'Some Folk Elements in the Elizabethan Madrigal', *Journal of the English Folk Dance and Song Society*, Vol. IV.

composers that dance rhythms are mostly to be found, but Thomas
Morley put a realistic description of a likely scene into a madrigal.

> Soft awhile piper, not away so fast! They melt them.
> Be hanged knave! See'st thou not the dancers swelt them?
> Stand out awhile! You come too far in, I say, in.
> There give the hobby-horse more room to play in.

They sat round the table after supper, those merry Elizabethans,
and sang their madrigals about fantastic nymphs and shepherds, but
for all their artistry they were not divorced from the common
tunes. Will Kemp's stage jig *Rowland* has been lost, but a text has
been found in a German translation,[1] with this tune to carry the lines.

Kemp was one of the Earl of Leicester's players, and his patron's
successor in the Netherlands was Peregrine Bertie, Lord Wil-
loughby. When the latter returned to England in 1598 the players
welcomed him with a ballad set to the tune they had made famous
on the stage both here and abroad. This tune William Byrd took for
a set of variations to be played on the virginals, calling it *Rowlande
—Lord Willobie's Welcome home*. Here is Byrd's arrangement of the
phrase quoted above; note in particular how the mind of William
Byrd develops the structure. The fingers on the keyboard decide
the lie of the parts, but see also how, as soon as Byrd begins to
elaborate the theme, the F sharps appear. The composer is pulling
the mode towards our modern conception of G minor, with its
sharpened leading-note.

---

[1] Rowland, *Hainhafer's Lute Book*, 1603. Cf. Baskervill, *The Elizabethan Jig*,
1929, p. 231.

This was the dawn of another phase of musical history—the development of keyboard music, with variations on *Sellenger's Round*, *The Carman's Whistle*, *Walsingham*, *The Woods so Wild* by William Byrd, or *Loth to Depart* and *Quodling's Delight* by Giles Farnaby. *O Mistress Mine*—which we know from *Twelfth Night*—is used by Morley in his *Consort Lessons* as an instrumental piece. *My Ladye Nevell's Booke* and the *Fitzwilliam Virginal Book* contain English hornpipes and Morris as well as the new continental dances. And why not? Were we not a nation of adventurers; and if we sailed to the New World in ships, was it not exciting in another way to explore the possibilities of new effects in music, and set the seal of human passion on imperishable verse?

Will Kemp's Dance.

V. Dissension and Distress

And the face of the King's Servants grew greater than the King:
He tricked them, and they trapped him, and stood round him in a ring.
The new grave lords closed round him, that had eaten the abbey's fruits,
And the men of the new religion, with their bibles in their boots,
We saw their shoulders moving, to menace or discuss,
And some were pure and some were vile; but none took heed of us.
We saw the King as they killed him, and his face was proud and pale;
And a few men talked of freedom, while England talked of ale.

G. K. CHESTERTON

THERE IS A MISCONCEPTION abroad that it is only of recent years that men have taken an interest in folk-songs and dances. This is not so, for folk-song enthusiasts draw for information on the printed collections of former centuries, compiled by writers who did not use the word 'folk-song'. The truth is that the modern enthusiast has a sense of responsibility towards folk-song to preserve it as it comes from the lips of the traditional singers, and not to transform it into something out of its kind. It is a practice easily ridiculed. Ben Jonson made fun of a connoisseur of popular ballads in his play *Bartholomew Fair*. Here we are introduced to a ballad-singer and a foolish squire who has a passion for ballads and a trust in itinerant singers not justified by their character. Ben Jonson's ballad-monger appears on the stage with his printed broadsheets flying, and sings the beginning of one of his songs to attract a crowd.

My masters and friends and good people draw near,
    And look to your purses, for that I do say;
And tho' little money in them you do bear,
    It costs more to get than to lose in a day.

'Ha, ha; this chimes!' says the witless squire who is the prototype of stage folk-song collectors. 'Good counsel at first dash.'

93

The ballad is *A Caveat against cut-purses,* and goes to the tune of *Paggington's Pound,* with verses like this.

> At Worc'ster, 'tis known well, and even in the jail,
>   A knight of good worship did there show his face,
> Against the foul sinners in zeal for to rail,
>   And lost *ipso facto* his purse in the place.
>   Nay, once from the seat
>   Of judgment so great,
> A judge there did lose a fair pouch of velvète;
> O Lord in thy mercy, how wicked or worse,
> Are those that so venture their necks for a purse!
> Youth, youth, thou had'st better been starved by thy nurse,
> Than live to be hangèd for cutting a purse.

And as the ballad-singer holds the squire's attention with his song, an accomplice tickles the squire on the ear with a straw; he removes his hand from his pocket to scratch himself, and the thief picks his pocket. Nothing could be simpler: only a fool would go to Bartholomew Fair with such credulity.

For if a man is not a rogue and vagabond, why does he hawk ballads at a fair? Once, the minstrel in the Saxon manor had been a man with his position recognized in society, but those days were over. The mediaeval wandering fiddler had come down in the world, inveigling himself into any company where free victuals were going. 'Not to fare as a fiddler or a friar, to seek feasts,' said *Piers Plowman,*[1] and where the fiddler and the friar went together the tumbler, juggler, cutpurse, and wanton woman were not far off. Nevertheless the mediaeval minstrel had been a musician; he made up his songs for the occasion and sang them, and played his fiddle, pipe, or bagpipes for the dance; but Ben Jonson's ballad-monger bought his ballads printed on broad sheets of paper which he sold for a penny, like a vendor of gingerbread or any other trifle: there was a difference.

It would be foolish to expect the printer not to cash in on the demand for ballads, and equally foolish to expect him to turn out superior productions for such a market; broadsheet (or broadside) ballads were often corrupted versions of songs which were better before they were printed, but they are part of the sum of popular literature. Many are without merit, but some have meaning for us.

[1] 1362-92.

One thing must be made clear before we proceed. The verse by Jonson just quoted is described as a ballad, but this is a very loose description; neither in form nor in spirit does it comply with the definition of a ballad given in Chapters II and III above. A ballad should relate a story impersonally, though in it the characters may speak their lines in the first person.

Queen Jane was in labour full six weeks and more,
And the women were weary, and fain would give o'er;
'O women, O women, as women ye be,
Rip open my two sides and save my baby.'

'O royal Queen Jane, that thing may not be;
We'll send for King Henry to come unto thee.'
King Henry came to her, and sate on her bed;
'What ails my dear lady, her eyes look so red?'

'O royal King Henry, do one thing for me;
Rip open my two sides and save my baby.'
'O royal Queen Jane, that thing will not do;
If I lose your fair body, I'll lose your baby too.'

She wept and she waild, and she wrung her hands sore;
O the flower of England must flourish no more!
She wept and she waild till she fell in a swound,
They opened her two sides and the baby was found.

The baby was christened with joy and much mirth,
Whilst poor Queen Jane's body lay cold under earth;
There was ringing and singing and mourning all day,
The Princess Elizabeth went weeping away.

This ballad of *The Bedding of Jane Seymour* (mother of Edward VI) is not strictly true to history, for Jane had a natural delivery but died twelve days later as a result of faulty aftercare. It is the dramatic force of the ballad which attracts us, however; the art had to vivify an event, not merely record it. Consider, then, how ballads vivify thought in a broader theme.

In March 1549 Hugh Latimer preached his first sermon before

Edward VI, entitled *Of the Plough*, wherein he spoke from his own experience of changing conditions.

My father was a yeoman, and had no lands of his own, only he had a farm of three or four pounds by year at the uttermost, and thereupon he tilled so much as kept half a dozen men. He had a walk for a hundred sheep, and my mother milked thirty kine. He was able, and did find the king a harness with himself and his horse, while he came to the place where he should receive the king's wages. I can remember that I buckled his harness when he went into Blackheath Field.

By this Latimer meant that his father was able not only to provide for his family but to do his duty as a defender of his king. By 'harness' he meant a suit of armour, and at Blackheath Field the Cornish rebels were defeated in 1497.

He kept me to school, or else I had not been able to have preached before the King's Majesty now. He kept hospitality for his poor neighbours, and some alms he gave to the poor. And all this he did of the said farm, where he that hath it now payeth sixteen pound by the year, or more, and is not able to do anything for his prince, for himself, for his children, or give a cup of drink to the poor.

Turn now from this sermon to a ballad, first printed about fifty years after Latimer delivered his sermon, but it tells the same tale.

> I read, in ancient days of yore,
>   That men of worthy calling,
> Built almshouses and spittles store,
>   Which now are all down falling;
> And few men seek them to repair,
>   Nor is there one among twenty,
> That for good deeds takes any care,
>   While Mock-Beggar Hall stands empty.
>
> Young landlords when to age they come,
>   Their rents they will be racking;
> The tenant must give a golden sum,
>   Or else is turned out packing;
> Great fines and double rent beside,
>   Or else they'll not content be,
> It is to maintain their monstrous pride
>   While Mock-Beggar Hall stands empty.

It may well be that some will muse
　　Wherefore, in this relation,
The name of Mock-beggar I do use
　　Without an explanation;
To clear which doubt before I end,
　　Because they shall all content be,
To show the meaning I do intend
　　Of Mock-Beggar Hall still empty.

Some gentlemen and citizens have,
　　In divers eminent places,
Erected houses, rich and brave,
　　Which stood for the owners' graces;
Let any poor to such a door
　　Come, they expecting plenty,
There they may ask till their throats are sore,
　　For Mock-Beggar Hall stands empty.

The decline of the good old days is a perennial theme, and varies according to the amount of change which is taking place at the time. No period is ever without change, but the Tudor period saw a dizzy seesaw of events which shook the people with many a sorry jolt. Monarchs had a lot to do with it, but not all. Economic forces were at work which were a heritage from the past. The Black Death of 1348-9 also, by its reduction of population, caused a scarcity of labour which induced landowners to let out some of their land for rent to anyone who could farm it. Sheep-farming was another way of employing the land with less labour. So there grew up a way of life in which great profits were made from sheep (as the fine churches of the Cotswolds indicate to this day) and a class of men who were small farmers and tenants of the landowners. Such a man was Bishop Latimer's father. Many of these tenants would hold their farms as leaseholds or copyholds; their rent was fixed according to the agreement; if prices rose the farmer prospered, but in this case the landowner was not so well off, because he would have to pay more for food and clothing out of a fixed income. He had to improve his lot by raising rents as leases fell in, and in fixing fines, or money payments, additional to the rent, when a farmer wished to come to a new agreement. The situation was one of 'pull devil, pull tailor'. Another method of dealing with the problem was to enclose common lands and add these to one's holdings, thus robbing the peasantry of common rights.

With the increase of trade in wool, merchants prospered; then, when in 1536–9 the monastic lands were seized, much more land was thrown on the market to be bought up by speculative townsmen and let out for rent. As if this were not enough, in the last years of his reign Henry VIII debased the coinage and prices again rocketed. The landlord had to force up rents by every device he could apply, or be ruined, but nobody had any sympathy for him. Then came another change, in Elizabeth's reign, when British sea-dogs harried the Spaniards and came home laden with cargoes of silver from the New World. Prices rose again. Some were rich, others poor; so at the one end of the social scale luxury increased (in some cases with extravagant spending) and at the other poverty gnawed with greater and greater ferocity. It was a disturbing situation. A children's rhyme preserves the memory.

> Hark, hark, the dogs do bark!
>   Beggars are coming to town.
> Some in rags, some in jags,
>   And one in a velvet gown.

No longer was the Church in a position to care for the poor. Church lands had been confiscated, and the many servants employed by the monks thrown out of work. Greed and vice had imperilled the monasteries before Henry VIII plundered them, however; he could not have done so had there not been many people in the Church itself desirous of reform. Latimer was one of those who expected that when the king took the monastic lands he would use these to endow schools and charities. How he was deceived! The State was no better than the Church.

When Latimer preached before Edward VI he must have been aware of certain disturbing signs. Beggars were condemned in 1531 to be 'tied to the end of a cart, naked, and be beaten with whips throughout the same market town or other place till his body be bloody by reason of such whipping'.[1] They were also ordered to go home to their parish of birth. Gradually the harsh treatment of vagrants increased, until in 1547 punishment went too far. Edward VI passed an Act by which vagrants could be made slaves if they

[1] 22 Hen. VIII, c. 12 (1530–1).

did not offer themselves for labour without wages (i.e. offer to work for meat and drink alone). They could be taken before the Justice of the Peace, who could order them to be branded on the chest with a large V, given in charge of a master who could give the slave only bread and water, or small drink, and only as much as he thought fit, drive him at work by beating, chaining, 'and otherwise in such work and labour how vile so ever it be as he shall put him into. And if any slave shall run away from his master the justices shall cause him to be marked on the forehead or ball of the cheek with an hot iron with the sign of an S, and shall judge the runaway to be the said master's slave forever. And if such slave shall the second time run away . . . such runaway to be taken as a felon and condemned to suffer pains of death, as other felons ought to do'. Further provisions were for the sale of slaves or their service, like the rest of a master's movable goods or cattle, and any man or woman slave may have 'a ring of iron about his neck, arm, or leg, for a more knowledge and keeping of him'.[1]

As it turned out, few were brutish enough to treat humans as harshly as this, and the Act, a failure, was repealed in the very year in which Latimer preached before King Edward. Above the law stood conscience; there was always another Judge to face when this life had run to its end. The Morality Plays told of inevitable judgment, and all men knew it anyway.

> Can you dance the shaking of the sheets,
>   A dance that everyone must do?
> Can you trim it up with dainty sweets,
>   And everything that 'longs thereto?
> Make ready then your winding-sheet,
>   And see how ye can bestir your feet,
> For Death is the man that all must meet,
> For Death is the man that all must meet.
>
> Bring away the beggar and the king,
>   And every man in his degree;
> Bring away the old and the youngest thing,
>   Come all to death and follow me;
> The courtier with his lofty looks,
>   The lawyer with his learned books,
> The banker with his baiting hooks.

[1] 1 Ed. VI, c. 3 (1547).

Merchants, have you made your mart in France?
   In Italy and all about?
Know you not that you and I must dance
   Both our heels wrapped in a clout?
What mean you make your houses gay,
   And I must take the tenant away,
And dig for your sake the clods of clay?

Think you on the solemn 'sizes past,
   How suddenly in Oxfordshire,
I came, and made the judges all aghast,
   And justices that did appear,
And took both Bell and Barham away,
   And many a worthy man that day,
And all their bodies brought to clay.

Think you that I dare not come to schools,
   Where all the cunning clerks are most?
Take I not away both wives and fools,
   And am I not on every coast?
Assure yourselves no creature can
   Make Death afraid of any man,
Or know my coming where or whan.

Where be they that make their leases strong,
   And join about them land to land?
Do you make account to live so long,
   To have the world come to your hand?
No, foolish nowle, for all thy pence,
   Full soon thy soul must needs go hence,
Then who shall toil for thy defence?

And you that lean on your ladies' laps,
   And lay your hands upon their knee;
'May think that you'll escape, perhaps,
   And need not come to dance with me.'
But no, fair lords and ladies all,
   I will make you come when I do call,
And find you a pipe to dance withal.

And you that are busy-minded fools,
　　To brabble for a pelting straw,
Know you not that I have ready tools
　　To cut you from your crafty law?
And you that falsely buy and sell,
　　And think you make your markets well,
Must dance with Death wheresoe'er you dwell.

Pride must have a pretty sheet, I see,
　　For properly she loves to dance;
Come away my wanton wench to me,
　　As gallantly as your eye doth glance;
And all good fellows that flash and swash,
　　In reds and yellows of revell dash,
I warrant you need not be so rash.

For I can quickly cool you all,
　　Or hot or stout soever you be;
Both high and low, both great and small,
　　I nought do fear your high degree;
The ladies fair, the beldames old,
　　The champion stout, the soldier bold,
Must all with me to earthly mould.

Therefore take time while it is lent,
　　Prepare with me yourselves to dance;
Forget me not, your lives lament,
　　I come oft-times by sudden chance.
Be ready, therefore, watch and pray,
　　That when my minstrel pipe doth play,
You may to heaven dance the way.

The reference to Justices Bell and Barham dying suddenly at the Oxford Assizes dates this ballad as later than 1577.[1] It is not the work of an illiterate man, and is indeed so much the expression of one mind that it may not stand as a good example of a common

[1] They held their court out of doors, in the castle yard, but they nevertheless caught the infection.

ballad. But undoubtedly it was well known, as was the song of
Greensleeves.

Alas, my love, you do me wrong,
To cast me off discourteously,
And I have lovèd you so long,
Delighting in your company.

Greensleeves was all my joy;
Greensleeves was my delight;
Greensleeves was my heart of gold,
And who but my Lady Greensleeves?

I have been ready to your hand,
To grant whatever you would crave;
I have both waged life and land
Your love and goodwill for to have.

Greensleeves, etc.

I bought thee kerchers to thy head
That were wrought fine and gallantly;
I kept thee booth at board and bed,
Which cost my purse well favouredly.

Greensleeves, etc.

I bought thee petticoats of the best,
The cloth as fine as might be;
I gave thee jewels for thy chest,
And all this cost I spent on thee.

Greensleeves, etc.

Thy smock of silk, both fair and white,
With gold embroidered gorgeously,
Thy petticoat of seldal right,
And these I bought thee gladly.

Greensleeves, etc.

Well will I pray to God on high
   That thou my constancy may'st see,
And that once more before I die
   Thou wilt vouchsafe to love me.

      Greensleeves, etc.

Greensleeves, now farewell; adieu!
   God I pray to prosper thee;
For I am still thy lover true;
   Come once again and love me.

     Greensleeves was all my joy;
     Greensleeves was my delight;
     Greensleeves was my heart of gold,
     And who but my Lady Greensleeves?

    The version here given is taken from *William Ballet's Lute Book*, and well fits the need of a singer in an Elizabethan home; but the tune was much more widely used. Did not Sir John Falstaff know it? 'Let the sky rain potatoes; let it thunder to the tune of *Greensleeves*!' In 1580 *Greensleeves* was 'moralized to the Scripture', though to be sure when Shakespeare wanted to point the difference between Falstaff's words and deeds he said 'they do no more adhere and keep pace together than the Hundredth Psalm to the tune of *Greensleeves*'. *Greensleeves* became the tune for innumerable parodies from the seventeenth century right on to the nineteenth, with a refrain on the last line to the words, 'Which nobody can deny'. Of the period with which we are now concerned anything might be parodied, for Puritans and Cavaliers were at each other's throats. The theatres were closed in 1642, yet this is not the full story of entertainment, for in that same year appeared *The Waits' Carol*, to the tune of *Greensleeves*. It bears puritanical influences, but it is neither doleful nor bad verse.

> The old year now away is fled,
> The new year it is enterèd,
> Then let us now our sins down-tread,
> And joyfully all appear.
>   And let us now both sport and play,
>   Hang grief; cast care away!
>   And so the year begin;
>   God send you a happy New Year.
>
> And now with New Year's gifts each friend
> Unto each other they do send,
> God grant we may all our lives amend,
> And that the truth may appear.
>   Now, like the snake, your skin
>   Cast off, of evil thoughts and sin,
>   And so the year begin;
>   God send us a happy New Year.

The waits have been disregarded by some writers on English music, unfortunately. They were for a long time a feature of our town life, with gowns and chains of office, sometimes of considerable value. Originally they had been merely the watchmen who patrolled the streets at night, marked the hours, and played upon the 'wayte', which was a popular name for the oboe.[1] There were also watchmen's horns, but these are of less importance in the later history of music.[2] An important part of the duty of the waits was to welcome distinguished visitors to the town with their band of music. Some waits were famous. The Norwich Waits were chosen by Sir Francis Drake to accompany him to Portugal, which the city fathers regarded as a great honour. Of the six waits, only two returned, so they must have shared the dangers of the expedition with the sailors. Orlando Gibbons, the great Elizabethan composer,

[1] Or its precursor, the shawm.
[2] A magnificent specimen is still used at Ripon, Yorks.

came of similar stock—his father was one of the waits of Cambridge.
John Banister, leader of the string band of Charles II, was originally
one of the waits at St Giles, London. The waits were not suppressed
during the Commonwealth, as has been stated in old books; in fact
they were not officially disbanded until the Municipal Reform Act of
1834. Anyway, Sir John Hawkins, who published a history of music
in 1776, has an interesting passage referring to the activities of these
men during the Commonwealth, which should be better known.

It is proposed to speak of those musical performances with which the
people in general were entertained at places of public resort, distinguishing
such as were calculated for the recreation of the vulgar, and those which
for their elegance come under the denomination of concerts. The first of
these were no more than the musical entertainments given to people in
Music-houses,[1] already spoken of, the performers in which consisted of
fidlers and others, hired by the master of the house; such as in the night
season were wont to parade the city and suburbs under the title of Waits.
The music of these men could hardly be called a concert, for this obvious
reason, that it had no variety of parts, nor commixture of different instruments: Half a dozen of fidlers would scrape *Sellenger's Round* or *John,
Come Kiss Me,* or *Old Simon the King* with divisions, till themselves and
their audience were tired, after which as many players on the hautboy
would in the most harsh and discordant tones grate forth *Greensleeves,
Yellow Stockings, Gillian of Croydon,* or some such common dance-tune,
and the people thought it fine music.

What Hawkins is trying to describe was a Cromwellian jam-
session. It differs from a modern jazz band because the players all
used the same type of instrument, but they played 'divisions', or
melodic variations improvised (which are what modern players call
'breaks'), and they 'had no admixture of parts'. By this Hawkins
means that their harmony was unlike that of conventional composers. They were in fact playing round a common tune, each in his
own original way, and all together. This is the practice of heterophony. Hawkins's contemptuous reference to their performance
should be noted, and also his contempt for the tunes they used as
the basis of their style. We shall meet it again.

Hawkins's intolerance of folk-music in 1776 was no worse than
religious intolerance in the Commonwealth, when all were forced
to take serious note of the Calvinistic doctrine and, except for the

---

[1] Inns or taverns where music was provided.

* D

elected few, were doomed to perdition. May Day customs were denounced as pagan, maypoles cut up for firewood. Those of us today who respect the pagan origins of Morris dances or Midsummer Night divination, when the young woman seeks to see the likeness of her beloved, should think on the attempts of seventeenth-century religious leaders to stamp out these 'godless' survivals, even as they would have stamped out the Mass or anything else associated with ancient ritual. We in the twentieth century may be comparatively irreligious, but we do not think ill of the White Paternoster.

> Matthew, Mark, Luke and John,
> Bless the bed that I lie on.
> Four corners to my bed,
> Four angels round my head;
> One to watch and one to pray,
> And two to bear my soul away.

In 1656, however, it was reported that there lived an old woman who had been a child as long ago as Bloody Mary's time, and during that accursed reign she had learned many Popish charms, of which one was, that every night when she lay down to sleep she would charm her bed with the words

> Matthew, Mark, Luke and John,
> The bed be blest that I lie on.

This she would repeat three times, 'reposing great confidence therein'.[1] Such was the tone adopted towards a simple woman's prayer. Nor was it the end. This story was repeated in later years with an addition. It was maintained that there was a witch in the years of the Commonwealth who was 'much addicted to nonsensical rhymes', including this:

> Four newks in this house, for haly angels;
> A post in the midst, that's Jesus Christ;
> Lucus, Marcus, Matthew, Joannes,
> God be into this house, and all that belongs us.[2]

---

[1] Thomas Ady, *A Candle in the Dark, or, a treatise Concerning the Nature of Witches and Witchcraft*, 1656.
[2] George Sinclair, *Satan's Invisible World Discovered*, 1661.

The White Paternoster had become the Black Paternoster. What happened to the poor woman I do not know, but one can guess. Trials for witchcraft increased rapidly during the Commonwealth, involving many poor people; people often very lonely, whose crimes included a fondness for pet animals.

In such a time let us turn to some who were true rebels against the order which prevailed. There was in Gloucestershire a secret club which had an apparently nonsensical song, which could be sung openly, but had a hidden meaning known only to its members. The song was called *Gaarge Ridler's Oven*. It was in local dialect. The songs started with everyone calling out 'The stwuns, the stwuns, the stwuns, the stwuns', in a great crescendo; then the verses followed.

> The stwuns [1] that built Gaarge Ridler's oven,
> And they quem from the Bleakeney's Quaar [2];
> And Gaarge he wur a jolly ould mon,
> And his yead it graw'd above his yare. [3]
>
> One thing of Gaarge Ridler's I must commend,
> And that wur vor a notable theng;
> He mead his braags [4] avoore [5] he died,
> Wi' any dree [6] brothers his zons zshould [7] zeng.
>
> There's Dick the treble and John the mean
> (Let every mon zeng in his auwn [8] pleace)
> And Gaarge he wur the elder brother,
> And therevoore he should zeng the beass. [9]
>
> Mine hostess's moid (and her neaum 'twur Nell)
> A pretty wench, and I lov'd her well;
> I lov'd her well—good reauzon why—
> Because zshe lov'd my dog and I.
>
> My dog has gotten zitch [10] a trick,
> To visit moids when thauy [11] be zick;
> When thauy be zick and like to die,
> Oh, thether gwoes my dog and I.

[1] Stones.   [2] Quarry.   [3] Hair.   [4] Brags.   [5] Before.   [6] Three.
[7] Should.   [8] Own.   [9] Bass.   [10] Such.   [11] They.

My dog is good to catch a hen,
A duck and goose is voor vor men;
And where good company I spy,
Oh, thether gwoes my dog and I.

Droo aal the world owld Gaarge would bwoast,
Commend me to merry owld England mwoast;
While vools gwoes scramblin' vur and nigh,
We bides at whoam, my dog and I.

Ov their furrin [1] tongues let travellers brag,
Wi' their fifteen names vo a puddin' bag;
Two tongues I knows ne'er told a lie,
And their wearers be my dog and I.

My mother told I when I wur young,
If I did vollow the strong beer pwoot,[2]
That drenk would pruv my auverdrow,[3]
And meauk me wear a threadbare cwoat.

When I have dree zixpences under my thumb,
O then I be welcome wherever I quem; [4]
But when I have none, oh, then I pass by;
'Tis poverty pearts good company.

When I gwoes dead, as it may hap,
My greauve shall be under the good yeal [5] tap,
In vouled earms [6] there wool us lie,
Cheek by jowl, my dog and I.

One verse of this song, quoted by Thomas Hughes in *Tom Brown's Schooldays*, has already been mentioned; to Hughes it meant exactly what it said, and it fitted perfectly with his conception of the ideal countryman, but there is a history of this song which throws another light on the matter. It belonged exclusively to the Gloucestershire Society, founded in 1657. This Society may seem at first to be the queerest mixture of political antagonists

---

[1] Foreign.   [2] Pewter.   [3] Overthrow.   [4] Come.   [5] Ale.
[6] Folded arms.

possible at that time, for it comprised some of the old influential families which had never betrayed their Roman Catholic sympathies, and some Dissenters who might be expected to betray the Catholics at any time. They were allies, however, because all of them were equally sick of Cromwell's dictatorship. Let it be remembered that the Presbyterians (who were the aristocracy of the Commonwealth period) stood always for law and order—for moral and political discipline—and they saw this in danger in the later years of Cromwell's life, and especially so at his death. It was they who were instrumental in fetching back Charles II from exile. No other party could have done it. This explains the strange union of opposites in 1657, and the characters in the ballad.

'George Ridler' was Charles I, whose 'oven' was the Cavalier Party; the stones with which the oven was built, and which 'came out of the Blakeney Quaar' were the followers of the Marquis of Worcester, who held out to the last at Raglan Castle, not surrendering until August 1646. George Ridler's head grew above his hair because the head of the State was the Crown, which the King wore. The King's boast before he died was that the British Constitution would recover, despite his adversity, in its true form of King, Lords, and Commons (the three sons who sang in harmony—treble, mean, and bass). 'Mine hostess' was the Queen, and her maid the Catholic Church of which she was a member. The 'dog' was a faithful adherent to the society; he would visit the 'sick', meaning desponding members, and prevent them from 'dying', or losing faith in the cause; he would also seek out any likely recruits to the society, whatever their opinions (hen, duck, or goose), provided they honestly wished the return of Charles II. 'The good ale-tap' was supposed by reason of a pun on 'ale' and 'aisle' to refer to the Church of England, and the final warning is about the timid, who gather round when things look prosperous (three sixpences under the thumb) but drop away when things looked ill (poverty). The singer therefore wishes in the end to be buried with his loyal companions in the church.

That these were perilous times nobody will deny, and plotting for the return of the King would have to be done in the greatest secrecy. Nevertheless there are gaps in the story which cannot be explained—symbols which have not come down correctly interpreted even through the Gloucestershire Society. Is there any truth in the whole interpretation? There have been other stories equally interesting which have been exposed as fictions of the over-zealous folk-lore fiend.

Of one thing, however, we can be sure. Whenever strict authority tries to suppress well-held beliefs, these will find a champion. In 1623 was born in Norwich John Playford, a bookseller, who as a young man set up shop at the entrance to the Inner Temple in London, selling the usual polemic literature of the day, but winning fame in February 1651 [1] with a music-book called *The English Dancing Master*. In it are to be found printed the tunes of many songs and ballads (without the words, which can, however, be got from other printed sources) which were then in use as dance tunes. Playford's object was to give 'Plaine and easie Rules for the Dancing of Country Dances, with a Tune to each Dance'. He was a young man of twenty-eight at the time, and intended his book to be used by young people of some social standing, such as the young lawyers who attended the Inns of Court. He states his case in the Preface.

TO THE INGENIOUS READER. The Art of Dancing called by the Ancient Greeks *Orchestice*, and *Orchestis*, is a commendable and rare Quality fit for yong Gentlemen, if opportunely and civilly used. And *Plato*, that famous Philosopher, thought it meet, that yong Ingenious Children be taught to dance. It is a quality that has been formerly honoured in the Courts of Princes, when performed by the most Noble *Heroes* of the Times: The Gentlemen of the Innes of Court, whose sweet and ayry Activity has crowned their Grand Solemnities with Admiration to all Spectators. This Art has been anciently handled by *Athenaus*, *Julius Pollux*, *Coelius Rhodiginus*, and others, and much commend it to be Excellent for Recreation, after more serious Studies, making the Body active and strong, gracefull in deportment, and a quality very much beseeming a Gentleman. Yet all this should not have been an Incitement to me for Publication of the Worke (knowing these Times and the Nature of it do not agree) But that there was a false and surreptitious Copy at the Printing Presse, which if it had been published, would have been a disparagement to the quality and the Professors thereof, and a hinderance to the Learner: Therefore for prevention of all which, having an excellent Copy by me, and the assistance of a knowing Friend; I have ventured to put forth this ensuing Worke to the View, and gentle censure of all ingenious Gentlemen lovers of this Quality; not doubting but their goodness will pardon what may be amiss, and accept the honest Intention

---

[1] 1651 New Style; the date on the book is given as 1650, this being the Old Style of reckoning.

of him what is a faithfull honourer of your Virtues, and *Your Servant to Command, J. P.*

So far the songs we have had to deal with have been considered mainly in relation to the country people, but now we have a book of country dances intended for the use of good-class town dwellers. There has actually been no great upheaval, however, for town and country were not so different in their ways of life as they are today. Towns were much smaller; London itself a small town by our own standards, with easy access to the fields. Playford's *Dancing Master* became a best seller almost overnight. The times appeared to be against frivolity, but it is in such periods that men have most need of light recreation. Playford, addressing his book to the respectable and well-to-do, was free from the suspicion that his publication would fan up enthusiasm for the traditional dances with pagan associations still danced on village greens (or, if prevented there, in the seclusion of the woods on Midsummer Eve), and he had at his back the prestige of the dancing-master.

The dancing-master was a product of a changing social environment. Time had been when the wealthy people had lived in grim castles and draughty halls (which can still be seen at the Tower of London, Windsor and Warwick castles, and in other places). Within these castles we can see how the necessity for defence gradually made way for higher standards of civilization, as men ceased to harass their neighbours by force of arms. Benches and stools give way to chairs, glass is put in the windows, and its quality improves; decorations acquire more elegance, and bed-chambers more comfort. In these circumstances it will be understood that the position of women in the household became more dignified, and a code of manners evolved in which the likings of ladies were given more consideration. The traditional teacher of good social behaviour in the sixteenth century was a new figure—the dancing-master. His influence as a teacher of manners was never in doubt until the nineteenth century, and may not, even today, be discounted utterly. His influence in the sixteenth century may be found in a book by 'Thoinot Arbeau' in 1588. It described the ballroom dances which a young Frenchman should know, their steps and tunes, and something more. Here is a passage on general behaviour.

You have executed your steps and movement well, and fallen properly into cadence, but when you dance in company never look down to examine your steps and ascertain whether you dance them correctly. Hold your head and body upright with a confident mien, and do not spit or blow your nose much. And if necessity obliges you to do so, turn your head away and use a clean white handkerchief. Converse pleasantly in a low and modest voice, let your arms fall by your sides neither in a lifeless nor in a restless manner, and be suitably and neatly dressed, your hose well drawn up and your shoes clean.[1]

Arbeau's book is rare, even in translation, but Sir John Davies's *Orchestra* can be obtained by those interested, without much trouble.[2] He describes

> The motions seven that are in nature found:
> Upward and downward, forth and back again,
> To this side and that, and turning round,
> Whereof a thousand brawls he doth compound,
> Which he doth teach unto the multitude,
> And ever with a turn they must conclude.

A 'brawl' was the French '*branle*'. There were many types of *branle*, to suit old and young, gentle and simple, and though the social scheme was developing so that for a time the common people would not know the refined steps taught by the dancing-master, the wealthier people knew the originals, of which the *branle* was a direct descendant. Of one type Arbeau says:

> This *branle* is danced by serving men and wenches, and sometimes by young men and damsels of gentle birth when they make a masquerade disguised as peasants and shepherds, or when they dance merrily among themselves.

Towards the end of the sixteenth century Italian dances became as popular as French dances in England, and the English Masque was at its height in the Jacobean age. In the better-class homes dancing and danced games were popular, with opportunities for kissing one's partner. *Trenchmore* was a merry chase, played throughout the house, in and out of rooms and under and over the furniture. Here is the tune which goes by that name in Playford's *Dancing Master*.

---

[1] Thoinot Arbeau, *Orchesography*, 1588, trans. Cyril W. Beaumont, 1925.
[2] Modern edition by Tillyard, 1945.

Playford's *Dancing Master* is an invaluable book, for it gives us many tunes we should not otherwise know. It gives us others which we know in various versions. Margaret Dean-Smith and Edward J. Nicol have written an excellent essay on *The Dancing Master*[1] in the course of which they trace through some of the dances.

The most curious of these disguises, illustrating also the association of Italianate figures with an old and vulgarized ballad, is *Kemp's Jig*. The dance, a *ruota a sei* with the grouping so often found in the Italian and French dances of one man and two women, provides the opportunities for behaviour—in Italy—'in the true gentlemanly manner', and—in England—for the man to kiss both his partners twice. The tune has no resemblance to our present-day notion of a jig; one must look for its derivation in the career of Will Kemp, whose contemporary fame rested not on his self-advertising Morris dance from London to Norwich, but as the member of Leicester's players who created the part of Dogberry, and who, taking a company of actors abroad, made famous all over Europe the peculiar English entertainment, the jig, which took root in Germany as the *Singspiel*. Kemp seems to have had a large repertory, but of all his jigs the most famous was *Rowland*, which had two sequels, *Rowland's Godson* and *The Third Part of Kemp's Jig*. Leicester's successor as governor of the Netherlands was welcomed back to England by the players with a new song based on their famous tune; Byrd made a set of variations on it, giving it the name of *Lord Willobie's Welcome Home*, and in parenthesis, *Rowland*. It is the tune of the country dance called by Playford *Kemp's Jig*.

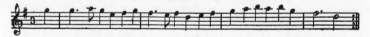

[1] *Journal of the English Folk Dance and Song Society*, Vol. IV, Nos. 4, 5, and 6.

A disguise it is, if we think of music in conservative terms, for not only is Playford's tune in the modern major mode, but it is in triple time.

Such, however, is to be expected. The tune which was once a vulgar ballad, hailing possibly from the country but being used on the stage to carry the entertainment of the Elizabethan jig, has now been adapted to a round dance. It takes on, therefore, the features required for such a recreation. If it seems melodically remote from the *Rowland* versions so far given, the link may be found in another version contained in a Lute Book at Cambridge, and called *Kemp's Jig*.[1]

But if Playford was retrospective, picking up tunes in general use among dancers, which they had drawn from all sorts of sources, composed or adapted from well-known songs, he was also a source for future musicians. His books are treasure-houses for lovely airs, and his *Dancing Master* [2] went through eighteen editions under him and his successors in business, and English composers throughout the eighteenth century owed much to the graceful styles he made so well known to the public. This subject is fascinating in itself, and must be left for other hands to describe, but one feature of interest which has recently come into prominence from across the Atlantic may be mentioned here; it is the practice of 'calling' in the square-dances, in which a singer tells the dancers the steps to make in going through their dance. The dance described is *Mr Lane's Maggot* (a 'maggot' was a quaint personal conceit, or private amusement), and the author of the lines Thomas d'Urfey; it appears in the ninth edition of *The Dancing Master*, in 1695.

> Strike up, Drowsie Guts Scrapers,
> Gallants be ready,
> Each with his Lady . . .
> ·I'll teach you all the dance.

---

[1] Cambridge MS. Dd. II, ii.   Cf. Baskervill, *The Elizabethan Jig*.
[2] First edition called *The English Dancing Master*, subsequent editions *The Dancing Master*.

Cast off, Tom, behind Johnny,
Do the same, Nanny,
Eyes are upon ye;
Trip in between
Little Dicky and Jane
And set in the second row:
Then cast back you must too,
And up the first row
Nimbly thrust through;
Then, then turn about
To the left, or you're out,
And meet your love below.
Pass, then cross,
Then Jack's Pretty Lass,
Then turn her about, and about, and about,
And Jack if you can will do so too
With Betty, whilst the time is true,
We'll all your ear commend.
Still there's more
To lead all four;
Two by Nancy stand
And give her your hand
And cast her quickly down below
And meet her in the second row,
The dance is at an end.

VI. Crime and Punishment

⸸⸸⸸

A famble,[1] a tattle,[2] and his popps,[3]
Had my boman [4] when he was ta'en,
But had he not boozed in the diddling-shops [5]
He'd still be in Drury Lane.

HARLEQUIN SHEPPARD, 1725

I

JAMES HIND was a man who moved with the times. He died in 1652—hanged, drawn, and quartered—but his soul went riding on; a chapbook of 1752 claimed to give combined accounts of 'two noted robbers and highwaymen—Robin Hood and James Hind'. This is fame indeed!

Hind was the son of a saddler of Chipping Norton in Oxfordshire, and was apprenticed to a butcher in that lovely little market town. He must have found butchery unexciting, however, for he left his master before his time was out and joined a gang of highway robbers in London. It is here that his enterprise was shown, for highway robbery was a trade with a future. The state of the roads in England was well described by Will Kemp as 'rotten' when he made his famous dance from London to Norwich; nor was there much chance of any improvement, for the upkeep of the roads was the responsibility of the parishes through which they ran. Parishioners were liable for their repair by statutory labour; those having horses and carts being obliged to loan these for six days each year to work on the roads, while those who had no property but were able-bodied were obliged to give six days' free labour on the roads, or pay someone else to do it. Waywardens were appointed to see that the work was done; they were obliged to serve for a year without pay in a capacity which, if carried out, would make them the enemies of their neighbours; so they did as little as possible; so did the parishioners, and so did the justices, who were expected

---

[1] Ring.　[2] Watch.　[3] Pistols.　[4] Lover (male).　[5] Ginshops.

to bring a parish to heel if it neglected its roads. As for repairing roads like Watling Street or the Great North Road, which served not the local parish so much as the country as a whole—well—the Bible commands us to love our neighbours, but reason forbids that a man should be so foolish as to love somebody else's neighbours. They passed through the village on their way to make money or to attend Parliament, and who knew what mischief they might be up to?

Travel was mainly on horseback, but for those who were infirm there were coaches. These lumbering vehicles, which were without springs, had broad wheels, leather curtains to keep out some of the weather, and were dragged through the mud by the sheer brute force of four huge horses. Their speed was decided by the state of the roads and the brutality of the driver. Imagine such a coach struggling painfully up a hill, the 'road' a deep rut in the local earth; round a bend the way passes between trees and some shaggy undergrowth; from the trees rides out a man on horseback with a pistol in his hand. The riders in the coach have no chance at all. He relieves them of whatever valuables they have, and is off across country at a speed they cannot hope to equal. The highwaymen were men with a future: men of enterprise; such was James Hind.

Had he stayed at home in Chipping Norton history would have passed him by, but as a highwayman he could acquire fame. He was apparently a selective thief, with a sense of humour and a grudge against Puritans; he was said to have robbed Colonel Harrison on one occasion and Oliver Cromwell on another. Certainly his sympathies were Royalist, for Sir William Compton gave him a commission in the King's Army. At the siege of Colchester he was taken prisoner, but escaped in a woman's clothes; he marched with Charles from Edinburgh to Worcester, fought there with the king in his last disastrous battle, and was afterwards taken prisoner. At his trial he denied that he was the man who accompanied Charles II across country in making his escape to France, but expressed gratification that His Majesty had got away. Throughout his trial he 'deported himself with undaunted courage, yet with a civil behaviour and smiling countenance'. They asked him had he read the disreputable blurbs which the common people were reading— *Hind's Ramble,* and *Hind's Exploits*; these he denied having seen, and said they were fictitious, but he readily admitted that he had had 'some merry pranks and revels'.

From the Puritan point of view the man was a menace not only for what he had done but for the hero-worship he inspired among the people. Robin Hood was dead and gone, but this man Hind was showing an example to his contemporaries; even in the dock at the Old Bailey he was a gentleman.

He was remanded while they sought another charge against him, then taken to Reading, where he was tried for manslaughter. This was for the death of a friend whom he had killed in a quarrel—a much less heroic deed. He was found guilty, sentenced to death, but pardoned under the Act of Oblivion of 1652. The justices would not let him go, however, and sent him to Worcester, where he was tried on a charge of High Treason, found guilty, hanged, drawn, and quartered. Such is the blindness of authority: the hero at this trial and execution was the criminal. He remained a hero to posterity.

> There's many a comical story you know,
>   With a hey down, down, and a down,
> Of valiant and brave Captain Hind;
> A song of them all, sing here now I shall,
> 'Tis jocular, pleasant, and fine.

This is the beginning of a ballad called *Captain Hind's Progress and Ramble,* which picks up the thread of several of his supposed adventures.[1] It is too long to be quoted in full, but here are two of his exploits—the one about a parson and the other about a distressed innkeeper. The refrain line is omitted to save space.

> Hind met with a Parson as he was pursued,
>   To whom he did merrily say;
> 'There's thieves behind, a-coming you'll find,
>   To take all your money away.'

> 'Sir, here is a pistol, pray shoot at the first.'
>   Which pistol the Parson receives,
> As knowing behold one saying of old,
>   'One honest man scares twenty thieves.'

---

[1] *Roxburge Ballads,* Ballad Society's edition (1871–99), Vol. VII, p. 644.

The Parson, being pot-valiant it seems,
  He shot, though it happened in vain;
Without more ado, the pistol he threw,
  At which he was presently ta'en.

Thus Hind got away, but the Parson was brought
  Unto an old justice, 'tis said;
Where soon he was cleared, for why? It appeared
  That he was no thief by his trade.

Hind's claim to popularity was that his adventures all had some spice of humour. The 'justification' of his crimes was that his victims had their money's worth of fun, if only they could see it.

Hind came to a town where the Bailiffs had got
  An innkeeper fast in the net;
An old Usurer, a crabbed old cur,
  Would send him to prison for debt.

Hind laid down the money and took up the bond;
  Then, finding the man was but poor;
He soon paid himself, for he robbed the old elf,
  Of that, likewise twenty pounds more.

Of all the great robbers that ever was known,
  He was the most frolicsome blade;
His merriment still did gain him goodwill,
  Tho' long he had followed his trade.

And many more frolics the Captain has play'd,
  Now if you will read them at large;
The book you may buy, good people for why?
  It is just but one penny charge.

So it happened that when a coach was robbed on the road, as likely as not the highwayman would adopt a 'gentlemanly' demeanour—provided he met with no resistance—and if there was any consolation in the thought that one had assisted to support an officer of 'the King across the water', well, one had it. Needless to say, all highwaymen were not gentlemen, but the trick worked.

A highwayman might have a wife in every county and a girl in every village and not be found out for years. When he was found out he was given away, the law took its course and his 'wife' the reward. At his trial he would emulate the manners of James Hind. Robbers not so romantic tried the same game, but their lot was not so happy: the highwayman was the aristocrat of criminals.

Therefore, when the poet John Gay needed money, he sought for a theme which would attract a large public, and the theme he chose was the Gentleman of the Road. The form he adopted was the ballad opera. This 'opera' he conceived as being the work of a London beggar, and true to life. There is no good character in it, but only the types known to the beggar—a highwayman, a receiver of stolen property who is also a thief-taker, an extortionate jailer, rogues in prison, rogues abroad, cutpurses, informers, harlots, and others, forming a state of society complete in all particulars but existing in a corrupt form—verminous, gin-sodden, within the shadow of the hangman's noose, and resigned to their ultimate fate. If the spectator sees in their behaviour something akin to the behaviour of the world at large, the world being what it then was, that would perhaps be justifiable; certainly the Beggar would understand.

Beggar: Through the whole piece you may observe such a similitude of Manners in high and low Life, that it is difficult to determine whether (in the fashionable Vices) the fine Gentlemen imitate the Gentlemen of the Road, or the Gentlemen of the Road the fine Gentlemen. Had the Play remained, as I at first intended, it would have carried a most excellent Moral. 'Twould have shown that the lower Sort of People have their Vices in a degree as well as the Rich: And that they are punished for them.

An ending true to life (in which the characters would all have been hanged or transported to the Colonies) could not be staged, because an opera must comply with the taste of the times and the taste of the times demanded a happy ending.

The Beggar's Opera was the work of a literary genius; musical historians have shown how it took up the tradition of the Elizabethan jigs,[1] but it is greatly superior to them in structure and in

[1] Cf. Edward J. Dent, *Foundations of English Opera*, 1928, and Eric W. White, *The Rise of English Opera*, 1951.

thought. The tunes John Gay chose to carry his satirical verses were well known, but not ballads in the strict sense of the term. Some are folk-songs, some tunes by famous composers like Purcell and Handel, some tunes taken from Playford's books, or from other collections of tunes—Thompson's *Orpheus Caledoniensis* of 1725 for example—children's songs, dances; but all were popular. The popularity of the tunes was part of the satire, for Gay depended on the tunes to carry his story, while at the same time being open to the criticism that they were as familiar in the gutters of St Giles as elsewhere. St Giles was a notoriously dangerous part of London by reason of the criminals who resorted there, for it was outside the jurisdiction of the City magistrates.[1]

What was true of the tunes was true also of the literary content. In his introduction the Beggar explains his idea.

This piece I own was originally writ for the celebrating the Marriage of James Chanter and Moll Lay, two most excellent Ballad-singers. I have introduced the Similes that are in all your celebrated Operas: The Swallow, the Moth, the Bee, the Ship, the Flower, &c. Besides, I have a Prison Scene which the Ladies always reckon charmingly pathetick. As to the Parts, I have observed such a nice Impartiality to our two Ladies, that it is impossible for either of them to take Offence. I hope I may be forgiven, that I have not made my Opera throughout unnatural, like those in vogue; for I have no Recitative: Excepting this, as I have consented to have neither Prologue nor Epilogue, it must be allowed an Opera in all its forms. The Piece indeed hath been heretofore frequently presented by our selves in our Great Room at St Giles's, so that I cannot too often acknowledge your Charity in bringing it now on the Stage.

The Beggar's Opera had in fact been offered to the managers of Drury Lane Theatre but rejected. John Rich (a master of mime, said to have been illiterate, but this I do not believe) accepted it for performance at his theatre in Portugal Street, Lincoln's Inn Fields, where his leading man, Quin, threw up the part of the Highwayman, Captain MacHeath, during rehearsals, as being sub-standard even for Lincoln's Inn Fields; it was taken over by a minor actor named Walker, and the part of Polly Peachum, the leading lady, was played by Lavinia Fenton, a small-part actress whose salary was

---

[1] Nearly all parishes dedicated to St Giles lie just outside city boundaries. St Giles is the patron saint of beggars, and beggars used to gather at the city gates. Many of the parishes of St Giles are still slum districts.

then fifteen shillings a week. With these resources John Gay was to shake the government of the day.

For Gay's satire was of social circumstances, with a sting intended for the Whigs, and especially for Robert Walpole, our first Prime Minister. The Tories had been in the wilderness, or practically so, since the time of Queen Anne, but in 1727 they gathered themselves together for an onslaught on Walpole and his adherents. They were not public benefactors, but politicians out for power; what they said about the Whigs need not be true provided it was plausible; a catchy tune was a well-known way of appealing to all and sundry.

> Ye circum and uncircumcised,
>   Come hear my song and be advised;
> Sell all your land, sell all your flocks,
>   And put your money in the stocks.

This is not by John Gay, but a political ballad brought out in 1720 to ridicule the folly of investing in the South Sea Bubble. Capitalist enterprise was at that time a fashionable craze fanned by Government promises of huge profits on a hare-brained scheme for sea-trading. The ballad went to the tune of *Over the Hills and Far Away*. It is not a narrative ballad, but the term ballad was used widely to describe pretty well anything a street hawker of rhymes could sell. The chorus ran:

> Hubble-bubble, Bubble-bubble now's in play,
> Come, buy our Hubble-bubbles while you may,
> For there's Hubble-bubble, Bubble-bubble night and day,
> At Jonathan's and Garraway.

At a time when insurance against risks was developing into a sound commercial undertaking the following verse would be of some interest:

> Come all who would large gain insure,
> Our ships upon the sea insure,
> And those the surest gain must find
> Who trust the faithless sea and wind.

> Hubble-bubble, etc.

One doubts if Lloyds would classify any ship A1 when owned by a man with that idea. He was on surer ground, however, when he turned his attention to the Royal Academy of Music, a company founded in that year to promote Italian opera. The project, in which Handel was employed, was of lavish proportions.

> Italian songsters, come away;
> Our gentry will the piper play;
> Come, hasten here, for before 'tis long,
> Opera stock will be sold for a song.

To this noble enterprise *The Beggar's Opera* was to deal the *coup de grâce* in 1728. When Handel said afterwards that his operas had been driven off the stage with lumps of pudding he did not mean it literally (for the audience never threw pudding—they threw oranges) but that he was referring to the final song and dance in *The Beggar's Opera*. It will be of interest to step back in time and see for ourselves how such a calamity can be brought about.

The Elizabethan jigs, it will be recalled, were based on well-known tunes to which satirical verses were written, and the ballads were relieved with dances and spoken dialogue. At the time this was going on in England, the Italian nobility was being treated to a new form of stage entertainment in which the play was sung throughout. With it went a new kind of song called recitative —a musical declamation with instrumental accompaniment. The characters represented on the stage were classical and heroic; gods, heroes, and mythological beings, whose virtues and misfortunes could be expected to lift up the drama beyond the plane of normal life. In England we had a master of blank verse—Shakespeare—to elevate human passion: in Italy they had the new music—recitative. As the Elizabethan jig was an inversion of the noble passion of the main drama which preceded it on the stage, so, regarded as musical entertainment, the jig can be an inversion of the noble style that was opera.[1] Opera exalted the passions; the jig debased them. *The Beggar's Opera* inverted also the social theme of the early eighteenth century; it made heroes of ruffians and villains of all in authority. Mr Peachum, a London magistrate, is a compound of all the foulest traits to be found in human character. He is receiver of stolen

---

[1] It could not be so regarded in Will Kemp's time, for the first opera came in 1601— in Florence—and the London audience in the playhouses would not know it.

property, master of the thieves who take it, insurer of those who might lose it, friend of the jailer, and a man of the world who expresses himself thus:

> In all the employment of life
>   Each neighbour abuses his brother;
> Whore and rogue they call husband and wife:
>   All professions be-rogue one another.
> The priest calls the lawyer a cheat,
>   The lawyer beknaves the divine;
> And the statesman, because he's so great,
>   Thinks his trade as honest as mine.

The characters of Peachum and his wife were founded on Mr and 'Mrs' Jonathan Wild, who were very much in the public mind in 1728. He had been instrumental in bringing to the rope a violent burglar named Jack Sheppard, who had three times escaped from prison. Wild was accused of having employed Sheppard, but to have found him unprofitable and therefore betrayed him for the reward that had been offered for his capture. All the underworld of London knew this, but Wild was too clever for them. He had an espionage system operating through the gin-shops. Gin was growing in popularity among the poor because it was cheap and could be obtained anywhere, and by the gentry because it increased the demand for grain—and the gentry were landowners. England was rotten, and was deliberately being made rottener to serve agricultural interests. By a lucky accident some stolen property was found on Wild's premises and he was tried, proved guilty, and hanged, amid genuine rejoicing of all parties, rich and poor alike.

Mr Peachum in *The Beggar's Opera* was a scapegoat for the accumulating vices of the age—a villain with no redeeming features. He was an ideal prototype for melodrama; ruler of an underworld where every human sympathy was flouted. Let us take the attitude towards love. The Peachums have just learnt from their daughter Polly that she has married Captain MacHeath the highwayman.

Peachum: And how do you propose to live, child?
Polly: Like other women, sir, upon the industry of my husband.
Mrs Peachum: What! Is the wench turned fool? A highwayman's wife, like a soldier's, hath as little of his pay as of his company.

Peachum: And had you not the common views of a gentlewoman in your marriage, Polly?

Polly: I don't know what you mean, sir.

Peachum: Of a jointure, and of being a widow.

Polly: But I love him, sir: how then could I have thoughts of parting with him?

Peachum: Parting with him! Why, that is the whole scheme and intention of all marriage articles. The comfortable estate of widowhood is the only hope that keeps up a wife's spirits. Where is the woman who would scruple to be a wife, if she had it in her power to be a widow whenever she pleased? If you have any views of this sort, Polly, I shall think the match not so very unreasonable.

Polly: How I dread to hear your advice! Yet I must beg you to explain yourself.

Peachum: Secure what he hath got, have him peach'd the next sessions, and at once you are made a rich widow.

Polly: What, murder the man I love! The blood runs cold at my heart with the very thought of it.

Peachum: Fie, Polly! What hath murder to do in the affair? Since the thing sooner or later must happen, I dare say, the Captain himself would like that we should get the reward for his death sooner than a stranger. Why, Polly, the Captain knows, that as 'tis his employment to rob, so 'tis ours to take robbers; every man in his business, so that there is no malice in the case.

Mrs P.: Ay, husband, now you have nicked the matter. To have him peach'd is the only thing could ever make me forgive her.

Polly drops on her knees, appealing to her parents. The tune of her song is one of those known as 'Chevy Chase.'

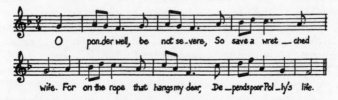

O ponder well, be not severe, So save a wretched wife. For on the rope that hangs my dear, Depends poor Polly's life.

Mrs P.: But your duty to your parents, hussy, obliges you to hang him. What would many a wife give for such an opportunity!

Polly: What is a jointure; what is widowhood to me? I know my heart. I cannot survive him.

Polly rises and comes down stage. She sings to the audience. The tune is that of a French air.

The tur—tle thus with plain—tive cry——ing, Her lo—ver dy—ing. The tur—tle thus, with plain—tive cry—ing, la—.ments her love. Down she drops, quite spent with sigh—ing, Pair'd in death as pair'd in love.

Polly: Thus, sir, it will happen to your poor Polly.

Mrs P.:   What! Is the fool in earnest then? I hate thee for being particular: why, wench, thou art a shame to thy very sex.

Polly: But hear me, mother. If you ever loved——

Mrs P.:   Those cursed playbooks she reads have been her ruin. One word more, hussy, and I shall knock your brains out, if you have any.

Now read through that passage again with the final speech in mind. This is common to all ages. Whenever magistrates find youth in rebellion against authority they tend to blame cheap literature. John Gay is laughing at his audience, which has just been hoaxed by an injection of sentimentality into the prevailing villainy. Polly's songs are the high lights of the sentimentality, contrasted with the 'no sentiment in business and life is a business' attitude of her parents. Gay was a master of comedy. There is a laugh in every line. The ·laughs are not produced, however, by empty absurdity, but by the inversion of fashionable behaviour. Marriage articles were truly intended as an insurance for the bride. Marriages were business arrangements among the socially superior classes. Only kitchen wenches married for love, or ladies who were headstrong young fools.

It was at this point in the play (for *The Beggar's Opera* is really a play with music and not an opera) that the success of the first production was determined. When Polly dropped on her knees and sang her sentimental song to the tune of *Chevy Chase* the audience grew quiet. This was more significant than the laughs at the satire. The Marquess of Queensbury exclaimed 'It'll do!' He had put money into the venture. Whether John Gay knew previously the accuracy of his judgment of theatrical taste cannot now be determined, but his skill was well employed. He used the simple beauty of the song as a set-off against the sordid social theme.

Throughout the history of art runs the principle of related contrasts. It is said that the dark and light colourings of the horns used in the Abbots Bromley dance are part of a forgotten symbolism of day and night, or summer and winter, or good and evil. In the Mummers' Play the Christian St George overcomes a dark heathen knight. In the short extract we have given from the Coventry Nativity Play the evil scene is contrasted immediately with the good scene of Joseph, Mary, and the Angel. Infanticide is contrasted with parental love. And this was still further demonstrated at the point where we left the play, when the serenity of the carol is immediately succeeded by the entry of the soldiers to kill the children. As the carol was used in the Nativity Play, John Gay used well-known songs in *The Beggar's Opera*. There are plenty of examples of this contrast of the ugly and the beautiful. There is the lovely tune of *Golden Slumbers Kiss your Eyes* set to these words.

Mrs Peachum: Not with a highwayman, you sorry slut!

Gay, and his collaborator Dr Pepusch, who arranged the music of the songs for use in the play, had a variety of ways by which music could be made to intensify the humour. Handel was good for a laugh in that anti-Whig company, for he was a King's man and enjoying the support of His Majesty at the opera-house in the Haymarket. One of Handel's most successful operas was *Rinaldo,* containing a heroic march. The characters of Italian opera were elevated to supermen and their parts were sung by special singers with unnatural voices. These men were castrated in boyhood in order to retain a soprano or contralto voice[1] in later life, and this voice was intensively trained in the Italian singing academies. It was not natural; nature was suborned to serve art. The Beggar twisted this back again to 'nature' by making Handel's heroic air serve a pack of scoundrels on their way to commit a highway robbery.

> Let us take the road.
> Hark! I hear the sound of coaches!
> The hour of attack approaches,
> To your arms, brave boys, and load.
> See the ball I hold.
> Let the chymists toil like asses,
> Our fire their fire surpasses,
> And turns all our lead to gold.

> *The Gang, rang'd in front of the stage, load their pistols and stick them under their girdles; then go off singing the first part in chorus.*

Everything in satire depends on association. The association of heroism with crime is here revealed by making Handel's march serve a pack of ruffians who think themselves brave boys, but whom the audience held in contempt. Similarly Sir Robert Walpole, who was present at the first performance, must have had a shock when he found a ballad tune, *The Happy Clown,* introduced into the overture. No words were sung at this point, but the audience could hardly fail to associate the tune with words sung about the streets, deriding

---

[1] The Italian words 'soprano' and 'contralto' are both masculine, though they apply now only to women's voices.

the Prime Minister. Later in the play the tune is heard again to the words

> I'm like a skiff on the ocean tost,
> Now high, now low, with each billow born,
> With her rudder broke and her anchor lost,
> Deserted and all forlorn.

This sort of thing has been said at some time about every government in power; that it has not been traditionally employed at political meetings can perhaps be explained by the low level of imagination shown at elections, and the popular expectation in former days of beer and bribery. Certainly John Gay knew how to strike home with a song.

There was a seventeenth-century political song well known to everyone. It was called *Lillibulero*, after a libel on the Irish contained in its refrain. This gibberish was said to have been used as a watch-word in the Ulster troubles of 1641. It was taken up in 1688 by Thomas, Lord Wharton, and given verses in which an Irishman congratulates another Irishman. ('Brother Teague' is slang, the word 'Teague' being then employed as we today say 'Paddy'.)

> Ho, brother Teague, hast heard the decree?
> Lillibulero, bullen-a-la;
> That we shall have a new deputy
> Lillibulero, bullen-a-la.
>> Lero, lero, lillibulero,
>> Lillibulero, bullen-a-la;
>> Lero, lero, lillibulero,
>> Lillibulero bullen-a-la.

It will be recalled that James II had proved stubborn in trying to force into law against the wish of the people his Declaration of Indulgence. The Church of England protested against his order to read this Declaration from the pulpits; seven bishops were arrested, taken to the Tower of London, tried, and acquitted; the army was expected to enforce the king's will on the Church, but showed itself unwilling; then came James's greatest stupidity. He broke up the camp at Hounslow Heath, sent the regiments back to their head-quarters, and tried to strengthen their ranks with Irish recruits. The Irish were Catholics and followers of Richard Talbot, Earl of

Tyrconnel; they would have no scruples about arresting the English clergy if necessary. The Irish peasantry, however, were the traditional enemies of the English and Scottish soldiers, and trouble was to be expected in the army as a result of this policy. At Portsmouth the soldiers declared they would not serve with the Irish recruits, and six of their officers supported their view. The officers were cashiered. No such outlet was available to the common soldiers, however, but they let their feelings go with the new song *Lillibulero*, then sweeping the country, which told how a prophecy had been made that Ireland would be ruled by a dog and an ass, which was now proved true, for 'Talbot's de dog, and James is de ass'. With this song echoing about the country James II escaped abroad.

The song, then, had rebel associations; these were enough for John Gay, but the words must be brought up to date. Gay was attacking the Whig government, which had the king's favour; it was not more corrupt than previous governments had been, but all members of Parliament sought their own advancement, so Gay's heroic highwayman sings:

> The modes of the Court so common are grown,
>   That a true friend can hardly be met;
> Friendship for interest is but a loan,
>   Which they let out for what they can get.

The nobility are mixed up with the new vogue of company promotion. There is no friendship in business—only interest.

>   'Tis true, you'll find
>   Some friends so kind,
> Who will give you good counsel themselves to defend;
>   In sorrowful ditty,
>   They promise, they pity,
> But shift you for money from friend to friend.

Such, then, was the way in which a popular street song might be used to stir up public opinion. It gave expression to an idea which had long been fostered. It takes a brave man to stand up for his rights in a corrupt world, but when a common wrong is bandied about the streets to the accompaniment of an infectious tune, cowards will whistle it, good men sing it, and rogues roar it. Thus it happened to *The Beggar's Opera*. It had a long initial run in the Lincoln's Inn Fields theatre and innumerable revivals. Men took this vulgar play to heart in various ways, according to temperament. It displayed abuses which some desired to remove. It ridiculed Italian opera, which was a highbrow entertainment and therefore subject to the wrath of the multitude. It glorified the highwayman, who was in their low-life literature a follower in the Robin Hood tradition. It made Gay rich and Rich gay.

Matt o' the Mint: We are heartily sorry, Captain, for your misfortune. But 'tis what we must all come to.

MacHeath: Peachum and Lockit, you know, are infamous scoundrels. Their lives are as much in your power as yours are in theirs. Remember your dying friend. 'Tis my last request. Bring those villains to the gallows before you, and I am satisfied.

Matt: We'll do it.

Small wonder then that if this sordid potboiler served the parliamentary opposition of its day to lambast the Prime Minister, it served also some who little deserved support. When Sir John Hawkins came to write his history of music [1] he had this to say:

The effects of *The Beggar's Opera* on the minds of the people, have fulfilled the prognostications of many that it would prove injurious to society. Rapine and violence have been gradually increasing ever since its first presentation. The rights of property, the obligation of the laws that guard it, are disputed on principle: every man's house is now what the law calls it, his castle, or at least it may be said that, like a castle, it requires to be a place of defence: Young men, apprentices, clerks, in public offices, and others, disdaining the arts of honest industry, and captivated with the charms of idleness and criminal pleasure, now take themselves to the road, effect politeness in the very act of robbery; And in the end become the victims of the justice of their country: And men of discernment who have been at the pains of tracing this great evil to its source, have found that not a few of those, who, during these last fifty years have paid to the law the penalty of their lives, have in the course of their pursuits been emulous to imitate the manners and general character of MacHeath.

[1] Published in 1776.

It is a pity the men of discernment he mentions had not more, or they would have gone back to James Hind, or even to Robin Hood. But therein lies a difficulty. Hood and Hind were of the past —their exploits were mellowed by tradition; *The Beggar's Opera* was on the stage, still a good box-office attraction; it was a current influence, and the law has always been a bit of an ass when it has become frightened. Could John Gay have foreseen the magistrates' objections to crime-plays? He put the very words into the mouth of Mrs Peachum. 'Those cursed playbooks she reads have been her ruin. One word more, hussy, and I shall knock your brains out, if you have any.'

Poor Polly! But what a list of followers she has had!

II

Yet *The Beggar's Opera*, for all its play on vulgar sentiments and tunes, was distinctive. It gave a new thrust towards moral criticism of society. For the full effects of this work we must look at subsequent developments in painting and in literature. Hogarth captured the spirit of *The Beggar's Opera* not only in his paintings on that subject, but even more surely in his other social satires. *Gin Street* and *Beer Lane* display in paint the essentials of Gay and Pepusch's principles of emphasis by contrast. The viewer is attracted to the art, but in admiring it receives a moral lesson. *Marriage à la Mode, The Rake's Progress, The Harlot's Progress, The Idle and Industrious Apprentices*, are further examples of Hogarth's skill. They were as rewarding financially to him as *The Beggar's Opera* was to Gay. Nor is this all. When Fielding turned to the novel, he acknowledged the debt he owed to Hogarth. He stated it categorically in the Preface to *Joseph Andrews*; but even had he not done so, the moral leaning, deliberate use of vices, sentiments, and nearness to contemporary characters and scenes, would have been sufficient. These things were not the products of skill alone, but depended on the wishes of many that public abuses should be removed. It is true that Parliament and the clergy were stubborn, and relied on the oppression of malefactors as a deterrent to crime, when all the time there was plenty of evidence that the people they sought to punish had as much fondness for a revolting spectacle as such malefactors have had at any time. Fielding and his brother were practical reformers who set up their rogation office in London, employing the celebrated Bow Street Runners of the Dick Turpin stories, who did much to bring criminals to justice. It could not be done with these resources alone, however; the improvement of communications and increasing popularity of travel were the highwayman's doom; long before he vanished from the roads he had lost his glamour.

This does not mean that he lost his appeal through popular fiction. Songs and stories gain a romantic flavour merely by telling of some hero of the past. Robin Hood will always stand as an example. The common mind does not hate a good murder in a song, but it hates treachery, injustice, deceit. Therein lies the appeal to the larger public. Some broadside ballads told credible stories, but all took care to denounce the traitor—man or woman.

A story I will tell you, it is of butchers three,
Gibson, Wilson, and Johnson, mark well what I do say;
Now as they had five hundred pounds all on a market day,
Now as they had five hundred pounds to pay upon their way.
>With my hey, ding, ding, with my ho, ding, ding,
>With my hey ding, ding, high day!
>May God keep all good people from such bad company.

Now as they rode along the road as fast as they could ride,
'Spur on your horse,' says Johnson, 'for I hear a woman cry';
And as they rode into the wood a scene they spied around,
For there they found a woman with her hair pinned to the ground.
>With my hey, ding, ding, etc.

'Oh woman, woman,' Johnson cries, 'oh pray, come tell to me;
Oh woman, woman,' Johnson cries, 'have you got any company?'
'Oh no, no, no!' the woman cries. 'Alas! how can that be,
When here have been by ten swaggering blades, and they have
>ill-used me?'
>With my hey, ding, ding, etc.

Now Johnson, being a valiant man, he bore a valiant mind,
He wropped her up in his great coat, and placed her up behind,
And as they rode along the road as fast as they could ride,
She put her fingers to her ear and gave a shriekful cry.
>With my hey, ding, ding, etc.

With that came out ten swaggering blades with their rapiers ready
    drawn
They rode up to bold Johnson, and boldly bid him stand.
'Oh, I cannot fight,' says Gibson, 'I am sure that I shall die!'
'No more won't I,' says Wilson, 'for I will sooner fly.'
    With my hey, ding, ding, etc.

'Come on, come on!' cries bold Johnson, 'I'll fight you all so free,
And, woman, stand you here behind; we'll gain the victory!'
The very first pistol Johnson fired was loaded with powder and ball,
And, out of these ten swaggering blades, five of them did fall.
    With my hey, ding, ding, etc.

'Come on, come on,' cries bold Johnson, 'there are but five for me,
And, woman, stand you here behind, we'll gain the victory!'
The very next pistol Johnson fired was loaded with powder and ball,
And out of these five swaggering blades there's three of them did
        fall.
    With my hey, ding, ding, etc.

'Come on! come on!' cries bold Johnson, 'there are but two to me,
And, woman, stand you here behind, we'll gain the victory!'
As Johnson fought these rogues in front, the woman he did not
        mind,
She took his knife all from his side, and ripped him down behind.
    With my hey, ding, ding, etc.

'Now I must fall,' says Johnson, 'I must fall to the ground!
For relieving this wicked woman she gave me my death wound!
Oh! woman, woman, woman, what have you been and done?
You have killed the finest butcher that ever the sun shone on.'
    With my hey, ding, ding, etc.

Now just as she had done the deed some men came riding by,
And, seeing what this woman had done, they raised a dreadful cry.
Then she was condemned to die in links and iron chains so strong,
For killing of bold Johnson, that great and valiant man.
    With my hey, ding, ding, with my ho, ding, ding,
    With my hey, ding, ding, high day!
    May God keep all good people from such bad company.

Many of these broadside ballads were the work of literary hacks, as this is. Sometimes they would invent a story, and sometimes— indeed, often—dress up a true episode just as the newspapers do with crimes today. The result was not always artistic but it can be so. There is the common tale of the gallant thief who fears nobody, but hates the authorities and sympathizes with the poor. He is a rebel, and the appeal of such ballads is largely to a sentimental public sympathetic to the hunted hero. This, incidentally, is the theme John Gay played on in *The Beggar's Opera*, but Gay was an educated man playing a political game, and he laughed at his hero even as he employed all the tricks of his supposed beggar-poet to glorify MacHeath. He was a master of the mock-heroic, with his fair share of the malice which contemporary poets could summon so readily. To be effective this needs a sense of purpose. A folk-song often carries a sense of wrong, but malice is not its strong suit. Robin Hood and James Hind ride on today, in company with Jesse James in America and Jack Dougan in Australia; with their company must be included William Brennan of the eighteenth century.

It's of a fearless highwayman a story I will tell;
His name was William Brennan and in Ireland he did dwell;
Upon the Libbery mountains he commenced his wild career,
Where many a wealthy gentleman before him shook with fear.

      Bold and undaunted stood Brennan on the moor.

A brace of loaded pistols he did carry night and day,
He never robbed a poor man all on the King's highway;
But what he'd taken from the rich, like Turpin and Black Bess,
He always did divide between the widows in distress.

      Bold and undaunted stood Brennan on the moor.

One day he robbed a packman and his name was Pedlar Bawn;
They travelled on together till the day began to dawn;
The pedlar found his money gone, likewise his watch and chain,
He at once encountered Brennan and he robbed him back again.

      Bold and undaunted stood Brennan on the moor.

When Brennan saw the packman was as good a man as he,
He took him on the highway his companion to be;
The pedlar threw away his pack without any delay,
And proved a faithful comrade unto his dying day.

Bold and undaunted stood Brennan on the moor.

One day upon the King's highway as Willie he sat down,
He met the Mayor of Cashel just a mile outside the town;
The Mayor he knew his features bold: 'O you're my man,' said he,
'I think you're William Brennan, you must come along with me'.

Bold and undaunted stood Brennan on the moor.

Now Willie's wife had been to town provisions for to buy,
And when she saw her Willie she began to sob and cry;
He said: 'Give me that tenpence!' And as quick as Willie spoke,
She handed him a blunderbuss from underneath her cloak.

Bold and undaunted stood Brennan on the moor.

Now with this loaded blunderbuss (the truth I will unfold)
He made the Mayor to tremble, and he robbed him of his gold;
A hundred pounds was offered for his apprehension there,
But he with horse and saddle to the mountains did repair.

Bold and undaunted stood Brennan on the moor.

He lay among the fern all day, 'twas thick upon the field,
And many wounds he did receive before that he would yield;
He was captured and found guilty, and the judge made this reply:
'For robbing on the King's highway you are condemned to die.'

Bold and undaunted stood Brennan on the moor.

This is in the true tradition of the romantic robber. It is a simple
fiction, with adventure but without malice. The date of this version
would probably be towards the end of the eighteenth century, for it
refers to Dick Turpin and calls a blunderbuss a 'tenpence'. It offers
no theory about the supposed practice of robbing from the rich to

give to the poor, but perpetuates the theme. MacHeath in *The Beggar's Opera* is different on this score: he and his gang are levellers.

Ben Budge: We are for a just partition of the world. The world is avaricious, and I hate avarice. A covetous fellow, like a jackdaw, steals what he was never made to enjoy, for the sake of hiding it. These are the robbers of mankind, for money was made for the free-hearted and generous, and where is the injury in taking from another what he hath not the heart to make use of?

If the countryman ever thought in such terms it was not with regard to fiscal policy but poaching. He simply could not agree that it was wrong to take wild animals, though the consequences were serious enough.

As I rode o—ver Ban-stead Downs, One mid-May mor-ning ear——ly, There I es-pied a pret-ty fair maid la—men-ting for her Geor-gie.

    Saying, 'Georgie never stood on the King's highway,
      He never robbèd money,
    But he stole fifteen of the King's fat deer,
      And sent them to Lord Navey.

    'Oh, come and saddle my milk-white steed,
      And bridle it all ready,
    That I may go to my good Lord Judge,
      And ask the life of my Georgie.'

    And when she came to the good Lord Judge,
      She fell down upon her knees already,
    Saying: 'My good Lord Judge, come pity me,
      Grant me the life of my Georgie.'

The judge looked over his left shoulder,
    He seemed as he was very sorry;
'My pretty fair maid, you are come too late,
    For he is condemned already.

'He will be hung on a silken cord
    Where there has not been many,
For he came of royal blood
    And courted a virtuous lady.'

'I wish I was on yonder hill,
    Where times I have been many!
With a sword and buckler by my side,
    I would fight for the life of my Georgie.'

In English versions Georgie is a thief, hanged on a silken cord according to the privilege granted to the nobility. This makes the story more romantic. The Scottish versions of the story made Georgie an Earl, sentenced to death as a result of political influence, who was saved by having his sentence commuted to loss of property.

VII. Glorious Albion

##

Go patter to lubbers and swabs, d'ye see,
About danger and fear and the like,
A tight-water boat and good searoom give me
And it's not for a little I'll strike.

CHARLES DIBDIN

HANDEL HAD NO REMEDY at law against John Gay and Christopher Pepusch for using his March from *Rinaldo* in *The Beggar's Opera,* but consciences were beginning to work, if we may trust a letter published in *The Gazette* at that time.

Sir A.D. 1728

The famous letter writers of *The Tatler* and *The Spectator* would begin with a quotation in Latin, or even Greek; but as I do not fully understand the first, nor understand the second at all, it is against my principles to quote other than in plain English.

Sir, if a man steals another man's horse and drive with it in his carriage, he is a thief. If he puts his own horse to grass in another man's field without his neighbour's permission, he is doing wrong. If he put his horse to grass on common land, why, he may do so.

Now, Sir, mark the plain and honest musical analogy. If Mr Gay in his *Beggar's Opera* steals an air from Mr Handel, then he is a plain thief. But if Mr Handel steals an air from an Italian composer, why, then, Sir, he is a thief too. If it be finely and vainly said he does this merely to obtain 'inspiration', then he is a man who puts his horse to grass in another man's field. To use the popular songs of the streets and the country taverns may show poverty of invention, but is not dishonest if the fact be admitted.

The Taste of the day allows composers to filch, but let us try to be as honest in our music as we ought to be in our politics.

I am, Sir,

Your humble servant,

AN HONEST MAN.

Let us indeed try, but personal interests were served first, either in politics or in the theatre, and, as Mrs Peachum would be the first to suggest: 'If I am wrong, my dear, you must excuse me, for nobody can help the frailty of an over-scrupulous conscience'. *The Beggar's Opera* made money, so what would you have? Fifteen ballad operas were produced in London in 1729, the number rising annually to twenty-two in 1733; then a decline set in until 1741, when no new ballad operas were written. *The Beggar's Opera* could not be stemmed, however, but went on from success to success, even after Walpole had gone out of office. The fact was that no man, by putting his horse to grass in a common field, could make a hack into a winner, but *The Beggar's Opera* was a winner from the start.

The flowers that bloom in the common fields come again year after year in all the miracle of their perfection, but how many species have become extinct before they settled to the necessities of the English climate no man can tell. So it was with songs. The same favourites held their place in men's affections, but how many have failed to take root in that soil we cannot even guess. Writers of tunes for the stage tried to graft their ideas on to any stem which seemed sturdy enough at the time. Henry Carey, for example, struck a good shoot in 1739 with a patriotic Interlude called *Nancy: or The Parting Lovers,* which sang of the glory of England and the honour of the jolly Jack Tar. This little comic opera had various revivals during the eighteenth century, and with them changed its name; for the revival of 1755 it was called *The Press Gang: or Love in Low Life,* and later *True Blue,* which is the name of its tenor character, a British lad pressed into the Navy by a Commodore named Dreadnought, with whose daughter True Blue is in love. Here are all the ingredients for a good story with the press-gang as the villains, and the wonder is that Carey did not treat it so. His public was at the time of its first performance wildly patriotic, and the British Navy could do no wrong.

One of the minor diversions of English history is the War of Jenkins's Ear. A British sea-captain named Jenkins had his ear cut off by a Spanish captain who boarded his ship. It was not so much the loss of the ear which troubled Britain as the loss of dignity, for the Spaniard gave back the ear to Captain Jenkins and told him to take it to England as a challenge to the country. The populace took up the gage despite the efforts of Walpole to avoid a war with Spain (for to tell the truth the British Navy was not what it ought to have been, and Walpole knew it).[1] Walpole, however, gave way to popular demand, though he told them they would regret it, and Admiral Vernon gained a victory at Porto Bello. We did regret the War of Jenkins's Ear, but not in 1739.

Then, in the midst of much national boasting, Carey wrote the Interlude of *Nancy*. He knew the trick the public would play on themselves, of projecting their own feelings into romantic characters on the stage, and he helped them by putting into his stage characters just what his audience wanted to feel. In the conflict of love and duty, in the classical plots, love had to give way; Carey could rely on this sentiment being made to work, but he knew his public would like to have their cake and eat it, so he devised an ending where both love and duty were satisfied. More—he skilfully manipulated a social convention, that marriage outside one's own class is wrong. This he did to the accompaniment of graceful and stirring tunes not stolen from other men, nor from the common pool, but so near to them that their acceptance was assured.

True Blue and Nancy are making love. Someone is heard approaching, and as True Blue is an honest working lad and Nancy a Commodore's daughter, she hides. It is the Commodore himself, come to press True Blue into the Navy. True Blue is willing to serve his country, but asks permission to say farewell to his lass. He sings a lovely air in her favour. Nancy's appearance, however, puts her father in a rage. 'Daughter,' he sings, 'you're too young to marry,' and as for True Blue, he tells him: 'You're beneath her. Don't aspire so high again.' It is all very laudable, for 'love to glory must give way'; this is sung with long runs on the word 'glory' with all the heroic figuration which Henry Purcell or Handel would have used in such a situation. Of course there then has to be a parting duet between True Blue and Nancy, he declaring his love for her and his obligation to his country, and she regretting to see him go. Who could resist so touching a scene? Not even the Commodore! But True Blue is still in that class to which God originally called him, which is well below Nancy's in the social scale; so the Commodore himself does a bit of calling, promoting True Blue on the spot

---

[1] Walpole's contempt was bitterest when the commercial interests deserted him in favour of war: 'They may ring their bells now, but they will soon be wringing their hands.'

to be a lieutenant on his ship. After this the way is clear for Cupid and a naval victory.

> Come away, my brave boys,
>   Hoist the flag, beat the drum,
> Let the streamers wave over the main;
>   When Old England she calls us
>   We merrily come,
> She can't call a sailor in vain.

Nor is all this entirely altruistic, for

> Undaunted we conquer, look death in the face,
> And return with a load of doubloons,

sung with great verve to a rousing tune. As for Spain,

> That proud race we'll entirely exterminate,
>   And be masters of our fate,

to a tune in triple time for all the world like those which used earlier to make Charles II tap his foot in church.

It is essential for success in comic opera that the music and sentiments make an immediate appeal. This we should always keep in mind when considering such music. It is in a way propaganda. Carey's *True Blue* was patriotic propaganda, and propaganda moreover for Carey's pocket. It caught on at the time, and has been enjoyed since, but none of his songs in this opera, pleasant as they are, entered into the common stock of songs to which *Chevy Chase*, *Lillibulero*, or *The Irish Trot* belonged. If we would put our hobby-horse to grass in the common field, we should feed him on things like this.

> Come all you seamen bold and draw near, and draw near,
> Come all you seamen bold and draw near;
> It's of an admiral's fame, O brave Benbow was his name,
> How he fought upon the main, you shall hear, you shall hear.

> Brave Benbow he set sail for to fight, for to fight,
> Brave Benbow he set sail for to fight;
> Brave Benbow he set sail, with a fine and pleasant gale,
> But his captains they turned tail, in a fright, in a fright.

Says Kirby unto Wade: 'We will run, we will run,'
Says Kirby unto Wade: 'We will run.
For I value no disgrace, nor the losing of my place,
But the enemy I won't face, nor his guns, nor his guns'.

The Ruby and Benbow fought the French, fought the French,
The Ruby and Benbow fought the French.
They fought them up and down, till the blood came trickling down,
Till the blood came trickling down where they lay, where they lay.

Brave Benbow lost his legs by chain shot, by chain shot,
Brave Benbow lost his legs by chain shot.
Brave Benbow lost his legs, and all on his stumps he begs,
'Fight on, my English lads, 'tis our lot, 'tis our lot'.

The surgeon dressed his wounds, cries Benbow, cries Benbow,
The surgeon dressed his wounds, cries Benbow:
'Let a cradle now in haste on the quarter-deck be placed,
That the enemy I may face till I die, till I die'.[1]

Here is a song in the true tradition. It tells of a hero who bears
the pains of death with fortitude. It tells also of men who avoided
fight. This is no sauce to appetize public opinion for warfare, but an
expression of admiration for a brave man. The causes of the war
matter not, nor is there any particular hatred of the French; the
latter were foreigners, and therefore not to be trusted; the common
sailor knew no French; he did not understand their language or
their ways, and what he did not understand he suspected of enmity.
He would fight the foreign foe to order, but his songs were about
the feeling he had towards warfare, and these were based on
personal experience.

The death of Admiral Benbow was in 1702, in the reign of
Queen Anne, but dates of battles do not make a song, nor does
defeat or victory by itself; the song depends on how a man feels
towards the theme. The following song is about a victory, and
refers to King George; but the name of the vessel may change, and
the name of the port to which she belonged; it matters not to the
singer.

---

[1] Collected and arranged by Cecil J. Sharp; by permission of Novello & Co. Ltd.

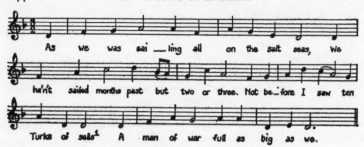

As we was sai—ling all on the salt seas, We ha'n't sailed months past but two or three. Not be-fore I saw ten Turks of sails[1] A man of war full as big as we.

'Pull down your colours, you English dogs!
Pull down your colours, do not refuse;
Oh, pull down your colours, you English dogs,
Or else your precious life shall lose!'

Our captain being a valiant man,
And a well-bespoken young man were he:
'Oh, it shall never be said that we died like dogs,
But we will fight them most manfully!

'Go up, you lofty cabin-boys,
And mount the mainmast topsail high,
For to spread abroad of King George's fleet,
To run a risk we must live and die.'

The fight began about six in the morning
And out to the setting of the sun;
Oh, and at the rising of the next morning
Out of ten ships we couldn't see but one.

Oh, three we sunk, and three we burned,
And three we causèd to run away,
And one we brought into Portsmouth harbour
For to let them know we had won the day.

If any one then should enquire
Or want to know our captain's name,
Oh, Captain Wellfounder, our chief commander;
But the *Royal Oak* is our ship by name.

[1] Turkish sails.

The version quoted was taken down by Iolo A. Williams from a singer in Surrey. Another version, in Gavin Greig's *Folk-Songs of the North-East* (1st series), has this conclusion:

> Would you know the ship that did it?
> And would you know the captain's name?
> 'Twas Captain Mansfield of Bristol Town,
> And the *Marigold* was the ship of fame.

Try to identify the vessel, the battle, and the captain, and you will find the folk-song as inaccurate as ever. There was a *Marigold* of Bristol given letters of marque to prey on the enemy's commerce in the early seventeenth century, and there was a *Royal Oak* sent to convoy the merchant fleet to Lisbon in 1707; she was boarded by the French and her captain (Wilde, not Wellfounder) was cashiered. Neither of these could have been of King George's fleet, but why ask? The story is equally human in whatever reign it took place, or even if it is purely imaginary.

In any case we may be wrong in assuming that the vessel was a warship, for right into the nineteenth century it was necessary for ships to fight their way through enemy raiders or pirates. The merchant ship carried guns and the crew had to man them. As British trade increased with the development of the American colonies and the East India Company, the interest of merchants and politicians centred more and more on its rapid extension. In the London theatres, as we have seen, patriotic fervour drew good audiences, and there is a style of art associated with these elegant productions (and the London pleasure gardens to which they were related) following the course of naval and military history and idealizing the common people. Scratch the surface of an eighteenth-century comic opera and the common people will be found, but they have to be dressed up for the stage to suit the demands of its patrons. If the songs are made for money, he who pays the piper calls the tune. A comic opera had to have a happy ending. Carey's *Nancy* told of a common lad in love with a girl of superior station. This was a good theme, but Carey's clever twist to the happy ending was an original piece of writing. The folk-songs often deal with this situation, but more realistically. It was not expected that a lad who found favour with a better-class young lady should have his way.

As I roved out one morning down by a riverside,
I heard a lovely maid lament, the tears fell from her eyes.
'This is a cold and stormy night,' these words I heard her say;
'My love is on the raging seas, bound for Americay.

'John Riley is my true love's name; he lives down by the quay;
He is as fine a young man as ever you did see;
My father he has riches great, but Riley he is poor,
Because I love my sailor dear they will not me endure.

'My mother took me by the hand, these words to me did say:
"If you are fond of Riley you must leave this countery;
Your father said he'd take his life, and that without delay,
So you must either go abroad or shun his company".

'"O mother dear, don't be severe, for where I send my love,
My very heart lies in his breast, as constant as a dove."
"O daughter dear, I am not severe, here is one thousand pound,
Send Riley to Americay to purchase there some ground."'

When she had got the money, to Riley she did run:
'This very night to take your life my father charged his gun;
Here is one thousand pounds of gold my mother sent to you;
Sail off unto Americay and I will follow you.'

When Riley got the money next day he sailed away,
And when he'd got his foot aboard these words I heard him say:
'This is a token of true love, I will break it in two,
You have my heart and half the ring, till I do find out you'.

In about a twelvemonth after she was walking by the sea,
When Riley he came back again to take his love away;
The ship got wrecked, all hands were lost, her father, grief full sore,
Found Riley drownded in her arms, and washed up on the shore.

He found a letter in her breast, it being wrote with blood:
'How cruel was my father, that thought to shoot my love!
Oh, this might be a warning to all fair maids so gay:
Don't never send your true love unto Americay'.

Thère is no elegance in this, but the human story is fundamental. The details of getting rid of the humble lover vary, but the tragedy is that he is made to suffer for a natural passion. The easiest way of removing an embarrassing suitor was by the press-gang. This hideous institution was liked by nobody, least of all the ship's company,[1] but since men would not willingly go to sea it was often the only means of manning the wooden walls that guarded Old England and her trade. Many folk-songs tell of the separation of lovers by the press-gang.

> Come all you brisk young seamen bold
>   That plough the watery main,
> And listen to my tragedy
>   Whilst I relate the same;
> Oh, pressed I was from my true love,
>   The girl I do adore,
> And sent I was to the raging seas,
>   Where foaming billows roar.

It is a great literary theme. Sometimes he is taken at the instigation of her parents, sometimes out of sheer chance, because the press-gang happens to drop on him. The tragedy may be that the girl does not know what has happened to him, and may, for all she knows, have been deserted. There are, then, the songs about the lonely woman expecting her child, the married woman suddenly left without a husband, and the songs of constancy—the latter among the most beautiful of folk-songs.

> My parents they chide me and will not agree,
>   That I and my sailor lad married should be,
> But let them deride me and say what they will,
>   While there's breath in my body he's the one I love still.

In some versions of this song the sailor has simply gone away to sea, but in a Dorset version he has been transported. Transportation need not have been for a villainy: one could be transported for poaching—a crime which the peasantry hardly acknowledged as such.

---

[1] Admiral ('Old Grog') Vernon tried to persuade the government to improve conditions of service, make recruiting more attractive, and abolish the press-gang, but in vain.

In the theatres England's glory was never sullied, but in folk-songs the glory and the shame intermingle. They offer a true picture of social history, however hazy the political and economic history of the singers may be. An understanding of the English is possible by combining the views of the politicians with those of the common people. William Pitt, Earl of Chatham, believed in the force of strong personalities, especially his own, and in capturing the world's trade. It had to be captured by conquest and by colonization; the end was to justify the means. India was a source of considerable profit, which went into private pockets through the trading of the East India Company, but a country like England was made up of individuals, and the more these prospered the greater would be the wealth of the whole. It happened that while British commerce was being wafted to prosperity on the waves of patriotism (and higher taxation for the furtherance of the Seven Years War) agriculture underwent a technical transformation. Lord (Turnip) Townshend (1674–1738) and Thomas Coke (1752–1842) improved the nature of low-yielding soil and introduced new root crops and methods of cultivation in Norfolk, while Robert Bakewell in Leicestershire demonstrated the benefits of scientific cattle and sheep breeding. Not only this, but with the wealth they acquired the landowning gentry built fine houses, and designed parks and gardens which transformed the face of the countryside, as did the hedges and ditches which were symbolic of the new farming methods. All these things needed capital in abundance, with the prospect of returns in future years, and were only achieved when the land could be enclosed and administered by one controlling mind. The old strip system of farming presented obstacles to agricultural reform which kept the yeoman farmer poor, and as time went on proved his bane. Either he had to find means to adopt the new methods or he lost his title to the land and became an employee of the larger landlords. Whichever way his fortune went there was a song to go with it; the theme of feminine constancy and the press-gang need not always be tragic, for here, combined with the new prosperity on the land, it starts a song which finds a happy ending.

Come all you pretty fair maids, and listen to my song,
While I relate a story that does to love belong;
'Tis of a blooming damsel walked through the fields so gay,
And there she met her true love, and he unto her did say.

'Where are you going, young Nancy, this morning bright and gay
Or why do you walk here alone? Come tell to me I pray?'
'I am going to yonder river-side, where fishes they do swim,
All for to gather flowers that grow around the brim.'

'Be not in haste, young Nancy,' this young man he did say,
'And I will bear you company, and guard you on the way.
I live by yonder river-side where fishes they do swim,
Where you may gather flowers that grow around the brim.'

'Kind sir, you must excuse me,' this maiden did reply,
'I will never walk with any man until the day I die;
I have a sweetheart of my own, and him my heart has won;
He lived in yonder cottage, a wealthy farmer's son.'

'And pray, what is your lover's name?' he unto her did say,
'Though in my tarry trousers, perhaps I know him may.'
She said: 'His name is William, from that I'll never run,
This ring we broke at parting. He's a wealthy farmer's son.'

The ring out of his pocket he instantly then drew,
Saying: 'Nancy, here's the parting gift; one half I left with you.
I have been pressed to sea and many a battle won;
But still my heart could ne'er depart from me, the farmer's son.'

When these words she heard him say, it put her in surprise,
The tear-drops they came twinkling down from her sparkling eyes.
'Oh, soothe your grief,' the young man said, 'the battle you have
        won.
For Hymen's chains shall bind us—you, and the farmer's son.'

To church then went this couple, and married were with speed.
The village bells they all did ring, and the girls did dance indeed.
She blessed the happy hour she in the fields did run,
To seek all for her true love, the wealthy farmer's son.

This is a variation of the song of the girl who wishes for a superior
lover. It may be compared with the Cinderella story. Cinderella is
imaginary, with fairy-lore and a most unorthodox Prince, but the
folk-song is remarkably near to life. No doubt it is fiction, but it

suits the wishes of folk-singers. If we would see the less presentable
side of eighteenth-century life it will be found in the numerous
songs about poaching. These often show pride in outwitting the
hare and the keeper, and end with a verse about a spree purchased
with the money got from the sale of the catch. Another ending
could be boastful:

> But let them say whatever they will,
> We'll have our hares and pheasants still.

Another version of the same song, with place-names changed to suit
another district, takes a glance at the consequences of being caught
by the gamekeeper.

> Over hedges, ditches, gates and rails,
> Our dogs followed after, behind our heels;
> If he had catched us, say what you will,
> He'd have sent us all to Abingdon jail.

While a broadsheet of later date goes deeper into the theme.

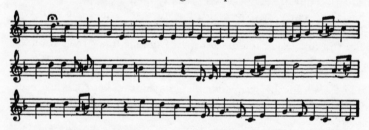

Come all you gallant poachers, that ramble free from care,
That walk out of a moonlight with your dog, your gun, and snare;
Where the lofty hare and pheasant you have at your command,
Not thinking that your last career is on Van Diemen's Land.

There was poor Tom Brown from Nottingham, Jack Williams, and
　　poor Joe,
Were three as daring poachers as the country well does know;
At night they were trepannéd by the keeper's hideous hand,
And for fourteen years transported were unto Van Diemen's Land.

Oh, when we sailed from England we landed at the bay,
We had rotten straw for bedding, we dared not to say nay;
Our cots are fenced with fire, we slumber when we can,
To drive away the wolves and tigers upon Van Diemen's Land.

Oh, when that we were landed upon that fatal shore,
The planters they came flocking round full twenty score or more;
They ranked us up like horses and sold us out of hand,
They yoked us to the plough my boys to plough Van Diemen's Land.

To see our fellows suffer, I'm sure I can't tell how,
Some chained us unto the harrow and some unto the plough;
They hooked us out by two and two like horses in a team,
And a driver standing over us with his long lash and cane.

There was a girl from England, Susan Summers was her name,
For fourteen years transported was, we all well knew the same;
Our planter bought her freedom, and he married her out of hand,
Good usage then she gave to us upon Van Diemen's Land.

Often, when I am slumbering, I have a pleasant dream,
With my sweet girl I am sitting, down by some puling stream,
Through England I am roaming, with her at my command,
Then waken, broken-hearted, upon Van Diemen's Land.

God bless our wives and families, likewise that happy shore,
That isle of sweet contentment which we shall see no more;
As for our wretched females, see them we seldom can,
There are twenty to one woman upon Van Diemen's Land.

Come, all you gallant poachers, give ear unto my song,
It is a bit of good advice, although it is not long;
Lay by your dog and snare; to you I do speak plain,
If you knew the hardships we endure you ne'er would poach again.

This ballad could be late eighteenth century, but is more likely
early nineteenth. Criminals were transported to Tasmania and
Australia [1] after the breakaway of the American Colonies, and until

[1] Van Diemen's Land is Tasmania; Botany Bay, of which there are also folk-songs,
was an Australian convict settlement equally feared.

1853. The song, nevertheless, serves to illustrate the attitude of the British Government for far too long; the colonies were places where undesirables might be sent, and if they did not come back, so much the better. Linked with this policy was the need for cheap labour in the areas being developed, and the moral opportunism of the legal mind which made an example of the lawbreaker in order to intimidate the wrongdoer.

There were, however, many, in the American Colonies in particular, who had emigrated voluntarily. To most of them England was not a land of sweet contentment, but a land in which they had been subjected to oppression, religious or economic. The American colonists had no love of British government, and when they found themselves liable to pressure from England they stood firm against it. They proved themselves slightly less inefficient than the British in warfare, and equally resolute in their determination on liberty. The United States of America were welded into a great independent nation.

How was the American War of Independence fought?

It was not fought without rancour, for the Americans were deeply enraged, and the British officers were in command of troops which had no sense of those traditions held in common by both British and Americans. Most of these were Germans hired out by their ruling princes to the British Crown, who fought because the consequences of failing to attack the enemy were worse than anything the enemy was likely to do. Of the English-speaking troops, some were men released from debtors' prisons and drafted into the army, some (and these the best) born in the garrison towns, some volunteers tricked into joining the army by the cajolery of the recruiting-sergeant, and others who joined in desperation.

> As I was a-walking down Newry one day,
> I met Captain Galligan by chance on my way;
> 'Will you take the bounty and come along with me
> To the sweet town of Newry happy hours for to see?'

> 'My mother is dead, and she never will return,
> My father's twice married, and a wife has brought home,
> My father's twice married, and a wife he's brought home,
> And to me she proves cruel, and does me disown.'

So I took the shilling and the bargain was made,
Then the ribbons were bought and pinned to my cockade,
Bad luck to all parents who have a bad son,   ,
For they don't know the hardships that they have to run.

Put in a cold guard-room all night and all day,
Put in a field of battle their enemies for to slay,
Bad luck to my uncle, wherever he may be,
For he's been the ruin and the downfall of me.

Out of the American War of Independence came a tune which has
persisted down the years—*Yankee Doodle*. A great deal of research
has gone into the origin of this tune, especially that undertaken for
the Library of Congress by Dr O. G. Sonneck in 1909. Nobody has
been able to say definitely whether the song was first used by the
Americans or the British. The British seem to have thought they
were using an American tune in derision against its creators. There
is a letter quoted by Iona and Peter Opie in *The Oxford Dictionary
of Nursery Rhymes*, from a British officer, which states that the British
troops in Boston had used the term 'Yankee' as a term of reproach,
but after the battle of Bunker's Hill the Americans gloried in it.

'Yankee Doodle is now their Paean, a favourite of favourites,
played in their army, esteemed as warlike as the Grenadiers' March
—it is the lover's spell, the nurse's lullaby. After our rapid successes,
we held the Yankees in great contempt, but it was not a little morti-
fying to hear them play this tune, when our army marched down to
surrender.' In fact, the British went out of the Thirteen Colonies
with the tune of *Yankee Doodle* rankling in their minds much as
Lillibulero must have rankled in the mind of James II.

So the United States started independent life to the accompaniment of a folk-song apparently of their own creation. Many of the
songs surviving in the New World, however, are of English origin,
as indeed are many of their ideas of other things. The importance of
the United States' contribution to folk-music will be discussed in a
later chapter, but while we are dealing with problems of British
colonization in the eighteenth century we may as well take a glance
at an interesting development recorded in the West Indies.

Transported criminals did not supply the whole of the labour force
for the plantations, nor indeed most of it; this was supplied by Negro
slaves. These unfortunates were taken in battle with neighbouring

tribes, or as a result of tribal raids, and sold to the white traders whose grim castles lay along the shores of the Gold Coast. The best of the Negro captives were chosen by the traders, the remainder being slaughtered without compunction by their Negro captors. Of all trades this was the most horrid; only the most brutal of men could stomach it, and of them the West African climate took heavy toll. The captains of these trading castles were as ruthless as those of a pirate ship, and their underlings for the most part men who had escaped from the law in their own countries and dared not return. The Negroes were shipped across the Atlantic and sold on the American mainland or in the West Indies. It did not matter to the planters what customs the Negroes had inherited in Africa, for whatever these were they must be heathen, and were therefore to be suppressed. There were two strong arguments in favour of taking a slave: the first of these was that his life was saved in Africa from his enemies, and the second was that in his new environment he would enjoy salvation from his heathen ways. It could also be argued that white men in their own countries were treated worse than slaves.

> The Negro 'gainst Negro who fights,
>   When conquered is bartered for gain,
> And tell me, pray would not the whites
>   Much rather be sold than be slain?
> Of barbarous usage, whate'er
>   May be the complaints of the West,
> From horrid transactions, 'tis clear,
>   There wants a reform in the East.
>
> That 'Britons shall never be slaves',
>   In Britain is frequently sung,
> And many times heard on the waves
>   When First Rates are rolling along;
> But what greater slaves can there be,
>   Than those hardy lads of the main,
> Who, when just returned from the sea,
>   Are dragged into service again?
>
> In Europe this much may be said,
>   So great a temptation has gold,
> For slaughter at so much per head
>   Have Germans by thousands been sold.

Too oft their ambitions to show,
  Crowned heads set their minions to work,
And Joseph the Emperor's view,
  A slave was to make of the Turk.

And so it to numbers appears,
  If commerce we aim to restrain,
Britannia but very few years
  The Empress will be of the main;
To lessen let's make it our care,
  The burdens upon our own backs,
For Britons too many there are,
  More miserable souls than the Blacks.

This ballad came from Birmingham, the work of John Freeth, a publican, who wrote political ballads to please his tavern customers. He had no experience of ways in the West Indies, but he would have been glad to know that though you may chain a Negro's body you cannot altogether chain his mind. The Negroes would relapse into ways which filled the white men with disgust. Above all the Negroes would dance strange dances.

These the planters at first prevented. They kept the Negroes at work continually, not only for profit, but for the good of the slaves' souls. This policy failed, however, because the slaves became apathetic to a marked degree. In this condition they were bad workers. The planters found that by letting the slaves have their own way on Sundays the slaves were more fit for work during the remainder of the week. They disapproved of their slaves' idea of enjoyment, but business necessitated that they did not obstruct this unduly.

So a curious situation arose. We can learn much from accounts left by those who studied the Negro slaves in these years. The first passage is by Père Lavat, who was on the French island of Martinique in 1698, and who says: [1]

The dance is their favourite passion. I don't think there is a people on the face of the earth who are more attached to it than they. When the master will not allow them to dance on the Estate, they will travel three or four leagues, as soon as they knock off work at the sugar-works on Saturday, and betake themselves to some place where they know that there will be a dance.

[1] Père Lavat, *Noveau Voyage aux isles de l'Amérique*, 1698, Vol. II, pp. 51f.

The one in which they take the greatest pleasure, and which is the usual one, is the Calenda. It came from the Guinea coast and to all appearances from Ardra. The Spaniards have learnt it from the Negroes and throughout America dance it in the same way as do the Negroes.

As the postures and movements of the dance are most indecent, the masters who live in a seemly way forbid it to their own people, and take care that they do not dance it; and this is no small matter, for it is to their liking, and the very children who are as yet scarcely strong enough to stand up, strive to imitate their fathers and mothers when they see dancing, and will spend entire days at this exercise.

The rhythm is provided by two drums, the larger to mark the time, and the smaller drum beaten more rapidly, with intricate rhythms, to arouse the passions, says Père Lavat.

The dancers are drawn up in two lines, one before the other, the men on one side and the women on the other. Those who are waiting their turns, and the spectators, make a circle round the dancers and drums. The more adept chants a song which he improvises on the spur of the moment, on some subject which he deems appropriate, the refrain of which, chanted by all the spectators, is accompanied by a great clapping of hands. As regards the dancers, they hold their arms a little after the manner of those who dance while playing the castanets. They skip, make a turn right and left, approach within two or three feet of each other, draw back in cadence, until the sound of the drum directs them to draw together again, striking the thighs one against the other, that is to say, the man against the woman. To all appearance it seems that the stomachs are hitting, while as a matter of fact it is the thighs that carry the blows. They retire at once in a pirouette, to begin again the same movements with altogether lascivious gestures, as often as the drum gives the signal, as it may do several times in succession. From time to time they interlock arms and make two or three turns, always striking the thighs and kissing. One easily sees from this abbreviated description how the dance is opposed to decency.[1]

Père Lavat was obviously as much disturbed by the Negro dancers as the early Christian missionaries must have been by pagan customs in tenth-century England, but his training did not allow of similar compromise. Nor was Lavat alone in his disgust; a century later Moreau de Saint-Mèry was equally disturbed in his mind.

Another Negro dance at San Domingo, which is also of African origin, is the Chica, called simply Calenda in the Windward Isle, Congo at Cayenne, Fandango in Spanish, etc. This dance has an air which is

[1] Ibid.

specially consecrated to it and wherein the measure is strongly marked. The proficiency in the dancer consists in the perfection with which she can move her hips and the lower part of her back while preserving the rest of her body in a kind of immobility, that even the slightest movement of the arms that balance the two ends of a handkerchief or her petticoat does not make her lose. A dancer approaches her. All of a sudden he makes a leap into the air and lands in measured time so as almost to touch her. He draws back; he jumps again, and excites her by the most seductive play. The dance becomes enlivened, and soon it presents a tableau, of which the entire action, at first voluptuous, afterwards becomes lascivious. It would be impossible to depict the Chica in its true character, and I will limit myself to saying that the impression it produces is so strong that the African or Creole (it does not matter of what shade) who comes to dance it without emotion, is considered to have lost the last spark of vitality.[1]

Saint-Mèry confirms Lavat's statement about the social attraction of dancing among the Negroes.

What enraptures the Negroes, whether they were born in Africa, or America is their cradle, is the dance. There is no amount of fatigue which can make them abandon going great distances, and sometimes even during the night, to satisfy this passion.

One Negro dance has come down with them from Africa to San Domingo, and for that very reason is common also to those who are born in the colony, and these latter practise it almost from birth. They call it the Calenda.

To dance the Calenda the Negroes have two drums made, when possible, from the hollow tree in a single piece. One end is open, and they stretch over the other a skin of a sheep or a goat. The shorter of these drums is called Bamboula, because it is sometimes made from a very thick bamboo. Astride of each drum is a Negro who strikes it with wrist and fingers, but slowly for one and rapidly for the other. To this monotone and hollow sound is joined that of a number, more or less great, of little calabashes half filled with small stones, or with grains of corn, and which they shake by striking them on one of the hands by means of a long haft which crosses them. When they wish to make the orchestra more complete they add the Banza, a kind of bass viol with four strings which they pluck. The Negresses arranged in a circle regulate the tempo by clapping their hands, and they reply in chorus to one or two chanters whose piercing voice repeats or improvises ditties. For the Negroes possess the talent of improvising, and it gives them an opportunity for displaying especially their tendency to banter.

[1] M. L. Moreau de Saint-Mèry, *Description topographique, physique, civile, politique, et historique de la partie française de l'isle Saint-Dominique*, etc., Philadelphia, 1797–8, Vol. I, p. 50.

The dancers, male and female, always equal in number, come to the middle of a circle (which is formed on even ground and in the open air) and they begin to dance. Each appropriates a partner to cut a figure before her. This dance, which has its origin upon Mount Atlas, and which offers little variation, consists of a movement where each foot is raised and lowered alternately, striking with force, sometimes the toe and sometimes the heel, on the ground, in a way quite similar to the English step. The dancer turns on himself or around his partner, who joins also and changes place, waving the two ends of a handkerchief which they hold. The dancer lowers and raises alternately his arms, while keeping the elbows near the body, and the hand almost closed. This dance, in which the play of the eyes is nothing less than extraordinary, is lively and animated, and an exact timing lends it real grace. The dancers follow one another with emulation, and it is often necessary to put an end to the ball, which the Negroes never abandon without regret.[1]

Actually there are two dances described in these passages from Lavat and Saint-Mèry. Saint-Mèry's first passage refers to the same dance as Lavat's two passages—the Chica, which was called Calenda in Martinique. The final passage from Saint-Mèry describes the true Calenda, which may be a development from the Chica, but is more of a social accomplishment. The Chica was apparently nearer to a simple fertility ritual. This is not the place to go fully into origins of Negro dances, nor to question the statement that one of these originated on Mount Atlas; our purpose in describing these is to show the importance of New World culture on future developments. Moreau de Saint-Mèry was a man of some merit. Born in Martinique in 1750, he went to Paris and was president of the *electeurs* when the Bastille fell. He received the key of the fortress in the name of the city. At the beginning of the Terror, however, he fled to America, and became a bookseller in Philadelphia. (William Cobbett, who knew him in Philadelphia, translated his *Topographical Description . . . of the Spanish District of Martinique.*)

William Cobbett was persecuted in America for daring to put forward a defence of British opinion. Like many of the active-minded English at that time he was by no means unsympathetic to the new United States. The inhabitants of the United States, however, were largely of British extraction, and a good percentage English. They had their forbears' stubborn Magna-Carta-and-Bill-of-Rights-for-ever mentality, for which they need hardly be blamed. If they detested English politics, however, they still loved

[1] Ibid.

English tunes. *The Beggar's Opera* was a steady American favourite from 1750 onwards, and not until the last years of the eighteenth century did foreign opera get a start in America: English comic operas were the vogue. The compositions of Arne, Attwood, Hook, Kelly, Shield, and Storace were as popular in the larger American towns as they were in England. Why should the English have all the good tunes? Why indeed!

The type of song favoured in these operas was elegant English. Carey's *Nancy* was an early specimen of the type. The florid runs of melody on words like 'glory' were part of the heroic figuration of the time; Arne, in *Rule, Britannia,* showed in music how Britain arose from the sea with an upward-curving figure on the word 'arose'. If we would seek examples of such tunes we can find them in Purcell, Handel, and of course innumerable composers of Italian opera, but this is art-music, not folk-song.

The simpler taste of the time can be shown in a verse of a song by Charles Dibdin, in his comic opera *The Milkmaid*:

> Sweet ditties would my Patty sing,
> *Old Chevy Chase, God Save the King,*
> *Fair Rosemy, The Sawny Scot,*
> *Lillibulero,* the *Irish Trot,*
> All these would sing my blue-eyed Patty.

Dibdin said he got the poetic style from Gay's *Trivia*. Of street music we have some excellent examples noted down by Malchair, leader of the orchestra in the Music Rooms at Oxford in the late eighteenth century. One of his notebooks contains this sentence: 'I heard a man whistle this tune in Magpie Lane, Oxon., December 27, 1789. Came home and noted it down.'

Then follows the tune.

Another popular song of this time is *The Girl I left Behind Me,* the tune of which, used for a dance, is known also as *Brighton Camp.* The character of the tune is modified for the purpose to which it is adapted. It may have been a flute tune. Drums and fifes were the traditional marching instruments of the soldiers, and there was a camp at Brighton from 1793 to 1795.

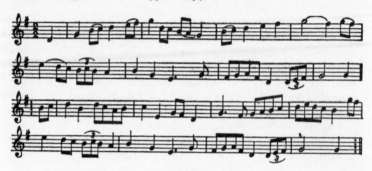

A Republic had been declared in France in 1793, the king executed, and the new Republic offered help to any nation wishing to depose its monarch. Conditions in the British Isles were probably worse for the peasantry than in France before the Revolution, and in the army and navy discipline was particularly brutal. The most perilous year was 1797, when the sailors at Spithead mutinied. Their wrongs were crying for redress—low pay and insufficient food even if they got all of it, which they did not. Shore leave was scanty, and flogging merciless—often for the most trivial offences. Some abatement of these harsh conditions was granted to the navy, the most unpopular of the officers dismissed, and the crews at Spithead then cheered and asked to be led against the French. That was one side of the picture. The other was that immediately afterwards the sailors at the Nore mutinied, but their leaders demanded political reforms derived from French and American ideas. To these the Government could not submit; the mutiny was broken and the leaders hanged. Nevertheless the remaining men fought bravely and loyally at Camperdown soon afterwards. Burning grievances and traditional loyalty were together alive in the hearts of the sailors. Recruits could not however be obtained. The situation for the country was serious.

Pitt conducted a war of ideas as well as a war of arms. He kept a

firm hand on the press. Editors who published matter prejudicial
to his policy were viciously penalized. One of these was William
Cobbett and another James Montgomery, the hymn writer and
editor of the *Sheffield Iris*. Most men toed the Tory party line for
safety's sake, others were resolute. But some there were who
believed absolutely in the cause of Glorious Albion, among whom
was the song-writer Charles Dibdin. His notion of the British
sailor was a man dauntless in battle but honest and kindhearted
to a fault when ashore. Moreover, Dibdin's patriotic songs were
popular.

> I say my heart, why here's your works,
>   The French have it now with the gravy;
> Why, what between the English and Turks,
>   They'll lose both their army and navy.
> Bold Nelson went out with deliberate view
>   To keep up our national glory,
> So of thirteen large ships he left mounseer two,
>   Just to tell the Directory the story.
> Then of England and England's brave tars let us sing,
>   As true as the keel to the kelson;
> Let's be loyal to truth, and honour the King,
>   And drink to the Navy and Nelson.

> But with France it's all up, they are meeting their fate,
>   They've thrown down their basket of crockery,
> And vengeance like this will o'ertake soon or late
>   All who make of religion a mockery.
> Then of England, that wonderful country, sing,
>   Where we've thousands of joys if we need 'em;
> Mild laws that protect us, a Protestant King,
>   Lovely women, grog, biscuit, and freedom.

This sort of thing may not be good art, but it appealed to the
imagination. It said what men wanted to believe. Recruits came into
the navy without being pressed; Pitt gave Dibdin an annual
pension of two hundred pounds.

Had Dibdin sold his pen? Not a bit of it; he had always believed
ardently in a Britain right or wrong. What is more, others believed
in it, however harshly their country treated them. The English were

not given to logic but to traditional defences, often amounting almost to paradox.

The conservatism of the English peasantry was something beyond reason, and a terrific force in world affairs. They sat knee by knee with their ale-mugs in their hands, and sang of *Boney's Lamentation*. If they knew any history, this was it.

Attend, you sons of high renown,
To these few lines which I pen down;
I was born to wear a stately crown,
And to rule a wealthy nation.
I am the man that beat Bello,
At Warmer's Hill did them subdue,
That great Archduke I overthrew,
On every plain my men were slain;
Grand traverse too I did obtain,
And got capitulation.

For to pursue the Egyptian shore,
Where the Algerians lay in their gore,
The rights of France for to restore
That long had been confiscated;
We pursued them close through mud and mire,
Till in despair my men retired,
And Moscow town was set on fire.
My men were lost through winter frost,
I ne'er before received such blast,
Since the hour I was created.

To Leipzig town my soldiers fled,
Mount Mark was strewed with Prussian dead,
We marched them forth inveterate streams
To stop a bold invasion.
So farewell, my royal spouse,
And offspring great whom I adore,
And may you reinstate that throne
That is torn away, without delay,
Those kings of me have made a prey,
And caused my lamentation.

This is not the work of a poet, nor yet an unlettered singer. More probably it came from some semi-literate hack. Anyway, it got into the folk tradition and was taken down in 1893 from Henry Burstow, bell-ringer, of Horsham, Surrey, who was then sixty-eight years old and had 'never left for a night, except once for a week'. Yet, was he uncultured? He knew four hundred songs and could sing them all from memory!

Boney's Lamentation dates apparently from after Napoleon's fall; the same is true of *The Bonny Bunch of Roses*; indeed it is later still, because it refers to his death at St Helena. The bunch of roses symbolizes the British Isles.

By the dangers of the ocean, one morning in the month of June,
The feathered warbling songsters their charming notes so sweet did tune,
It was there I spied a female, seemingly in grief and woe,
Conversing with young Bonaparte concerning the bonny bunch of roses O.

'O then,' said young Napoleon, and grasped his mother by the hand,
'Do, mother, pray have patience, till I'm able to command.
I will raise a terrible army, and through tremendous dangers go,
And in spite of all the universe I'll gain the bonny bunch of roses O.

'When first you saw great Bonaparte you fell upon your bended knee,
You asked your father's life of him, he granted it most manfully.
'Twas then he took an army and through frozen realms did go,
He said, "I'll conquer Moscow, then wear the bonny bunch of roses O."'

'Now son, never speak so venturesome. England is the heart of oak.
England, Ireland, and Scotland, their unity has never been broke;
And son, look at your father! in St Helena his body lies low,
And you will soon follow after, so beware of the bonny bunch of roses O.'

'O mother, adieu for ever! Now I am on my dying bed;
If I had lived I should have been clever, but now I droop my
　　youthful head,
But while our bones do moulder, and weeping willows o'er us grow,
The deeds of bold Napoleon will sting the bonny bunch of roses O.'

Napoleon's only son died in 1832, aged 21!

VIII. The Romantic Revival

❊❊❊

The child is father of the man;
And I could wish my days to be
Bound each to each by natural piety.

WORDSWORTH

I

CHARLES DIBDIN was not only a popular song-writer, but a
man with a fondness for travel. His first tour of England was undertaken in 1787 and 1788 with the object of raising money to go to
India, for he was at that time disgusted with his treatment in the
London theatres. Ten years later he made tours of Scotland and the
South of England, right to Land's End, publishing his opinions on
these places and his experiences of the roads. He started as a dis-
gruntled man, but learned to like his countrymen better as a result
of his travels. His books are worthy of republication. Passing
through Gloucester he left a ballad in remembrance of his visit. He
had a facile mind, which nevertheless reflects much of the thought
of the time.

George Ridler's oven, I've been told, contains some curious jokes,
    sirs,
And very much of it is said by many Glo'ster folk, sirs;
But ovens now are serious things, and from my soul I wish, sirs,
Your ovens here may ne'er want bread to fill the poor man's dish, sirs,
    sirs.

The tune is *Yankee Doodle*; the words are to be found on two
ballad-sheets dating from the beginning of the nineteenth century,
one of which bears the imprint of Robert Raikes. Tradition ascribes
the words to Dibdin.

In his wanderings Dibdin called upon Raikes because he, Raikes,
was the local printer, but we know him also as a pioneer of Sunday

schools for poor children, and as a prison reformer. Though Dibdin himself took no part in such reforms, they were part of the English social scene, and he had his opinions on them, which, to his credit, were sympathetic. In 1787 he visited Coalbrookdale, where he saw the new methods of smelting and working iron. (The famous Iron Bridge, which still stands, had just been completed.) The workers were grimy and possibly misshapen, which caused Dibdin's companion to remark that he would be sorry to meet one of these 'dingy gentlemen' in a dark lane. Dibdin answered, however, that he had himself made such a mistake when first he saw the miners at Kingswood, near Bristol, but that he soon learned that the men were God-fearing, and no doubt the Coalbrookdale iron-workers were too, for their employers were Quakers. On inquiry he discovered that there were many Methodists also in Coalbrookdale.

Quakers won converts by their unwavering honesty: Methodists by the fervour of their preaching and the soul-compelling ardour of their hymns. At a time when poets were given to classical aloofness what must have been the effect of lines like these?

> I cannot see Thy face and live,
>   Then let me see Thy face, and die!
> Now, Lord, my gasping spirit receive;
>   Give me on eagle's wings to fly,
> With eagle's eyes on Thee to gaze,
> And plunge into the glorious blaze!

Such devotion must have sounded to the polite scholars of 1749 much as Pope regarded the preaching of Whitefield.

> So swells each wind-pipe; Ass intones to Ass;
> Harmonic twang! of leather, horn, and brass;
> Such as from lab'ring lungs the Enthusiast blows,
> High sound, attemper'd to the vocal nose.

But whatever success *The Dunciad* earned among the educated, it could make no effect on the uneducated. To both classes went the Methodists; they sought out the rich in Bath and the poor in Kingswood; they knew no parish boundaries, nor did persecution by the distressed themselves turn back the Wesleys. 'They sought them out in garrets and cellars, prisons and work-houses; they visited them in lonely places of squalor and crowded areas of destitution, in highways and byways; they carried to the despised the gospel of divine love and compassion.' [1] What Gay's Beggar had spurned in an 'opera' these preachers brought to God.

Singing was as important to the Methodists as preaching, and secondary only to prayer. In the new hymns religious emotion was amplified by communal participation until it became irresistible, especially to souls starved of the finer passions. The music John Wesley favoured was simple; music in which all could take part. He had a fondness for German chorale-tunes, some of which were in their beginning religious folk-songs, but he was not narrow in his outlook. His strong objection was to such tunes as only a few were able to sing, or those where different voices sang different words at the same time. His argument was that the meaning of the words was obscured by the confusion of sounds. It was a reasonable argument, but could he get conformity among his followers? Not he. They liked bold, independent entries in the second and third lines of a tune. This practice they called 'fugueing'; an example is to be found in the tune *Cranbrook*. Unless you are elderly, you will not know the name 'Cranbrook' for a hymn-tune, but you will know a corrupt version of the tune, which you sing to the Yorkshire dialect verses of 'On Ilkla Moor Baht 'At'.

In order to understand why John Wesley found his converts fond of music more complex than he would have wished, we must go back in history a long way. At the Reformation churchmen found a difficulty in preparing the minds of the congregations in church for the new style of music. The skilled singers in the cathedrals could be trained to sing the new settings of the services and the English anthems, but the congregations in the parish churches were required to sing metrical versions of the Psalms. These were cast in metrical form so that the common people might learn them easily and remember them (for these common metres have the quality that they are easily memorable). Nevertheless, more progress could be made if the ordinary members of the congregation could be taught to read music-script. So, from the 1561 edition of Sternhold and Hopkins's metrical settings of the Psalms, introductory chapters were printed in books of psalmody teaching the readers how to sing and how to read musical notation. They learnt by this means

[1] Dr R. F. Wearmouth, *Methodism and the Common People of the Eighteenth Century.*

how to sing in parts; teachers in due course began to establish themselves in the towns, and to travel the country districts for the
purpose of instructing the parishioners wherever the squire and
parson approved their introduction. Addison in *The Spectator* made
Sir Roger de Coverley an employer of an itinerant singing-master
for his villagers, and claimed that the singing was much improved in
consequence. By the end of the eighteenth century the wide range of
vestry interests included payments for the purchase of books for
societies of psalm-singers, contributions to funds to encourage
psalm-singing associations, and payments to teachers. 'The rules
and articles of association of the psalm singers of Wysall, Notts,
1773, are to be found in the Parish Chest there. . . . Cardington,
Beds, invited over the Luton psalm-singers in 1779, rewarded them
with 22½ quarts of beer for their labours (since evidently it was
considered that psalm-singing was thirsty work) then, apparently
fired by a spirit of emulation, it formed a band of its own in 1785,
spending five shillings for a "psalms pipe" to give the musicians
their pitch.' [1]

The only thing wrong with Cardington would seem to be
lethargy, for why, after so entertaining a hint, did it take them
seven years to start their own association? Anyway, the paying of
such sums from the parish rates shows clearly enough that the
vestries were alive to the need for better congregational singing. It
may well be that they were answering the challenge of the Methodists,[2] whose singing was soul-stirring anyway, and often soul-
shaking.

The spending of parish funds on beer may seem unusual today,
but it was not so at that time. Abstinence from liquor was a doctrine
being preached, but beer-drinking had not the same sinful associations that began to cling to it in the nineteenth century. Hogarth's
paintings of *Gin Street* and *Beer Lane* denounce gin but approve
good honest beer, and this must be regarded as the general point of
view. The inns were musical: there one might sing with the men
impromptu, or belong to a private club, meeting in a special room
on a prearranged night, to sing psalms, catches, and glees. At these
meetings men read their music-books, sang in full harmony,

---

[1] W. E. Tate, *The Parish Chest*, 1946, p. 168. See this book also for many other
references to psalm clubs.

[2] Complaints were made by clergy that church congregations were influenced by
Methodist style.

smoked, drank, chaffed, and frequently subscribed to a fund by which a member in difficulties could be temporarily assisted. These clubs were democratic in management, with a chairman, and decisions of conduct were made by votes operating round a code of rules similarly decided.

Folk-singing as we understand the term was not the function of the glee clubs. They fostered music in three or more parts, and the wealthier clubs offered prizes to composers for new works in this style. Heterophony—with each man singing his own variations on a tune together—would not suit them. There is a dramatic setting of *The Erl King* by Dr John Wall Callcott, which will illustrate the style they strove to accomplish satisfactorily; it is written for three voices in combination, the singers taking the parts of the three characters in the ballad—the father, the child, and the Spirit of Death which is the Erl King. Where the story is told in the third person the three voices sing together.

3 Voices: Who is it that rides through the forest so fast,
           Whilst night glooms around him, whilst chill roars the blast?
           The father who holds his young son in his arm,
           And close in his mantle has wrapped him up warm.

2nd Alto: Why trembles my darling? Why shrinks he with fear?

1st Alto: My father! my father! the Erl King is near,
           The Erl King with his crown, and his beard long and white!

2nd Alto: My child, you're deceived by the vapours of night.

Bass: If thou wilt, dear baby, with me go away,
           I'll give thee fine garments, we'll play a fine play;
           Fine flowers are growing, white, scarlet and blue,
           On the banks of yon river, and all are for you.

1st Alto: My father! my father! and dost thou not hear,
           What words the Erl King whispers soft in my ear?

3 Voices: Oh, hush thee, my child, set thy bosom at ease;
           Thou hear'st but the willows when murmurs the breeze.

Bass: If thou wilt, dear baby, with me go away,
           My daughters shall nurse thee, so fair and so gay;
           My daughter, in purple and gold who is dressed,
           Shall love thee and kiss thee, and sing thee to rest.

1st Alto:　My father! my father! and dost thou not see,
　　　　　The Erl King and his daughter are waiting for me?

3 Voices:　Oh! shame thee, my infant, 'tis fear makes thee blind,
　　　　　Thou seest the dark willows which wave in the wind.

Bass:　　I love thee, I doat on thy features so fine;
　　　　　I must and will have thee, and force makes me thine.

1st Alto:　My father! my father, oh! hold me now fast,
　　　　　He pulls me, he hurts me, he'll have me at last!

3 Voices:　The father trembled, he doubled his speed,
　　　　　O'er the hills and through forests he spurr'd his black steed;
　　　　　But when he arrived at his own castle door,
　　　　　Life throbb'd in the poor baby's bosom no more.[1]

There is an artificiality of diction here which belongs neither to folk-song nor to the English theatrical style of *The Beggar's Opera*. The English Glee, however, was an art-form existing in its own right, and its merit must be in accordance with criticism based on the rules of that style. It came from companies of men predominantly middle class, met together to sing for their own recreation, and aided by musicians like Dr Callcott, Spofforth, the two Samuel Webbes (father and son), and many more. The faculty of reading music and singing it in true parts was now an accomplishment which almost anyone might acquire. There were many artisan clubs, mainly for the singing of catches (which were rounds or canons, often set to base sentiments, but capable of clever satire or good humour), but the same singers often sang in the church choirs, and psalms, anthems, and at least one oratorio were within their ken. Once these singers had gained such experience they were, from the point of view of a modern folk-song purist, like Adam and Eve after eating the fruit of the tree of the knowledge of good and evil. They could not go back to their previous state of innocence, and would undoubtedly continue to make decisions, some wrong ones. It is only fair to say that nobody thought this at the time. Has there ever been a time when men did not make choice of the songs they sang? The opinion most favoured by collectors of popular and national songs in the first three-quarters of the nineteenth century was that

---

[1] The verses quoted here are inferior to Scott's translation. Schubert's setting of Goethe's *Erlkönig* is well known. The original folk-legend was Danish.

when the songs showed errors of construction or taste the common people were responsible for these; and undoubtedly many fine songs suffered corruption.

This corruption was not brought about by any one class, however, but was of various odours, some smelling of the gutter and some of the musty study. Religion, the most common influence on the art of the time, could not but be involved, and all sects which employed music must bear their share of responsibility for what was to happen to folk-song.

We have seen already how Charles Dibdin wrote popular songs to inspire men with bravery and a love of their country, or to seek favour with those whose commercial or political theories supported a notion of expanding Empire. He did this believing sincerely in the cause, and in the superior merit of music which everyone could understand. Writing of highbrow musicians Dibdin said:[1] 'One would think these dogmatic musicians knew their own defects and encouraged them; like callous-hearted lawyers who dare not indulge the softer feelings lest they should incline them to pity and compassion. I am told there is a certain great harmonist who wears the hind part of his shirt before, by way of armour against Cupid, fearing lest anything tender and natural should get into his compositions.' If Dibdin's opinion be considered that of a prejudiced man, we can quote the poet Wordsworth.[2] 'The poetry of the period intervening between the publication of *Paradise Lost* [1667] and *The Seasons* [1726] does not [with a few unimportant exceptions] contain a single new image of external nature, and scarcely presents a familiar one from which it can be inferred that the eye of the poet had been steadily fixed upon his object, much less that his feelings had urged him to work upon it in the spirit of true imagination.'

Against this prevailing artificiality James Thomson reacted in a seriously poetical way, Gay employed satire, and the evangelical preachers a religious fervour. In Scotland, towards the end of the century, a voice of the people was being accepted in aristocratic circles—however much he disdained them—and the common songs he knew he refurbished for a literary circle. In the pages of Burns's works may be found *John Barleycorn*, for instance, and poems which use traditional symbolism with conviction.

[1] *Musical Tour*, 1788.
[2] *Essay, Supplementary to the Preface to the Poems*, 1815.

O my Luve's like a red, red rose
   That's newly sprung in June:
O my Luve's like the melodie
   That's sweetly played in tune!

As fair thou art, my bonnie lass,
   So deep in luve am I:
And I will luve thee still, my dear,
   Till a' the seas gang dry:

Till a' the seas gang dry, my dear,
   And the rocks melt wi' the sun;
I will luve thee still, my dear,
   While the sands o' life shall run.

And fare thee weel, my only Luve,
   And fare thee weel a while!
And I will come again, my Luve,
   Tho' it were ten thousand mile.

The use of flower-symbols has been mentioned earlier; [1] to these we can add similes of the love that will go on for ever—until the seas go dry and the hard rocks melt. These are found in folk-songs like *The Turtle Dove*.

Poets, however, like to re-create whatever they touch, for theirs are fertile minds. Scholars, too, will alter things which they find incorrect when subjected to the test of analysis. Between the two, that which was truly natural had much of the life squeezed out of it. As we shall see later, however, they could not crush everything. Meanwhile, another trick grew in favour. Many of us are familiar with Wallis's painting of *The Death of Chatterton*, showing a youth with face and hair rather like Shelley lying dead on a couch in a ramshackle garret. This picture was in its time very popular indeed, for one's sympathy went out at once to the tragedy of a promising life cut off in the bud. The death of Chatterton was not his only tragedy, however, for he had written poems which he passed off as the work of a fifteenth-century monk named Thomas Rowley. This Chatterton did while still at school. Horace Walpole, when he discovered the deception, advised him to put off the writing of

[1] Cf. Chapter IV, pp. 79–83.

poetry until he should have made a fortune, which is good worldly advice, but not that which poets take.

Society was predisposed to poetry with an antique flavour. In 1762–3 appeared Macpherson's 'Ossian', which purported to be taken from Gaelic sources. They were forgeries, but before this fact was made generally known the poems had received wide acclamation.[1] They found their way into German universities at a time when Shakespearian studies were greatly in favour, and young Germans who had undoubted genius were on the brink of their careers. While Goethe and Schiller were lifting high the bright torch of romantic inspiration in Germany, Macpherson's *Lays of Ossian* found their way into most of Europe, being translated into French, Spanish, Italian, Dutch, Danish, Swedish, Polish, and Russian. Even after the original was proved to be a fake, the literary influence went on, for Macpherson, like Chatterton, was not the *fons et origo* of antiquarian romanticism, but one who took advantage of a new demand.

The reaction against formal classicism was complete when Dr Johnson died in 1784. During his lifetime he had been an authority on literature: ask him a straight question and he would give you a straight answer. Literary men, moreover, accepted the judgment. After his death no such figure dominated the literary scene, and the general tendency was towards subjective interpretations of natural belief. Scholars being what they were, they could not let a simple tale be told without bringing to bear on it a mass of editorial comment. In such a way did Thomas Percy, later Bishop of Dromore, present to the world his *Reliques of Ancient English Poetry* in 1765. But however erudite the commentary might be, the ballads of which his book was composed were genuine. The manuscript from which they were taken is thought to date from the same year as Playford's *Dancing Master*—1651—so these two sources give us tunes and ballads, but separately, for Playford wanted only the tunes for dancing while the compiler of the manuscript collection of ballads was interested only in the words. Bishop Percy's *Folio Manuscript* was not made available until well into the nineteenth century, but the edited version—the *Reliques*—was known to literary men from the time of its publication, and its influence was widespread. Sir Walter Scott's *Border Minstrelsy*

[1] There may be a basis of Celtic legend in 'Ossian' but, if so, Macpherson so edited, expanded, and interpolated, that Ossian (if he ever lived) would not have recognized it.

came out in 1802-3, Motherwell's *Minstrelsy* in 1827, the nine volumes of Roxburghe Ballads appeared from 1871 to 1899, and Child's *English and Scottish Popular Ballads*, 1882-98. More important than these collections of popular ballads were the original contributions of English men of letters like Wordsworth, Scott, Byron, Shelley, Keats, Coleridge, and their contemporaries, creating a romantic world in literature; the opera-houses likewise demanded romantic operas and ballets on the themes of Scott and Byron. Art had reputedly gone back to nature.

The eighteenth century also was famous for the transformation of the congregational singing in English churches, which happened as hymns were adopted to supplement or take the place of the old metrical psalms. Here was a great opportunity for musicians to produce tunes which were sincere and easy to sing. Their sources of inspiration, however, were scholastic or theatrical (in which latter class we must put the oratorios), and if there is any folk-song similarity this is probably accidental. It has been pointed out that the hymn-tune *St Theodulph* [1] is a square-cut version of *Sellenger's Round*, but the immediate source is nevertheless seventeenth-century German. Methodists liked some tunes with lines that could be repeated, taken up by the women's and men's voices alternately, and hymns with a refrain.

The scope of congregational music was widened. In America variety was far greater than in England, for they had there a national character largely opposed to orthodoxy. So many of their people had emigrated in order to obtain freedom to worship in their own way that it would be illogical to expect them to conform to estab-lished church styles. Even those who did (and metrical psalmody was deeply rooted in the New England Puritans) turned it on the Old Country, as did William Billings.

> Let tyrants shake their iron rod,
> And slavery clank her galling chains;
> We'll fear them not, we'll trust in God;
> New England's God for ever reigns.

In which, however, he followed in the steps of the English, for Tate and Brady's version of the Psalms (1696) turned to account Psalm cvii, verse 40—'Though he suffer them to be evil intreated

---

[1] Sung to *All glory, laud, and honour*.

through tyrants: and let them wander out of the way in the wilderness'—which became, with a sideglance at the deposed James II:

> The prince who slights what God commands,
>   Exposed to scorn, must quit his throne;
> And over wild and desert lands,
>   Where no path offers, stray alone.

It was not in deviations from biblical purpose that the Americans really showed their freedom, then, but in the way they strove to enliven the service of God. The Americans were not fundamentally different from their British ancestors, but were more determined. They seem on their own showing to have droned their metrical psalms slower than the English and Scottish congregations did, and, since this was extremely difficult to do, the breaking-up of the melody with ornamental twiddles was carried further into practice than in Britain. In the backwoods the roaming preacher was widely welcomed, with hell-fire doctrine and scintillating music to catch the imagination of the ungodly. Camp meetings became a feature of American life, attended by thousands of worshippers (mourners, they called themselves) who sang religious songs of the simplest structure, with much repetition.

> O brothers will you meet me,
> O sisters will you meet me,
> O mourners will you meet me,
> On Canaan's happy shore?
>
> By the grace of God I'll meet you,
> By the grace of God I'll meet you,
> By the grace of God I'll meet you,
> Where parting is no more.[1]

Under the influence of a rocking rhythm, sung by thousands, the 'mourners' worked themselves into a hysteria in which many fell swooning to the ground, some burst into tears, others fled into the forest.

The basis of some of these hymns was Methodist, but the style was altered to intensify the hypnotic effect. In the following (taken

[1] Mintz's *Hymns and Spiritual Songs*, North Carolina, 1806.

from Charles Wesley, who got the idea from a ballad of Carey) [1] the
refrain lines are the addition of the Americans.

> He comes, he comes, the Judge severe,
> Roll, Jordan, roll.
> The seventh trumpet speaks him near,
> Roll, Jordan, roll. [2]

There were records of hysteria at Methodist meetings in England
in the pioneer days of the movement, but the original field preaching
must not be confused with Methodist camp meetings. These did not
start in England until 1807, when they were introduced to a small
Methodist community in North Staffordshire by an American
named Lorenzo Dow. So emotional were the camp meetings held
under their auspices on the nearby hill called Mow Cop, that the
respectable, well-established Wesleyans opposed them. The result
was a split in Methodist ranks; the 'ranters' set up their own
organization, calling themselves Primitive Methodists. They spread
rapidly throughout the midlands and north, especially in the towns.
Their founders were Hugh Bourne, a carpenter, and William
Clowes, a potter. Lorenzo Dow dropped right out of their history;
though he was in the country in 1818, when the Home Office
received a report from one of their spies that Dow was 'an alarmist
and endeavouring to decoy manufacturers to America'. He had been
'instrumental of mischief . . . I think it necessary to watch his pro-
ceedings'. [3]

The mission hymn, however, had come to stay; for good or for
ill it was to become a link between religion and the music-halls.

II

Religion has been blamed for bolstering up a form of nineteenth-
century puritanism which was but a distorted version of the old
puritanism which had moved in the hearts of Milton, Bunyan, and
the Pilgrim Fathers. The Christian religion was not itself the cause,
however, for it was twisted to fit into theories which would have

[1] See R. Nettel, *The Englishman Makes Music*, 1952, Chapter III.
[2] Mintz, op. cit.
[3] Dr R. F. Wearmouth, *Some Working-class Movements of the Nineteenth Century*,
1948, p. 144.

convulsed the Fathers of the Church. One of these was the nine-teenth-century secular theory of the purity of Art—always spelt with a capital A. In a novel by Miss Sara Sheppard (a girl of seventeen) published in 1853, the holiness of the true art of music is implicit in passages such as the following, describing a German musical academy.

The school of Cecilia was not only at the summit of the hill, it was the only building on the summit; it was isolated, and in its isolation grand. There were cottages in orchards, vinegardens, fertile lands, and an ancient church, sprinkled upon the sides, or nestling in the slopes; but itself looked lonely and consecrated, as in verity it might be named. A belt of glorious trees, dark and dense as a Druid grove, surrounded with an older growth of modern superstructure; but its basis had been a feudal ruin, whose entrance still remained; a hall, a wide waste of room, of rugged symmetry and almost twilight atmosphere. . . . The doorway of the hall was free; we entered together; and my companion left me one moment while he made some arrangements with the porter, who was quite alone in his corner. Otherwise silence reigned. . . .[1]

This dreamwork of a girl has the rare beauty of the refined age in which she lived; an age in which the well-to-do young woman might blush when first she saw the legs of a ballerina, but who would feel it her duty to reclaim the poor from their vulgar ways. Sara Sheppard dedicated her book to Benjamin Disraeli, who said of it: 'No greater book will ever be written upon music, and one day it will be recognized as the imaginative classic of that divine art'. Disraeli's own literary style was much nearer to earth, however, and in *Sybil* there is a scene set in a Victorian tavern, which reveals the way in which romantic art was employed to refine the taste of the working classes. The tavern was no sordid cell, but a gilded hall outside which flickered in jets of flaming gas its name—'The Temple of the Muses.'

The walls were painted, and by a brush of considerable power. Each panel represented some well-known scene from Shakespeare, Byron, or Scott: King Richard, Mazeppa, the Lady of the Lake were easily recognized: in one panel Hubert menaced Arthur; here Haidee rescued Juan; there Jeanie Deans curtsied before the Queen. . . . In general the noise was great, though not disagreeable; sometimes a bell rang and there was comparative silence, while a curtain drew up at the further end of the

[1] Sara Sheppard, *Charles Auchester*, 1853, opening of Chapter XXVIII.

room, opposite the entrance, and where there was a theatre, the stage raised at a due elevation, and adorned with side scenes from which issued a lady in a fancy dress who sang a favourite ballad; or a gentleman elaborately habited in a farmer's costume of the old comedy, a bob-wig, silver buttons and buckles, and blue stockings, and who favoured the company with that melancholy effusion called a comic song.[1]

This description of the comic farmer of the music-halls should be compared with Dickens's description in the essay on *Vauxhall Gardens by Night*.[2] In the urban places of entertainment the old rural ballads were comic partly because of their length. The rustic singer liked his song to go on and on, with all the evening before him, but the townsman liked speed and change. So Dickens tells how 'we really thought that a gentleman, with his dinner in his pocket-handkerchief, who stood near us, would have fainted with excess of joy'. Obviously a rustic!

A marvellously facetious gentleman that comic singer is: his distinguishing characteristics are, a wig approaching to the flaxen, and an aged countenance, and he bears the name of one of the English counties, if we recollect right. He sang a very good song about the seven ages, the first half-hour of which afforded the assembly the purest delight; of the rest we can make no report, as we did not stay to hear any more.

In prime of years, when I was young, I took delight in youthful toys, not knowing then what did belong Unto the pleasure of those days, At seven years old I was a child, And subject for to be beguiled.

At twice seven I must needs go learn
What discipline was taught at school;
When good from evil I could discern
I thought myself no more a fool.
My parents were contriving then
How I might live when I became a man.

[1] Benjamin Disraeli, *Sybil*, Chapter X.
[2] Charles Dickens, *Sketches by Boz*.
The singer was Paul Bedford

At three times seven I wexèd wild,
And manhood led me to be bold;
I thought myself no more a child,
My own conceit it so me told.
Then I did venture far and near
To buy delight at a price full dear.

At four times seven I must take a wife
And leave off all my wanton ways,
Thinking thereby perhaps to thrive
And save myself from sad disgrace.
So fare ye well, companions all,
For other business doth me call.

At five times seven I would go prove
What I could gain by art or skill,
But still against the stream I strove,
I bowled stones up against the hill.
The more I laboured with might and main
The more I strove against the stream.

At six times seven all covetness
Began to harbour in my breast,
My mind then still contriving was
How I might gain all worldly wealth,
To purchase lands and live on them
To make my children mighty men.

At seven times seven all worldly care
Began to harbour in my brain,
Then I did drink a heavy draught
Of water of experience plain.
Then none so ready was as I,
To purchase, bargain, sell, or buy.

At eight times seven I wexèd old,
I took myself unto my rest,
My neighbours then my counsel craved
And I was held in great request.
But age did so abate my strength
That I was forced to yield at length.

At nine times seven I must take leave
Of all my carnal vain delight,
And then full sore it did me grieve,
I fetched up many a bitter sigh.
To rise up early and sit up late
I was no longer fit, my strength did abate.

At ten times seven my glass was run,
And I, poor silly man, must die,
I lookèd up, and saw the sun
Was overcome with crystal sky.
And now I must this world forsake,
Another man my place must take.

Now you may see within the glass
The whole estate of mortal man;
How they from seven to seven do pass,
Until they are three score and ten,
And, when their glass is fully run,
They must leave off where they first begun.[1]

To return however to Disraeli's *Sybil*. The comic farmer was melancholy, but there was Art to be had as well.

Some nights there was music on the stage; a young lady with a white robe and a golden harp, and attended by a gentleman in black moustachios. This was when the principal harpist of the King of Saxony happened to be passing through Mowbray, merely by accident, or on a tour of pleasure and instruction, to witness the famous scenes of British industry. Otherwise the audience of the Cat and Fiddle—we mean The Temple of the Muses—were fain to be content with four Bohemian Brothers, or an equal number of Swiss Sisters.

Continental influences were the rage not only in the opera-houses and concert-halls, but in the vulgar haunts of the proletariat, and the reason is evident in the name of this music-hall—'The Temple of the Muses'. As the proprietor said: 'Must have a name, Mr Morley; name's everything; made the fortune of the Temple; if I had called it the Saloon, it would never have filled, and perhaps the magistrates would never have granted a licence'.

---

[1] Dickens does not quote the song in *Sketches by Boz*, but this probably is the one he heard.

It was Paul Bedford's favourite.

'Now ladies, now gentlemen, if you please; silence if you please for a song from the Polish Lady. The Signora sings in English like a new-born babe.'

The Polish lady sang *Cherry Ripe* to the infinite satisfaction of her audience. . . . The lady as she retired curtsied like a prima donna; but the host continued on his legs for some time, throwing open his coat and bowing to his guests, who expressed by their applause how much they approved his enterprise. At length he resumed his seat; 'It's almost too much,' he exclaimed; 'the enthusiasm of these people. I believe they look on me as a father'.

It is a fact of geography, which even the dullest children can be taught, that by raising yourself you will see a wider horizon. This proves that the earth is not what it seems.

The vulgar ballad was a product of the thought of the age—whether intended seriously or satirically. Other forms of art, however, became debased through circumstances. We may recall Dickens's description of May Day, with its sordid parody of what had once been a healthy rural custom. He saw a procession start out from a hovel somewhere down Maiden Lane, composed of a 'lord' dressed in a cocked hat and a costume much the same as that of the comic singer he saw at Vauxhall Gardens, attended by a 'lady'.

Her head was ornamented with a profusion of artificial flowers; and in her hand she bore a large brass ladle, wherein to receive what she figuratively denominated 'the tin'. The other characters were a young gentleman in girl's clothes and a widow's cap; two clowns who walked on their hands in the mud, to the immeasurable delight of all the spectators; a man with a drum; another man with a flageolet; a dirty woman in a large shawl, with a box under her arm for the money—and last, though not least, the 'green'.

The man hammered away at the drum, the flageolet squeaked, the shovels rattled, the 'green' rolled about, pitching first on one side and then on the other; my lady threw her right foot over her left ankle, and her left foot over her right ankle, alternately; my lord ran a few paces forward, and butted at the 'green', and then a few paces backward upon the toes of the crowd, and then went to the right, and then to the left, and then dodged my lady round the 'green'; and finally drew her arm through his, and called upon the boys to shout, which they did lustily—for this was the dancing.

How has May Day decayed!

Apart from the mud and the poverty, other things have marred the custom. The man-woman has become a true woman, though she retains her ladle for the practical purpose of collecting money, and the subsidiary characters are theatrical clowns. The Jack-in-the-Green remains, and the practice of getting drunk, but now there is nothing divine in the custom. Dickens abhorred the spectacle, and he knew what his readers wanted. To this would the common folk descend if their superiors did not take heed. Everything was done to encourage the poor to cultivate a taste for romantic painting and literature, to sing in harmony and attend places of worship, but their own traditional arts were doomed.

Vauxhall Gardens by Day.   Cruikshank.

IX. The Age of Progress

##

Here's luck to the duck that crosses the brook;
Here's luck to the house of industry.
Here's luck to every poor man's wife
That drinks health to her country.
If life was a thing that money could buy,
The rich would live and the poor might die.
Here's oceans of wine, rivers of beer,
A nice little wife and ten thousand a year.

HARVEST HOME TOAST SUNG IN THE
VALE OF THE WHITE HORSE

THERE WERE MANY things wrong in 1832, but nobody could honestly say we lacked excitement. The ringleaders of the Reform Riots of the previous year were tried in January; in February the cholera broke out; in June the Reform Bill was passed, the Duke of Wellington was knocked from his horse in Fenchurch Street, and King William IV was hit on the head by a stone flung from the crowd at Ascot; in July Parliament granted £15,000 towards the cost of building the National Gallery and the Public Record Office; in August a waterman from Waterloo Bridge rowed ninety-nine miles in twelve hours. In September Sir Walter Scott died, but the same year saw the appearance of Disraeli's first novel, *Contarini Fleming*, Letitia Landon's *Drawing-room Scrap-Book,* and an anonymous trifle called *The Young Lady's Book,* which had a poetic *Ouverture,*

> Minerva and the Graces here display
>   The charms of taste with woman's lore combined;
> And willing Sylphs their various arts essay,
>   To raise, improve, and gratify the mind.

'Mental improvement should always be made conducive to moral advancement,' asserts the anonymous author; 'to render a young woman wise and good, to prepare her mind for the duties and trials of life, is the great purpose of education. Accomplishments, however desirable and attractive, must always be considered as secondary objects when compared with those virtues which form the character and influence the power of woman in society.' Music was, of course, an essential part of education, and closely related to goodness. 'The influence of the temper upon tone deserves much consideration. Habits of querulousness, or ill-nature, will communicate a cat-like quality to the singing, as infallibly as they give a peculiar character to the speaking voice.' A music teacher must be zealous to prevent wilfulness in the young: 'The neglect of laying a foundation of musical knowledge, and the too great dependence on the feeling or ear, hinder many from becoming fine performers; and these errors, therefore, cannot be too zealously combated'.

Dancing was equally valuable as an aid to manners and deportment. The author quotes the blue-stocking Mrs Chapone [1] as saying that 'dancing is now so universal that it cannot be dispensed with in the education of a gentlewoman; it is indeed, both useful and ornamental, as it forms and strengthens the body, and improves the carriage'. Apparently a rival to the dancing-master was in evidence in 1832, against whom readers must be warned. 'The employment of soldiers to teach young ladies how to walk, which, we are sorry to say, is a practice adopted by many parents and heads of seminaries, is much to be deprecated. The stiffness acquired under regimental tuition is adverse to all the principles of grace, and annihilates that buoyant lightness which is so conducive to ease and elegance in the young.' [2]

Buoyant lightness and the principles of graceful walking were desired in the large houses, but their occupants had only to look out of their windows to see the principles naturally demonstrated. To London in the early summer came thousands of young girls from the country; they found employment in the strawberry gardens which then surrounded London, and while the fruit-picking season lasted these girls were a familiar sight in the streets, carrying on their heads large baskets of freshly picked fruit for immediate sale in the markets and shops. They wore their country garb, with a coloured handkerchief round the neck; they walked with a natural grace, head and body upright, hands on hips, but with no trace in their walk of the stiffness of a soldier. Small boys no doubt jeered at their apple cheeks and unfamiliar dialects—for the girls came from many

[1] A friend of Dr Johnson.
[2] Cf. Mark Edward Perugini, *The Omnibus Box*, 1933.

counties, even from the borders of Wales—but the girls were safe
from the attentions of the rich bucks; for though these might turn to
stare in admiration of the swing of the hips and the steady carriage
of the head, they would not address a bumpkin with red rough hands
and country ways. London offered plenty of scope for the buck's
distraction among the 'Cyprian' ladies who haunted the West End.
The strawberry-carriers lived in tents in the fields and made two or
three journeys a day into the capital with their loads of fruit; they
spent little of their earnings, and, when the season was over, back
they went to their villages with some five or more pounds saved.

Such girls were models of comely grace, if they were noticed in
the city, but it is likely that at home they were not the best girls in
the village. They were the leavings, after the gentry had taken their
choice of the villagers for domestic duties. The *Reports of the
Commissioners on the Employment of Women and Children in Agriculture*, submitted in 1843, say that women might work on the land
because they bore some moral blemish which the lady of the big
house would not approve among her servants. In any case agricultural work was a second choice for a woman; domestic service
was preferable. So the strawberry-girls came to London for a season,
or perhaps more; they saved their earnings; and when he met a girl
with such a dowry as, say, ten pounds, what young labourer could
resist the lure of marriage?

That, no doubt, is the truth of the matter, but in a folk-song the
wish-process idealizes the theme; the lover is superior but asks for
gifts which money cannot buy.

> As I was going to Strawberry Fair,
>   Singing, singing, buttercups and daisies,
> I met a maiden taking her ware,
>   Fol-de-dee!
> Her eyes were blue and golden her hair,
> As she went on to Strawberry Fair.
>   Ri-fol, ri-fol, tol-de-riddle-lido,
>   Ri-fol, ri-fol, tol-de-riddle-dee.
>
> 'Kind Sir, pray pick of my basket,' she said,
>   Singing, singing, buttercups and daisies,
> 'My cherries ripe or my roses red,'
>   Fol-de-dee!

'My strawberries sweet I can of them spare,
As I go on to Strawberry Fair.'
>   Ri-fol, ri-fol, tol-de-riddle-lido,
>   Ri-fol, ri-fol, tol-de-riddle, dee.

'Your cherries soon will be wasted away,'
>   Singing, singing, buttercups and daisies,
'Your roses wither and never stay,'
>   Fol-de-dee!
''Tis not to seek such perishing ware
That I am tramping to Strawberry Fair.'
>   Ri-fol, ri-fol, tol-de-riddle-lido,
>   Ri-fol, ri-fol, tol-de-riddle-dee.

'I want to purchase a generous heart,'
>   Singing, singing, buttercups and daisies;
'A tongue that neither is nimble nor tart,'
>   Fol-de-dee!
'An honest mind, but such trifles are rare,
I doubt if they're found at Strawberry Fair.'
>   Ri-fol, ri-fol, tol-de-riddle-lido,
>   Ri-fol, ri-fol, tol-de-riddle-dee.

'The price I offer my sweet pretty maid,'
>   Singing, singing, buttercups and daisies;
'A ring of gold on your finger displayed,'
>   Fol-de-dee!
'So come, make over to me your ware
In church today at Strawberry Fair.'
>   Ri-fol, ri-fol, tol-de-riddle-lido,
>   Ri-fol, ri-fol, tol-de-riddle-dee.

The dream of Cinderella, with the social background adjusted, is in the song (though it may be doubted if this is of peasant origin). The dream persists in many folk-songs, however, with variations according to the state of the singer. The singer is poor, but by some generously disposed person is relieved, not with the cold charity of the parish, but through means by which he can live his normal life happily. Such sentiments run through the song of the *Nobleman and the Thresher*.

A nobleman lived on a fine estate,
And he kept a thresher whose family was great;
He'd a wife and seven children, the most of them small,
With nought but his labour to maintain them all.

This nobleman went to the thresher one day,
Said he, 'Honest thresher, come tell me, I pray!
Thou hast wife and seven children, I know it is true,
How do you maintain them as well as you do?'

'Why, sometimes I reap, and sometimes I mow,
And sometimes a-dredging and ditching I go;
There's nothing comes amiss to me—cart, harrow, or plough,
So my living I get by the sweat of my brow.

'I go to my house when my day's work is done,
My children come round me with their prattling tongue;
My children come round me with their prattling toys,
Now this is the comfort a poor man enjoys.

'My wife she is willing to join in the yoke,
We never do one or the other provoke;
There's nothing to wonder at our being poor,
Though we manage to keep the wolf from the door.'

'Now, as you speak so well of your family and wife,
I will make you happy for the rest of your life;
Fifty bright acres of land will I give unto thee,
To maintain thy wife and thy dear family.'

This is a character-sketch of the ideal farm-worker, and some may say that it reveals the wishful thinking not of the worker but of his master—a labourer content to live on the simplest fare obtained by hard work, and believing in a master who will prove benevolent, whatever the facts at the time may be. The facts were grim indeed throughout the nineteenth century. Nevertheless the thought is rightly expressed: just as men, for love of England, voluntarily joined the Navy to man Nelson's ships, knowing full well the brutality to which they would be subjected in the course of discipline, so they believed in the *status quo* of the countryside, with squire, parson, and farmer each doing his duty in the state to which it should please God to call him. Some there were who revolted and burnt ricks, but for the most part the labourer was a conservative man even in misfortune. He did not think it right that he should be compelled to work for less than the cost of his keep, and have his earnings grudgingly made up by parish relief, but he suffered the indignity as part of his lot in life. The city worker was an appalling figure in hardship, for his environment made the picture worse, but the country labourer, equally oppressed, and a lonely figure helpless against the accumulated mass of parish customs, had a traditional belief in fate—a belief natural to all who live near to the soil and are dependent on the weather. It gave him dignity in adversity. It is a fact that when the Speenhamland system of subsidizing farmworkers' wages from the rates was at its worst, the labour of some men was put up for auction, as though they were slaves, and others were obliged to go round to the farms in the hope of being given temporary work at whatever wage was offered.

The labourer's lot earned sentimental sympathy, if we are to judge by drawing-room entertainments. Folk-songs, however, were not always so sure. While the Victorians listened to the drawing-room ballad of *The Farmer's Boy* who came to seek casual employment and remained to marry the farmer's daughter and inherit the farm, another ballad was sung in the village inn.

In former days you all must know,
The poor man cheerful used to go
Quite neat and clean, upon my life,
With his children and his darling wife;
And for his labour it is said,
A fair day's wages he was paid,
But now to live he hardly can—
May God protect the working man.

There is one thing we must confess,
If England finds they're in a mess,
And has to face the daring foe,
Unto the labouring man they go
To fight their battles, understand,
Either on sea or on the land;
Deny the truth we never can,
They call upon the labouring man.

Some for soldiers they will go,
And jolly sailors too we know,
To guard Old England day and night,
And for their country boldly fight,
But when they do return again
They're looked upon with great disdain;
Now in distress throughout the land
You may behold the labouring man.

When Bonaparte, and Nelson too,
And Wellington at Waterloo,
Were fighting both by land and sea,
The poor man gained these victories!
Their hearts are cast in honour's mould,
The sailors and the soldiers bold;
And every battle, understand,
Was conquered by the labouring man.

The labouring man will plough the deep,
Till the ground and sow the wheat,
Fight the battles when afar,
Fear no dangers nor a scar;

> But still they're looked upon like thieves,
> By them they keep at home at ease,
> And every day throughout the land,
> They try to starve the labouring man.
>
> Now if the wars should rise again,
> And England be in want of men,
> They'll have to search the country round,
> For the lads that plough the ground.
> Then to some foreign land they'll go,
> To fight and drub the daring foe;
> Do what they will, do what they can,
> They can't do without the labouring man.

This song was sung to Miss Lucy Broadwood in 1898 by Mr Sparks of Dunsfold, Surrey, and his friends. He told her he got the words from a ballad-sheet, but the tune he made up himself. This at any rate should be a reminder to some of us that rural singers did not dry up in the nineteenth century. Mr Sparks sang it 'like a rhythmical chant that could be harmonized throughout with the same simple chords. His friends sang the chorus with extraordinary vigour and with a good attempt at partsinging', says Miss Broadwood.

The last sentence should be noted. It simply is not true that folk-songs were always sung unaccompanied. They were generally so sung because the singers had not the instruments of accompaniment, but when a fiddle, pipe, or harp [1] was available in the old days it would be used; when the concertina was invented, this was substituted for the fiddle in many places where folk-dancing went on, and with the concertina (as with the harp in olden times) harmonies were available. During the eighteenth and nineteenth centuries the cultural horizon was widening. Psalm-singing, hymn-singing, the band of instruments in the west gallery of the church, glee-singing and the singing of part-songs (in many cases not far from secular hymn tunes) were becoming part of the common stream of culture. The catch was a back number because of its rudenesses, but canons and rounds of unimpeachable purity persisted and were encouraged. We are concerned not so much with these as with the way the

[1] The harp was uncommon in England in the lower classes, but common enough in Wales.

catches influenced solo song. Catches were for three or more voices, in canon, with, in many cases, a playful juggling with the words. Here is one published in 1780.[1]

Now let us return to the researches of Lucy Broadwood.[2]

Sussex singers of the past generation seem to have been especially fond of catch or forfeit-songs. Whilst sitting together over their beer and cider they usually included such songs as tests of quick-wittedness or—as time waxed late—of sobriety. The solo singer having given forth his phrase, it was the duty of his companions each to sing the syllable or word that fell to his lot, all taking part in the chorus. The singer who failed to supply the right word at the right moment had to pay for a pot of beer on behalf of the company.

Similar forfeits were part of the fun of the old glee and catch clubs. The following song Lucy Broadwood took down from the singing of John Burberry, a gamekeeper at Lyne, in 1892.

---

[1] James Sibbald, *A Collection of Catches*, 1780.
[2] 'Songs Connected with Customs,' *Journal of the Folk Song Society*, Vol. V, No. 19.

The tune is not that of the catch, but the trick of splitting up the words 'cobbler' and 'tinker' is transferred to a one-part song. This is not all. At Swannington in Leicestershire Miss Broadwood found a miner named Wardle singing the verse of *Cobbler and Tinker* to a different tune, and miners there had added a verse which appealed to their own sense of humour.

Now let us follow Miss Broadwood in her comparative studies. She writes: [1]

Compare the above Leicestershire air with *Since we are met, let's merry be*, to the 'Cobbler and Tinker' words, in Rimbault's *Nursery Rhymes*. It is in its first phrase just the same as the tune *Y Blotyn Du* in *Alawon fy Ngwlad*, Old Welsh Airs collected by N. Bennett (Bailey and Fergusson, Glasgow, 1897). The air *Y Blotyn Du* appears, in considerably altered form, in the *Scottish Students' Song-Book* (Bailey and Fergusson, Glasgow, 1897) under the title *Come, Landlord, fill the Flowing Bowl*. My copy of the latter book, which is apparently the second edition, gives a different version from *Come, Landlord, fill the Flowing Bowl* quoted in the recent number of the *Journal of the Welsh Folk Song Society* (Vol. ii, Part I, 1914) where it is given as a note on *Can y Ffon*. The latter should be compared with the Leicestershire tune. Chappell's air to *Come, Landlord, fill the Flowing Bowl* has nothing in common with the above tunes. In any case, the melody under discussion is probably of foreign origin. In its *Y Blotyn Du* form, it seems a mixture of the old French air *Le Petit Tambour de la Guarde Nationale* by Meissonier (long popular in England and still sung in nurseries to the rhyme

> The brave old Duke of York,
> He had a thousand men.)

and the drinking-song *Vive la Compagnie*. There are also a large number of German folk-airs of the same type. Cf. particularly the Westphalian song *Die Rosen* and the Lower Rhenish song *Schlechte Besserung* (both of which are for alternate voice and chorus) in Zuccalmaglio's *Deutsche Volkslieder* (1840) and the tune of a child's song in Boehme's *Deutsches Kinderlied und Kinderspiel*, p. 89. In the late Mr E. D. Hammond's manuscripts there are two tunes, noted by him in Dorset to *John Barley-corn*, which are variants of this Leicestershire air. I have noted the children's game of 'Bingo' to the same air, from a Derbyshire singer; and Lady Gomme gives it as a Leicestershire 'Bingo' tune in her *Traditional Games*.

Within that short quotation are glimpses of life in many lands and in many social settings—the nursery, the public-house, the coal-mine, and the countryside. Miss Broadwood shows how a song in various forms is made to serve social requirements. A change had come over writers on this subject, however, which must be understood.

Miss Broadwood was a member of a family famous in the music trade, and we may call to mind another family equally famous—the house of Chappell. William Chappell (*b.* 1809) took an interest in antiquarian musical research, and edited in 1838–40 a *Collection of National English Airs*. There followed in the years 1855 to 1859 his *Popular Music of the Olden Time*, with the songs arranged in historical order and with much erudite information wrapped round each song in the best early nineteenth-century tradition of romantic scholarship. The tunes and words were often taken from different sources and wedded for Chappell's edition; the sources were literary, and when the tunes took unorthodox turns Chappell put them carefully back on the rails, believing that unskilled musicians had at some time corrupted them. His researches nevertheless are valuable; from our twentieth-century point of view, however, they need to be taken after studying the results of modern researches like those of Miss Broadwood, and even then with a pinch of salt.

Lucy Broadwood had an uncle named John Broadwood, who was rector of Lyne in Sussex in the eighteen-forties. He was struck with the peculiar nature of the songs his parishioners sang, not in church, but at harvest feasts and at Christmas, when they went about the neighbouring houses singing, or 'wassailing', as they called it. He decided to set down these airs exactly as they were sung, believing them to be the true Old English Melody, but for this he had to request the organist to write them down. Then the trouble started.

'That can't be right, sir; this must be a sharp,' would say the organist, for the tunes did not always fit into the accepted scale system. He would have altered it, but the rector was firm.

'Musically it may be wrong, but I *will* have it exactly as my singers sang it,' said the Reverend John, and as he was paying for the printing, down the tunes went in the book, sixteen of them, 'wrong' notes and all, much as Cromwell's wart went on the painter's canvas.[1] 'The words are given in their original Rough State,' says the compiler, 'with an occasional slight alteration to render the sense intelligible.' What a clergyman would have done with really rough words is not for us to ask, but we know what Broadwood did with rough tunes: he left them as they were. The seventh song in his little collection [2] is *The Privateer*, which has an excellent melody with a final tonal centre on F, and an upper tonal centre on C. Note, however, the sharpened B, D, and E.

The tunes the Rev. John Broadwood had printed in 1843 were what he heard sung at harvest home celebrations and at Christmas wassailing. These were not customs which he would celebrate in his church, but secular customs carried out by the parishioners and not to be confused with our modern harvest festival within the church. When the harvest had to be gathered in everybody able to work in

[1] See the Centenary article by Frank Howes in the *Journal of the English Folk Dance and Song Society*, December 1943.

[2] There is a copy in the British Museum catalogued under the name G. A. Dusart, who harmonized the tunes for the collector. Broadwood's name does not appear. The date of publication was 1843.

the village was pressed into service, for harvesting is always in England a race against the weather. The farm workers had to cut the hay or corn with scythes and sickles; it had to be turned with forks or stacked in sheaves, loaded and carted. This had all to be done in hot weather, and work went on from dawn until dusk. Thirst was quenched with beer and cider provided liberally by the farmer. When the last sheaf was gathered in, the whole party would sit down to a meal in one of the farm buildings and rejoice that they had saved the crop. Sometimes the farmer would invite the village wheelwright and the blacksmith to attend the feast, the parson often looked in, and the village constable.[1] Then all would sing together.

> Here's a health unto our master, the founder of the feast,
> I hope to God with all my heart his soul in heaven may rest,
> And all his works may prosper, whatever he takes in hand,
> For we are all his servants and are at his command.
> Then drink, boys, drink, and see you do not spill,
> For if you do you shall drink two, it is our master's will.

> Here's a health unto our master, our mistress shan't go free,
> For she's a good provider—provides as well as he;
> For she's a good provider, and bids us all to come,
> So take this cup and sip it up, for it is our harvest home.

Sometimes they put a threat in it for good measure.

> Here's a health unto our mistress, prosperity and happiness,
> Prosperity and happiness and plenty of store;
> And he that doth refuse the same,
> To drink a health unto our dame,
> We'll turn him out of doors for shame,
> And own him no more.

It was a time for jollity, and there were puritanical people who thought the merriment went too far. They lied. Alfred Williams described a scene from his own experience.[2]

---

[1] Petty or Parish constable.   Not a County Council policeman.
[2] *Round About the Upper Thames*, 1922.

'Lar! faather,' says the good wife, 'byent ee gwain to say grace?'
Whereupon the farmer stood up, shut his eyes, and said:

> O Lard, make us able
> To eat all on table,

and the young men bellowed 'Amen'. Maybe some of them would
have to be carried home that night, but if a lad has sweated with a
scythe in the sun for sixteen hours a day for a fortnight, surely he
has a right to his tipple afterwards? For those who did not like
much beer—women in particular—tea with cream would be
provided.

It would be idle to pretend that these songs give a complete
picture of English life. There were bad years and good ones, and
government policies which caused at times great hardship. The
introduction of the New Poor Law in 1834 ended the Speenhamland
system, and, since farmers now had to pay their workers enough to
keep them alive or see them enter a workhouse, wages rose. There
was also a boom in that year. But the townsmen were not in the
same circumstances, and the removal of outdoor relief (used
previously to tide over a period of bad trade) proved a great hardship. Moreover, the boom ended in 1835, and in 1836 depression in
the industrial areas grew severe. The year 1837, which saw the New
Poor Law being extended to northern industrial towns, coincided
with a commercial crisis which continued until 1842. Feeling ran
high. 'If the musket, and the pistol, the sword and the pike are of no
avail,' said Rev. J. R. Stephens, 'let the woman take the scissors,
the child the pin or the needle. If all fails, the firebrand—ay, the
firebrand, I repeat.'

The Government, wishing to bring home to everyone the
necessity for economy, proclaimed every Wednesday a fast day.
This was too much for the ballad-singers. A broadside told what the
country thought of the prospect of politicians obeying their own
suggestions.

There was such a jolly game, you know, on Wednesday last;
Some did swear and some did dance, but very few did fast.
For Lord John Russell eat a pig, like-wise a large cow-heel,
And old Duke Nosey swallowed a gun and a bushel of barley
    meal.

Chorus:

Oh, fasting is a curious game and to some it is a treat,
But I shall never fast till I can nothing get to eat.

Little Billy ate his trap, and poor old Joey Hume
Had three cartloads of cabbage-plants put into his bedroom,
And invited Tommy Duncombe to dine on Wednesday last,
And when they'd bolted all the greens Tom Wheatley holloed 'fast'.

Lords Palmerston and Derby cried: 'We very hungry be',
And Radnor eat a sausage as big as a chestnut tree;
He was so hungry in the night he started up from bed,
And swallowed the pantry furniture and fourteen loaves of bread.

Lord Morpeth he had such a gorge of salmon, sprats, and eggs,
And finished off the dainty dish with fourteen wooden legs;
Then in steps young Disraeli with a belly like a whale,
And drank six quarts of shandygaff and a dozen of bottled ale.

The Bishop of St Asaph's unto the Lords did prate,
And told them what a sin it was to touch a bit of meat;
Then Lord George Bentinck he jumped up with a bun as big as a
    mask,
And drank eleven pots of beer, and that's the way they fast.

Chorus:

Oh, fasting is a curious game and to some it is a treat,
But I shall never fast till I can nothing get to eat.

'Duke Nosey' was the Duke of Wellington; Joseph Hume a
Radical who had planned with Francis Place the parliamentary
tactics by which the Combination Acts were repealed in 1824, thus
making trade unions legal; Thomas Slingsby Duncombe was
another Radical, favourable to Chartism; Lord Derby and Disraeli
were Tories, Lord Palmerston a Whig; the ballad was therefore
non-party, but painted all politicians with the same brush.

Visitors to quiet country towns should make a point of looking
at the cast-iron objects to be found in the streets—such things as
water-pipes and pumps. It will often be found that these were made

at local foundries. Such foundries often made farm machinery also. One at Fairford in Gloucestershire made threshing machines to be operated by horse power, and the threshers who had previously beaten the corn with flails found themselves unemployed. Five hundred labourers in 1830 armed themselves with scythes, pitch-forks, and sledge-hammers, and broke up the machinery in the Fairford foundry. It was but one of numerous riots which happened at that time. The rioters went round to the farms, smashing property wherever they went. The mob was completely out of hand when the Swindon Yeomanry arrived to restore order.

Not a drop of blood was spilt in the ensuing 'battle'. The Captain of the Troop, looking down at his ankle, saw that his gaiter was unbuttoned. Battle could not be joined in such a state. He shouted to the leader of the mob; a villainous-looking man with a scythe-blade fastened on a pole.

'You—fellow—put that thing down and come and button up my gaiter!'

Taken by surprise, the leader laid down his weapon and advanced. The Captain stuck out his foot and the gaiter was fastened. Traditional authority was stronger than mob law; the mob dis-persed and the foundry was not afterwards molested.

Rioting with the approval of the squire and the parson, however, was another matter. The fact that the workers had no votes would not prevent them from smashing the windows of anyone voting against squire. Afterwards it would be impossible to find out who started it or why; in any case nobody was interested; a riot was something to be enjoyed for its excitement, and for any plunder that might be found at the time. Folk-songs had their place at elections, with words written for the occasion. Everyone knows the North Country song *Bobby Shafto*.

> Bobby Shafto's gone to sea,
> Silver buckles on his knee,
> He'll come back and marry me,
>   Bobby, Bobby Shafto.

> Bobby Shafto's fat and fair,
> Combing down his yellow hair,
> He's my love for evermair,
>   Bobby, Bobby Shafto.

The man this is supposed to commemorate died in 1737, but in 1761 a certain Robert Shafto,[1] who actually was fat and had yellow hair, put up for election to parliament. His friends saw to it that nobody wanted for beer, and they added a verse to the folk-song:

> Bobby Shafto's looking out,
> All his ribbons flew about,
> All the ladies gave a shout,
> 'Hey for Bobby Shafto!'

By such devices was election assured. In 1820 a 'political Christmas card' was issued by friends of Lord Castlereagh. It went to the tune of *God rest ye merry, gentlemen*, and is given here with the tune printed in Hone's *Political Tracts*.

There was more reason to be thankful for being left alive than one would imagine from a glance at this song, for Castlereagh and his cabinet had that year been threatened by a gunpowder plot. A group of malcontents, led by an insignificant person named Thistle-wood, met in a house in Cato Street to devise means of blowing up

---

[1] Robert Shafto of Whitworth. He certainly won the election, and a Miss Bellasyse, heiress of Brancepeth, pined and died for love of him, or so they said.

the Cabinet in session; they were betrayed and rounded up before doing any harm, but the incident is still known as the Cato Street Plot, and Cato Street, a mean alley, may still be seen.   Our interest lies not with Cato Street and Castlereagh, however, but with the music quoted.

This is elegant variation of the tune such as was fashionable at the time. The politicians were not responsible. In fact the cut-and-thrust of politics had no effect on tunes. Politicians will steal ideas from anywhere, provided they show signs of making a popular appeal, but the creative work is left to others. Much work in the cause of music and moral uplift was undertaken by social reformers, but these were only indirectly related to political life, and the most effective of them were not allied to any political party. The elegant variation we have observed could be heard in the concert rooms and in the churches and chapels. ('Graces'—which were the addition of ornamental notes to a melody—could be heard in some nonconformist chapels until the early twentieth century.[1]) At the beginning of the nineteenth century an old custom among trained choirs, of singing the melody of a hymn or metrical psalm in the tenor, with parts above and below it, had almost gone out of fashion, but was lingering on in places. Where the old custom persisted the tendency was for the top part—the treble—to steal the attention of the listeners. This led to an interesting development.

In Henry Playford's [2] *The Divine Companion* of 1701 is *An Hymn for Christmas Day*, beginning:

> What words, what voices can we bring,
> Which way our accents raise,
> To welcome the misterious [*sic*] King,
> And sing a Saviour's praise?

It is set to a tune by Jeremiah Clarke (in itself a much elaborated version of his tune to Psalm cxvii in the same book, which we know under the name *St Magnus*). Clarke's melody appears again in a MS. tune book which bears a watermark of 1796 and the date 1807, once

---

[1] Cf. Dr Percy A. Scholes, *The Oxford Companion to Music*, 1950, article on 'Methodism and Music'.

[2] Henry Playford (1657–1706) succeeded to his father's business in 1684. He continued to issue books his father had first published (including *The Dancing Master*) and added others.

used by the singers in the church choir at Orton, in Westmorland. It is in the tenor book.

The treble book, written in the same hand, has a watermark of 1810 and a date 1820. It has this melody to go with the above tenor.

The interesting fact about this melody is the second half, which bears a resemblance to the tune of *The First Nowell*, the words of which are traditional. The tune we know is first published in Sandys' *Collection of Christmas Carols*, in 1833, where it takes this form.

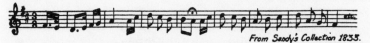

From Sandys Collection 1833.

It may be that the similarity of the prevailing motive in *The First Nowell* tune and the treble of the west gallery version of the older hymn is fortuitous, or it may be that the modern tune was built up from the third phrase of the treble counterpoint found in the old tune-book.[1] From the ending on the mediant it seems likely that the *Nowell* tune was originally a counterpoint or added part. It is not a good tune, but it is infinitely better than the first half of the west gallery treble melody, and would therefore be the section likely to be remembered. Once a snatch of tune 'catches fire' anything may happen.

The tune of *The First Nowell* was issued by Novello & Company in a collection by Bramley and Stainer published in penny numbers.

[1] Cf. Anne A. Gilchrist in *The Journal of the Folk Song Society*, Vol. V, pp. 240–2, where the matter is fully discussed.

If it is true that a tune can 'catch fire' in the hearts of singers, it is equally true that the conflagration can be spread rapidly by the cheap press. This was a factor of the most vital importance in the nineteenth century, when cheap 'steam' printing multiplied the literature and music—good and bad—which was available to anybody who could read. Even if you had not the penny to spend on it, there were plenty of philanthropists ready to support free libraries, reading rooms, literary societies, and singing classes. One of the most respected teachers of the mid-nineteenth century, Dr John Pyke Hullah, had this to say in 1841.

A nation without innocent amusements is commonly demoralized. Amusements which wean the people from vicious indulgences are in themselves a great advantage : they contribute indirectly to the increase of domestic comfort, and promote the contentment of the artisan. Next in importance are those which, like the athletic games, tend to develop the national strength and energy; but the most important are such as diffuse sentiments by which the honour and prosperity of the country can be promoted. The national legends, frequently embodied in songs, are the peasant's chief source of that national feeling which other ranks derive from a more extensive acquaintance with history. The songs of a people may be regarded as an important means of forming an industrious, loyal, and religious working class.[1]

This is a big subject, liable to draw us off from the consideration of the peasantry to the artisan in the new towns, so for the present it must be left.[2] Here we are concerned with the widening horizon of everybody interested in music in the nineteenth century. The cheap press was not only an aid to philanthropy, but a great source of profit. All classes except the illiterate were directly affected by it. *The Young Lady's Book* we have already mentioned. Its reader must know the principal operas, and herself be able to dance, sing, play the harp or the piano. Millions of easy and effective pianoforte solos rolled from the presses, sure of a ready sale. Of these we may mention *The Battle March of Delhi*—a piece of descriptive music of no musical merit, but popular because it pictured in sound the alleged background to life in Delhi during the Indian Mutiny. A form of composition called the Patrol was related to this, but simpler. A Patrol was a march which started quietly, increased in

[1] J. P. Hullah, *Wilhem's Method of Teaching Singing*, etc., 1841.
[2] Cf. R. Nettel, *The Englishman Makes Music*, for fuller treatment.

loudness until it reached its middle section, and then decreased until
it faded away at the end. The idea was to give the impression of a
band on the march approaching and passing. There was a tune
known in Scotland as *The Band at a Distance*, which used to be
played on the piano in this way. The tune became associated with
Sir Walter Scott's poem *Bonnie Dundee*, in which association it is
now generally known. This union dates apparently from 1840, the
singer Miss Dolby (afterwards Madame Sainton Dolby) being
responsible. Be that as it may, the tune is well known in the north
as the accompaniment to a children's game. At Loch Awe, Miss
Gilchrist heard it sung thus:

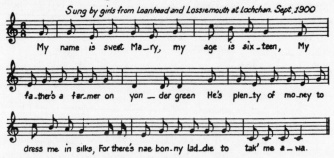

At Southport, Lancashire, it varied slightly from the Scottish
version both in words and music. The tune here is a little better in
its curve. The Scottish words must have puzzled Lancashire
children, so 'For there's nae bonny laddie to tak' me awa'' was
changed to 'Come along, bonny Lassie, and give me a waltz'.

But this is not all. Some of us may remember *Hemy's Pianoforte
Tutor*, which had an enormous vogue for over a century, though
few of us ever tried to find out who Hemy was. Henri Hemy was

organist at a Roman Catholic Church in Newcastle upon Tyne, and he wanted a tune for the hymn, *Hail, Queen of Heaven, the Ocean Star*. The word 'star' made him think of the Latin *stella*, and Stella was the name of a village four miles from Newcastle, where Hemy had heard children singing the tune *Sweet Mary* or *Queen Mary*, and with Mary he associated the Virgin Mary; *Ave maris stella*—the circle was complete. He adapted the children's tune to the hymn and named the tune *Stella*.[1]

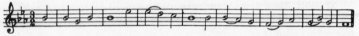

Did the little girls of the village of Stella sue Henri Hemy for breach of their copyright? Not a bit of it. If they had known they would have been proud that their tune had found so good a home. Religion was the keystone to the Victorian social structure. Politicians thundered, but they obeyed the dictates of religious belief or went out of office. Only the scientists could stand firm against a literal interpretation of the Bible, and they suffered many hard words. Nevertheless sectarian differences could be overridden by the successful musical educationists. Music served God in every house—or should have done so. Hullah's views we have mentioned.

Another great teacher of the century was John Curwen, who advocated a system called Tonic Sol-fa. The system was easy to learn and to teach, consequently classes sprang up rapidly all over the country. It caught on first in England and Scotland, and then in Wales, which is a stronghold of the system to this day. Curwen started with the resolution that all religious congregations should learn to sing and read music; if they chose to give concerts also, well and good, but the beginning must be in congregational singing. He trained teachers, who took classes, and they trained other teachers. The system spread naturally and paid its way, even among the poor. It was not restricted in its application, but from simple beginnings went into hymn-singing, part-songs, Anglican and Gregorian chanting, and with the last Curwen had to lead his followers into a study of the Ecclesiastical Modes.

All this was done in the simple notation he advocated. He toured the country to see for himself how his system was being applied, and the year 1864 found him in Wales. He was a man of his time,

[1] Cf. Anne G. Gilchrist, 'Notes on Children's Game Songs', *Journal of the Folk Song Society*, Vol. V, pp. 221-3.

living as he well knew in an age of progress. What educationist today, visiting an industrial district, would say things like this of a local industry?

The Taff Vale Railway

This, the best paying line in the kingdom, carries coals and iron from Merthyr Tydfil and all the mines of that beautiful Welsh valley to the port of Cardiff, where docks cannot be made fast enough to accommodate the shipping which flock from all parts of the world to obtain these valuable minerals.*

Prosperity was not round the corner; it was present. We were an example to the world.

Mr Curwen's reception was cordial and hearty, and the singing of the hardy workers in coal and iron something grand to hear. They sang, at Mr Curwen's request, a fine old minor tune. It was in the Ray Mode [i.e. Dorian †], and Mr Curwen was delighted to notice that when (according to the written music before them) the people ought to have sung | l : se | l :,[1] they, with united voice, sounded out clearly and vigorously | l : s | l :.[2] Perhaps it ought to have been written | r : d | r :.[3] The tune was No. 51 in the Rev. John Robert's *Llyfrtonau*. We noticed the same determined preference for the Ray Mode to the Lah Mode, i.e. the modern Minor Mode whether ancient or modern, on two other occasions. On one occasion, a true-hearted Welsh lady, notwithstanding all her English education, sang at family worship.

r | f : m | r : r' | d' : t | l [4]

---

* *Tonic Sol-fa Reporter*, March 1864, p. 219.

† The Mode which runs

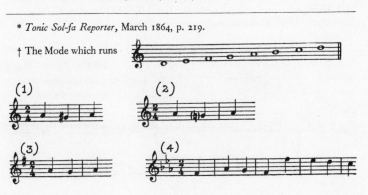

when the book would have made her sing:

$$l \mid d : t \mid l : l' \mid s' : f' \mid m :{}^{(5)}$$

This was evidently no mistake of hers, but simply the fine old Welsh habit of ear and voice. The mistake was in the book. On another occasion we heard a Welsh congregation in Cardiff singing the tune *Eifionydd*, No. 70 in *Llyfrtonau*. It commences thus:

$$\mid l : l . t \mid d' : t . l \mid se : l \,{}^{(6)}$$

We had no book before us, but in trying to interpret this manly Minor (which the whole congregation—men, women, and children were singing) into the Tonic Sol-fa Notation, we made quite sure of the last note above quoted. Except in one verse of the hymn it was as certainly and clearly the 'weeping Lah' as that Lah could possibly be given.

The good minister and his wife kindly brought us the music, next morning, when we found it to be written as above, *without the weeping Lah*. We sang it as thus written, and asked our friends if that was the way the congregation had sung it the night before. They seemed doubtful. We then sang it as follows:

$$\mid r : r . m \mid f : m . r \mid d : r \mid m : l_1 \,{}^{(1)}$$

They answered promptly that that was the true way—the way in which the congregation had sung.

The exceptional verse in which the Lah Mode was sung, was one which the choir (who practise their tunes after church on Sunday evenings as well as on other occasions) had the start of the congregation, and so succeeded in getting the Lah Mode sung in accordance with the book, but plainly against the mind and will of all the people. We thought that this also might be an old Welsh minor, wrongly written, but it proved to be a modern tune, intended to be sung in the modern Lah Mode. It was evident that Welsh ears prefer the Ray to the Lah Mode. This raises the question whether these two minor modes can co-exist in the popular ear.

It raises also a lot of other problems. Curwen knew nothing about the Rev. John Broadwood's little book. Tunes were being wrongly written; twisted by musicians into a modern scale-system.

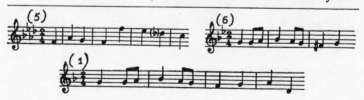

But modern tunes were being twisted also into an old and traditional idiom by singers who evidently could not read music. (Even, it would seem, by the lady with an English education.) Here are folk and academic traditions in conflict, and we see what is about to happen when we glance at the trained choir. To them the written music was correct. When all could read, what then?

X. Westward Ho!

✸ ✸

With my 'Hya! Heeya! Heeya! Hullah! Haul!'
(O the green that thunders aft along the deck!)
Are you sick o' towns and men? You must sign and sail again,
For it's 'Johnny Bowlegs, pack your kit and trek!'

RUDYARD KIPLING

TUCKED AWAY in a drawer at our house, when I was a child, was a small black leather-covered pocket-book, much frayed, and stained with sea-water; within was my father's name—James Reginald Nettel, A.B.—and a list of ships' names and dates of signing on and off. This little book and a Bible are all that came with him through three shipwrecks, a bad attack of Yellow Jack in Santos, and a three months' silence in Calcutta about which my mother would never speak, but which I believe followed on a row with the mate, who had injured the ship's boy who acted as cook's assistant. I imagine that my father, being ship's cook at that time, thought he ought to have some say in how the lad should be treated. Of course he was wrong; the crew always were, as any shantyman would tell you.

> They gave me three months in Calcutta town,
> To me way-ay, blow the man down,
> For kicking the mate and blowing him down;
> Give me some time to blow the man down.

To blow a man down was to knock him down. This incident is all the more shameful because my father was not a hooligan; he was a lad who took an interest in books and religion before he went to sea, and at one time seriously thought of studying to be a nonconformist minister. Circumstances were against him; his father had married twice, and my father had a rough time at home. He became friendly with a ne'er-do-well character who lived down by the canal—this being the only place in that midland town where any sort of floating thing arrived—and from him learnt something of the ways of ships and life on foreign shores. Need we ask what followed? If a youth felt himself to be unwanted at home, a cog in the wheels of industry at work, and unable to gain anything better by reason of educational limitations, should he despair? Smiling prairies beckoned from the New World, one could join the Royal North-West Mounted Police or settle in Australia, where the land was not over-populated, or likely to be. He made his way to Liverpool and signed on aboard a windjammer. It was in the nineties, but he never sailed in steam.

He knew certain songs which I have not heard elsewhere, picked up at sea, but songs which the collectors of sea-songs tend to ignore; songs which I imagine must have been sung in the fo'c'sle during the watch below, songs about the Homeland.

> If we all heave with a will boys,
>   Soon our anchors we will trip,
> And we'll cross the briny ocean,
>   In our good and gallant ship.

Chorus: Rolling home, rolling home,
                  Rolling home across the sea;
              Rolling home to merry England,
                  Rolling home, dear land to thee.[1]

It may well be he picked it up from men who picked it up in public houses, singing with improvised harmonies. At such improvisation my father was an adept, for he had played second cornet in the local Temperance Band before he went to sea, and always reckoned he had a musical ear. Any authority on sea-songs will tell you that sailors do not talk about 'good and gallant ships' or about 'the briny ocean' or 'merry England'. Any authority can be wrong. My father sang them and my mother did not object.

There were other songs, however, to which she did object.

> In Cardiff town there lived a maid,
>   Mark well what I do say.
> In Cardiff town there lived a maid,
> And she was mistress of her trade,
>   I'll go no more a-roving with you, fair maid.

[1] The words are based on a poem by Charles MacKay (father of Marie Corelli) published in 1858. John Masefield says he heard it sung at the capstan.

> A-roving, a-roving,
>   Since roving's been my ru-i-in,
> I'll go no more a-roving
>   With you, fair maid.

Though life at sea was fraught with hardship it was difficult to leave. The sailor had his own ways, a great deal of acquired skill, and resource in danger. He knew, moreover, that the world ashore was against him. The man of the sea is unmistakable; not to be confused with a landsman; his figure, his gait, his way of thinking, are his own. The sea was his province; the places ashore he touched on he generally left without regret, thanks to the wiles of sailors' boarding-house keepers: Sailors' Homes were not much better.

> But when we'd spent my hard-earned screw,
>   Mark well what I do say;
> And the whole of the gold from Timbuctoo,
> She cut her stick and vanished too;
>   So I'll go no more a-roving,
>   With you, fair maid.

This is nineteenth-century satire, easily to be distinguished from the dream-song of the old tradition, where, after all is spent, the ladies remain friendly.

The gallant frigate *Amphitrite* she lay in Plymouth Sound,
Blue Peter at the foremast head, for she was outward bound.
We were waiting there for orders for to send us far from home,
Our orders came for Rio and thence around Cape Horn.

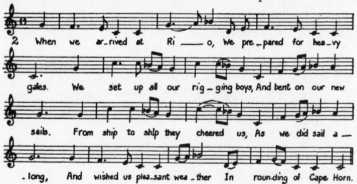

2 When we ar-rived at Ri — o, We pre-pared for hea-vy gales. We set up all our rig-ging boys, And bent on our new sails. From ship to ship they cheered us, As we did sail a-long, And wished us plea-sant wea-ther In roun-ding of Cape Horn.

While beating off Magellan Straits it blew exceeding hard,
Whilst shortening sail two gallant tars fell from the tops'l yard;
By angry seas the ropes we threw were from their poor hands torn,
And we were forced to leave them to the sharks that prowl around Cape Horn.

When we got round the Horn, my boys, we had some glorious days,
And very soon our killick dropped in Valparaiso Bay;
The pretty girls came down in flocks—I solemnly declare,
They were far before the Plymouth girls with their long and curly hair.

They love a jolly sailor when he spends his money free;
They'll laugh and sing and merry-merry be, and have a jovial spree.
And when your money is all gone, they won't on you impose;
They are not like the Plymouth girls that'll pawn and sell your clothes.

Farewell to Valparaiso, farewell for a while,
Likewise to all the Spanish girls all on the coast of Chile;
And if ever I be paid off, I'll sit and sing this song:
'God bless those pretty Spanish girls we left around Cape Horn.'

Alas, such girls are always foreigners in the songs, but Plymouth or Portsmouth may learn.

The tune is a variant of that used by countrymen for *The Faithful Plough*; as for the words, they are true to the sailors' world. The hardships of the voyage are in their true perspective, and the song moves on to a process of wishful thinking about girls and their ways. Are the girls in Spanish seaports free from the faults of those in England? Well might the Plymouth girls answer with the chorus that is sung at the end of *The Derby Ram*.

It's a lie; it's a lie;
It's a tiddy-fa-lal lie.

The Amphitrite was taken down from the singing of an old sailor at Southport in 1907. It is old; quite different from the following, which has a nineteenth-century rake to its outline.

As I strolled out one evening, out for a night's career.
I spied a lofty clipper, and after her I steered;
I hoisted her my signals which she very quickly knew,
And when she seed my bunting fly she immediately hove to.

Chorus:
She'd a dark and roving eye, and her hair hung down in rinkerlets;
She was a nice girl, a fancy girl, but one of the rakish kind.

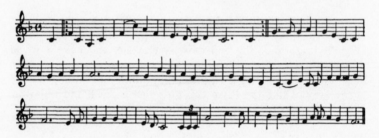

'Oh sir, you must excuse me for being out so late,
For if my parents knew of it then sad would be my fate;
My father he's a minister, a true and honest man,
My mother she's a Methodist and I do the best I can.'

She'd a dark and roving eye, etc.

I took her to a tavern and I treated her to wine,
Little did I think that she belonged to the rakish kind;
I handled her, I dandled her, and found to my surprise,
She was nothing but a fireship rigged up in that disguise.

She'd a dark and roving eye, etc.

Such songs as these must not be confused with sea-shanties, which are work-songs. *Rounding Cape Horn* is a folk-song which actually goes better ashore than aboard ship. It deals with the navy rather than with the merchant service. The same is true of the well-known *Spanish Ladies*.[1]

> Farewell and adieu to you, fair Spanish ladies,
> Farewell and adieu to you, ladies of Spain,
> For we've received orders to sail for old England,
> But we hope in a short while to see you again.

Chorus:
> We'll rant and we'll roar all o'er the wild ocean;
> We'll rant and we'll roar all o'er the wild seas;
> Until we strike soundings in the Channel of Old England,
> From Ushant to Scilly is thirty-five leagues.

In some way the magic of the song works better than the whipped-up enthusiasm of the theatrical sea-songs. The verses describing the entry to the Channel and the depth of the soundings use true facts as literary images; the happiness, too, at the approach to familiar landmarks—Rame Head off Plymouth, Start, Portland, Wight, Beachy Head, Fairlee, and Dungeness, before anchoring in the Downs, is natural and artistically revealing, as is the satisfaction of arrival.

> The signal was made for the Grand Fleet to anchor,
> We clewed up our fores'ls, stuck out tacks and sheets,
> We stood by our stoppers, we brailed in our spanker,
> And anchored ahead of the noblest of fleets.

> Then let every man here toss off his bumper,
> Then let every man here toss off his full bowl,
> For we will be jolly, and drown melancholy,
> With a health to each jovial and true-hearted soul.

Spanish Ladies and *Rounding Cape Horn* are folk-songs, simple and honest, yet with character. Beauty they have, but not fashionable elegance. As for the sea-shanties, one has no right to look for elegance, since these were songs used for a practical purpose. The styles are fitted to the job in hand—hauling on the halyards or pushing round the capstan.

[1] Collected and arranged by Cecil J. Sharp; by permission of Novello & Co. Ltd.

Whisky is the strength of life.
Whisky, Johnny, whisky!
Whisky made me leave my wife.
Whisky, Johnny, whisky!

The word 'whisky' is good for a sharp haul. The shantyman improvises the narrative lines and the men pull together in the refrain lines. The shantyman had the best job afloat, for he was worth the weight of an extra couple of haulers if he had a sense of rhythm. He was valuable too as a strengthener of morale, especially if his sense of humour could invent new treatment for a drunken sailor which no publisher of songs dare print. He had a contempt for landsmen, for bad sailors, and the ships they manned.

Reuben Ranzo was no sailor,
So he shipped aboard a whaler.

His songs were sung for men, with their own way of life and a common heritage of culture—for theirs was a culture just as much as the life of the concert-halls, only it differed in style. The refrain lines of a shanty can have terrific power when allied to the right narrative lines.

I thought I heard the old man say,
Leave her, Johnny, leave her.
You can go ashore and take your pay,
It's time for us to leave her.

The winds were foul, the work was hard,
Leave her, Johnny, leave her.
From Liverpool Docks to Brooklyn Yard
It's time for us to leave her.

She would neither steer nor stay,
Leave her, Johnny, leave her.
She shipped it green both night and day,
It's time for us to leave her.

She shipped it green and made us curse,
Leave her, Johnny, leave her.
The mate was a devil and the old man worse,
It's time for us to leave her.

The winds were foul, the ship was slow,
  Leave her, Johnny, leave her.
The grub was bad, the wages low,
  It's time for us to leave her.

We'll sing, oh, may we never be—
  Leave her, Johnny, leave her.
On a hungry bitch the like of she,
  It's time for us to leave her.

Sea-shanties went out of use when steam power did away with the
manual work the songs were designed to facilitate, but they were
not allowed to die. They had sufficient character to endear them to
landrooted singers and their audiences. For a short time they could
be heard on concert platforms, then they gravitated to camp-fire
gatherings and community singings, where they are preserved and
even loved after a fashion. They are not dead things, like objects in a
museum, because these songs do not die easily, but they are made
orderly—like cheering the Queen at a Naval Review. Such orderli-
ness is not to be compared with the discipline of a shanty, spontaneously undertaken with the will to do the job in hand.

O, the smartest vessel that you can find.
  Ah-ho, way-o, are you most done?
Is the *Marg'ret Evans* of the Blue Cross line,
  So clear the track, let the bullgine run.

O, the *Marg'ret Evans* of the Blue Cross line,
  Ah-ho, way-o, are you most done?
She's never a day behind her time,
  So clear the track, let the bullgine run.

Into the songs come snatches of thought from anywhere the sailors
have in mind.

Tibby hey, rig-a-gig, in a jaunting-car,
  Ah-ho, way-o, are you most done?
With a Liza Lee all on my knee,
  So clear the track, let the bullgine run.

Liza Lees could be picked up anywhere, but a jaunting-car belonged to Ireland. It mattered not to a sailor; the obscure General Santa Ana became 'Santy Anny' even 'Susianna', with no relevance to the context of a song; a ballad about the Oneida chief Shenandoah, who died in 1816, and his daughter's elopement with a white trader, starting among the frontiersmen of Western U.S.A. was taken up by cavalrymen posted to Western forts, and snatches of it appear much later among sailors, remodelled for the purpose of a worksong in the style we know as the shanty *Shenandoah*.

Oh, Shenandoah, I long to hear you, A — way, you rolling river. Oh, Shenandoah, I long to hear you, A — way I'm bound to go 'Cross the wide Missouri.

Many of the sea-shanties most popular nowadays are of American origin; *Santy Anna*, *The Rio Grande*, Johnny coming up or down from Hilo, and songs like *The Hog-eye Man*. The 'ditch-hogs' were river sailors, and so to be held in contempt by blue-water men, but the river traffic of the Mississippi-Missouri Valleys nevertheless opened up the Middle West of the U.S.A., and provided the quick transport necessary for the economic expansion of the greatest country in the world. Railways and aircraft are merely carrying on there the work the 'ditch-hogs' started. Distances have lost much of their hardship with the years, and much of their mystery to us, though to the sailors they were always a common factor in life, and the girls behaved according to type anywhere; a Scottish ballad, *Jock Hawk's Adventures in Glasgow*,[1] had a nautical parallel in this:

> As I walked down the Broadway, one evening in July,
> I met a maid who axed my trade: 'A sailor John', says I.
> And away, you Santee, my dear Annie;
> Oh, you New York girls, can't you dance the Polka!

[1] Ord's *Bothy Ballads*, 1930, p. 278.

To Tiffany's I took her, I did not mind expense;
I bought her two gold earrings; they cost me fifty cents.
    And away, you Santee, my dear Annie;
    Oh, you New York girls, can't you dance the Polka!

Says she: 'You lime-juice sailor, now see me home my way'.
But when we reached her cottage door she unto me did say:
    And away, Santee, my dear Annie,
    Oh, you New York girls, can't you dance the Polka!

'My flash man, he's a Yankee, with his hair cut short behind;
He wears a tarry jumper and he sails on the Black-Ball line.'
    And away, Santee, my dear Annie;
    Oh, you New York girls, can't you dance the Polka!

The Black-Ball line was famous the world over. It was an American company. The wages and conditions of service aboard were notoriously bad and their ships often carried sailors on the run from the law. Even that might have its humour in a shanty.

As I was a-walking down Paradise Street,[1]
    To me way-ay, blow the man down.
A brass-bound policeman I happened to meet.
    Give me some time to blow the man down.

He says: 'You're a Black-Baller by the cut of your hair';
    To me way-ay, blow the man down.
'I know you're a Black-Baller by the clothes that you wear.'
    O give me some time to blow the man down.

'O p'leeceman, O p'leeceman, you do me great wrong';
    To me way-ay, blow the man down.
'I'm a Flying Fish sailor just home from Hong Kong.'
    O give me some time to blow the man down.

So for a time the sailor lived his life afloat and knew the seamen's world, but it was not an isolated life except on long voyages. Ashore he learned the songs of the landlubbers in the streets, the taverns, the music-halls and (for there were plenty of such places, and some gave free coffee) the mission-halls. He was afloat with the white

---

[1] In Liverpool.

man and the Negro, who took his pay like a white sailor at the end
of the voyage, though not so much of it, and was a free man
provided he did not go back to the Southern States Stephen Foster
sang about so dreamily. (There never was a Swannee River except
in nineteenth-century imagination.) The pentatonic [1] lilt of *Johnny
Come Down from Hilo* or *The Rio Grande* could be heard in the
cotton plantations, but not among the sham niggers who entertained us in England with *Old Black Joe*. Let us not abuse them, for
they painted themselves blacker than they were, but let us rid our
minds of cant; the Harriet Beecher Stowe conception of American
Negro life was not unbiased, though *Uncle Tom's Cabin* was a
social force in England and America. There was an opinion prevalent
that the Negro slave was a simple soul with a love of religion and
music. Musical reformers were as sure of themselves as social
reformers, and it will perhaps be worth our while to glance at one
of them in contact with the Negro at his devotions in 1863. The
passage is quoted indirectly from the *New York Musical Review*.

While in Richmond, Va., lately, I went half a day to the African Church,
which is attended mostly by slaves. . . . Mr Van Meter and myself were
told that there would be singing by the choir at two o'clock, so we were
there punctually. There was, however, some mistake, and we found but
one person in the church—a respectable-looking old Negro, who, in
answer to our inquiries, said there would be 'no singin' till de folks come'.

'Yes, but doesn't the choir sing before meeting?'

'No, mas'r. All de folks sing de solemn old tunes fit to do yo soul good.'

We found the old gentleman decidedly in favour of congregational
singing and not much pleased with the choir. I should have said that the
choir in this church has the reputation of being the best in Richmond, and
of this they are a little proud (a state of things, by the way, not at all
confined to that particular church). We asked where we could sit.

'Oh, anywhar yo please. I allus come 'fo de time myself 'cos I likes to
get this yer seat.'

The seat referred to was exactly behind a pillar, so that the occupier
could not see the preacher except by stretching his neck considerably one
way or the other. Whether it was a good place to sleep in or not I did not
inquire. . . .

[1] Pentatonic = a scale of five notes within the octave.

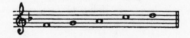

About half an hour before the time for the service to commence, and when the church was perhaps half-full, an old man near me commenced singing *My God, the spring of all my joys*, to a slow, quaint melody; one after the other joined in, until all seemed to be singing. This was congregational singing out-and-out, no mincing the matter. No humming the melody two octaves below pitch for fear of being conspicuous, but strong, mellow tones, full of pathos, singing 'as unto God, and not unto men'.

The tune was not altogether appropriate, and they filled it with odd turns and embellishments, and did not keep remarkably well together; but notwithstanding this, and their uncouth pronunciation, there was so much real devotion and soul in their tunes—so much solemnity and humility in their manner—that I must confess to being more affected than ever I remember to have been by anything of the kind before.

We today could give technical names to the devices used by the Negroes in elaborating their tunes, and of the rhythm, which the observer of 1863 found 'did not keep remarkably well together'. These styles were unstudied, however, by New York editors of musical journals at that time. He writes, however, of what he saw.

I was a little discomposed by the grin of satisfaction on the face of my old friend who had been observing my emotion from behind the pillar. They next struck up *Come, Holy Spirit, Heavenly Dove*, to a melody often heard in Western Methodist meetings, but the name of which I do not know.

After the service had begun, their pastor called on one and another of his flock to lead the congregation in prayer, and again the emotional rise and fall of the voice governed the style of utterance, the sentences rising by a minor third and declining to the original note.[1]

O Lord, bless our Pa_stor,   Stand by him and pre_serve him.

We may be tempted to say that the Negro had come under the influence of Catholic missionaries and had taken to the basic principle of early Christian chant, but this is not so. Apparently whatever efforts the orthodox priests made had failed to win over the Negroes. If they sang with the rise and fall characteristic of early

---

[1] He may have heard a flat minor third (what the jazzmen call a 'blue' third) but we cannot tell. It could not be written down in simple notation.

Christian chant, that was because it was as natural to them as it had been to early Christians and to the ancient Hebrews before them.

Actually the extent of religious influence on Negro song has been exaggerated in some quarters. Negroes were also passionately fond of dancing, which was a social custom. There is no doubt about the slaves' style of dancing; it was a Sunday attraction for visitors to New Orleans and similar centres of transport. The dancing was very like that described by Père Lavat in 1698 and Moreau de Saint-Mèry in 1798. It was still regarded with contempt by the white man, but permitted because such recreation kept the slaves in good humour.

Then came the American Civil War and the subsequent liberation of the slaves, without any established code of conduct, or state policy capable of carrying out the change efficiently. A sailor ashore in the U.S.A. would see razor fights in the Southern States, lynchings, and a condition of moral corruption in the towns as bad as that to be found in any port in the world. If you would read of this behaviour in simple English, do not go to erudite historians but to *The Autobiography of a Super-tramp,* by W. H. Davies the Welsh poet. Davies saw American life from an even lower viewpoint than the sailors; his own voyages were done in cattle-boats sailing between Baltimore and Liverpool, on which the crews were drawn from the dredgings of longshore society. Ashore he begged, worked as a navvy on the Chicago Canal, sailed down the Mississippi in a ramshackle houseboat, and was knocked on the head by a gang of Negroes out to rob one even as destitute as he. Low as he was, there were men lower; men who would not work on the railroads or canals, but lay in wait to rob and murder any who passed by with a month's wages. The U.S.A. was weak in administration but strong in character; it is evident from the songs of this period—songs of the river, the railroad, the chain-gangs, bawds, prostitutes, and the American hobo. In the English music-halls the black-faced singer yearned for the Mississippi and 'de ole folks at home', but that river was in fact an uncontrolled monster, a spreading waste of waters with, in places, only a narrow navigable channel, though the width of shallows might be two miles; the swamps adjacent were malaria-ridden. Here the Negroes improvised their Mississippi blues.

Not all blues were mournful, nor songs of the destitute whining. The American hobo was capable of a satirical dreamlife which comes out in the following well-known song.

Oh, the buzzing of the bees, and the cigarette trees,
   And the soda-water fountain,
Where the limonade springs and the blue-bird sings
   On the big rock-candy mountain.

Like many another satirical song of adults, it can be taken up and sung in all innocence by children. Not so, however, a song of the American bum, or migratory worker, which spotlights the economic humbug of the modern world.

Hallelujah, I'm a bum!
Hallelujah, bum again!
Hallelujah! give us a handout
To revive us again.

The tune is a relic of a dance in the tradition of the London pleasure gardens; it will be found in the overture to *The Miller and his Men*, an English opera by Sir Henry Bishop dating from 1813, where it takes this form:

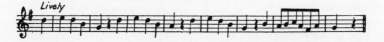

The verses of the American song (which are twentieth-century with a decided slant towards Marx)[1] cannot all be quoted, but here are some.

The lady came out when I knocked at the door.
'You'll get nothing here, for I've seen you before.'

Hallelujah, etc.

'Oh, why don't you work, as other fellows do?'
'How the hell can I work when there's no work to do.'

Hallelujah, etc.

[1] Perhaps I am wrong in this. American syndicalism is more likely, derived through the Industrial Workers of the World movement from the revolutionaries Proudhon and Bakunin.

'Oh, why don't you pray for your daily bread.'
'If that's all I did I should damn soon be dead.'

Hallelujah, I'm a bum!
Hallelujah, bum again!
Hallelujah, give us a handout
For Christ's sake, Amen.

This verse was saved to the last in obedience to an artistic recognition of the emotional force of blasphemy. It was not a song intended for society at large, but for the limited society which the migratory workers composed. Begging songs are quite different; for this purpose a sentimental hymn paid the biggest dividends, at any rate in England. Among tramps this occupation was called 'gridling'; W. H. Davies had one experience of it, but found the situation too degrading for his conscience; the style did not suit a poet, though his tutor's intentions doubtlessly were good.

'Friend,' he began, 'before we commence again, let me give you a word or two of advice. First of all, you sing in too lusty a voice, as though you were well fed, and in good health. Secondly, you are in too much of a hurry to move on, and would get out of people's hearing before they have time to be affected. Try to sing in a weaker voice: draw out the easy low notes to a greater length, and cut the difficult high notes short, as though you had spasms in your side. Your object is to save your voice as much as possible, indifferent to the demands of music, or the spirit of the song. When we start in another street,' he continued—but at this admonitory point I cut him short, telling him I had had enough of gridling.
'What! enough of chanting?' he cried in amaze. 'Why, my dear fellow, it's the best thing on the road, bar none.'[1]

Not only on the road, either, if we consider the fortunes of successful crooners. Their art being quite 'respectable', however, falls outside our scope.
Among the best of American traditional songs are the ballads commemorating some hero of labour:

John Henry drove his fifteen feet
And the steam-drill drove but nine.

[1] W. H. Davies, *The Autobiography of a Super-tramp*, 1907.

Who was John Henry? He may have been an individual, but he lives as a legend; the wishful thinking which created giants of old created the superstrong hammerman of the construction camps. Probe beneath the surface and it will be found that the tradition of the popular hero works the same all the world over, and at all times.

> Would you know the ship that did it?
> And would you know the captain's name?
> 'Twas Captain Mansfield of Bristol town
> And the *Marigold* was the ship of fame.[1]

This is eighteenth-century English, but the following is late nineteenth century American:

> If anyone asks you who was it sang this song,
> Just tell 'em Stalebread's done been here and gone.

'Stalebread Charley' was a zither-player and blues-singer, known in New Orleans. Another player of the time was Buddy Bolden, who set the standard for trumpet-players in the early days of jazz; he improvised hysterically and drank himself into a madhouse, yet you may know the veneration he has inspired if you listen to the intricate heterophony of Jelly Roll Morton's New Orleans Jazzmen.

> I thought I heard Buddy Bolden say:
> 'You're nasty but you're dirty—take it away.
> You're terrible—you're awful—take it away.'
> I thought I heard him say.

The horror was, presumably, music not in the authentic tradition of hectic heterophony.

> I thought I heard Buddy Bolden shout:
> 'Open up the window—let that foul air out.'

Here, however, is the vulnerable spot in jazz, when it depends on a

[1] Cf. Chapter VII, p. 145.

common prejudice for its popularity (like the opinion that orthodox music stinks) yet depends for its treatment on a group of highly skilled professionals among whom only is it truly communal. Nevertheless it is indigenous to a country where an eighteenth-century conception of freedom is commonly accepted; out of that tradition we should look for our explanation of the American way of life and its distinctive application to the arts. To seek the origins of modern American art in a short period just after the American Civil War is senseless.

There should therefore be some reconsideration of old formulas regarding the purity of folk-style. When Cecil Sharp and Maud Karpeles went to Kentucky in 1916 they found a community of people in the Southern Appalachians singing hundreds of folk-songs known to old singers in rural parts of Britain. These songs had been taken to Kentucky in the late eighteenth century by those pioneers who followed Daniel Boone westward, but who had become culturally isolated, conservative, stickers to the old habits, preservers of old ideas, whether these led to blood-feuds or traditional sing-songs. They disliked strangers as much as the English countrymen among whom Sharp had previously worked, but he had a way with him and they withheld nothing. To one of these songs we have already referred—the American version of the ballad of *Edward*.[1] Another, equally well known, is the riddle song which runs:

I gave my love a cherry that has no stones. I
gave my love a chicken that has no bones. I
gave my love a ring that has no end. I
gave my love a baby that's no cryen.

---

[1] Cf. Chapter I, p. 36.

How can there be a cherry that has no stones?
How can there be a chicken that has no bones?
How can there be a ring that has no end?
How can there be a baby that's no cryen?

A cherry when it's blooming it has no stones;
A chicken when it's pipping it has no bones;
A ring when it's rolling it has no end;
A baby when it's sleeping there's no cryen.[1]

There were two distinct forces at work in folk-song—one conserving and the other bringing up to date. In an expanding society geographical boundaries did not matter so much as mental boundaries. Folk-songs were preserved in their old-time perfection in the Southern Appalachians because of the conservative minds of the people—elsewhere they were brought into line with modern requirements. We may call to mind the way in which John Playford's readers were taught the sequence of a dance with the rhyme sung out by a 'caller'.[2] This custom was popular in the U.S.A. The people would come from miles around to dance. Their dances were jolly and in no way 'arty'. They would romp round in a barn to the sound of fiddle, guitar, accordion, while a caller gave them instructions for the next figure in their square-dance. These dances were of the common people, but were not vulgar in the modern derogative sense of that word. They are modern folk-dances based on a mixture of styles, being partly derived from the round and chain-dances of long ago, and partly from nineteenth-century ballroom dances like the quadrilles, cotillions, and Caledonians. In a country containing a mixture of many peoples, knit by choice into a great liberty-loving fellowship, these dances became part of the social scheme in a way which did not happen in countries like England. What is true of the U.S.A. in this respect is true also of Canada, where, before her accession to the throne, Queen Elizabeth II and the Duke of Edinburgh learnt to dance square-dances. By doing so they gave an impetus to the establishment of these dances in Britain, where they had not previously been very well known. Such is the way the British respond to a social stimulus at once un-American and yet unartificial. These dances are now well in favour in Britain.

[1] Collected and arranged by Cecil J. Sharp; by permission of Novello & Co. Ltd.
[2] Cf. Chapter V, pp. 114–15.

The lead in folk-song and dance among English-speaking peoples passed undeniably to America during the nineteenth century. Well may we ask why this was not noticed at the time, but in fact the English themselves were largely under the impression that there were no English folk-songs. The respectable portion of the population in Britain believed they had the sole right to leadership in taste, and disdained 'vulgarity'. Knowing that some songs of the common people were obscene, they condemned too widely. In fairness to the English, however, we ought to point out that in America there were plenty of puritans, and they were as zealous to clean up the store of social music as anyone. In some cases their efforts gained considerable approval in Britain, as in the case of the nineteenth-century chorus-song *There's a Tavern in the Town*. The basis of this is in an old English folk-song.

'There is an ale-house in the next town,
Where my love goes and sits him down;
He takes another girl on his knee,
Pray, don't you think it a grief to me?

'A grief to me, I will tell you why;
Because she's got more gold than I;
His gold will melt and his silver will fly,
In time he'll [*sic*] be as poor as I.

'I wish my little babe was born,
Sat smiling on her dadda's knee,
And I myself in the bed of clay
With the green grass growing all over me.

'There is a flower, I've heard folks say,
That's called a heartsease by night and day;
I wish I could that flower find,
Would ease my heart and cure my mind.'

Then round the flowery fields she ran,
Gathering fine flowers all as they sprang;
Of every sort she plucked and pulled
Till at length she gather'd her apron full.

Then down she sat and no more spoke,
At last they thought her poor heart was broke;
Soon as they found her corpse was cold,
They ran to her false love, and told:

'Oh, cruel man I know thou art,
For breaking of thine own child's heart!
Now she in Abram's bosom shall sleep,
While thy tormenting soul shall weep!'

Dig her grave both wide and deep,
Two marble stones at her head and feet,
And in the middle a turtle-dove
To show the world that she died of love.

I wish, I wish, but all in vain;
I wish she was a maid again;
No rest for me wherever I be;
I wish I'd died instead of she.

There, surely, is a song which touches the heart of all humanity.
It treats the facts of life with candour and a natural delicacy. Why,
then, should anyone, American or British, think it in need of
bowdlerizing? It is one of the mysteries of the nineteenth century
that puritanical corruptions of art were profitable. An American
musician took this song, cut out the heart of it and applied a blend of
musical cosmetics to the corpse, in the American manner. It went
well with cocoa in young ladies' seminaries!

XI. The Folk Song Society

░░

For oh, the honest countryman
Speaks truly from his heart;
His pride is in his tillage,
His horses and his cart.

OLD SONG

OF ALL THE TOWNS in the West Riding of Yorkshire, Leeds was the most prosperous and rapidly expanding in the nineteenth century. Once the Yorkshire farmers had spun and woven the wool they sheared from the backs of their sheep, but now the work was done in factories on a scale undreamed of a century previously. Water power had made the factory system profitable, and Giant Steam had outspun the water-wheel. Power was concentrated in urban centres comprising employers and employed, with the factories, civic buildings, and houses built to accommodate them. The streets were dirty, drainage improving but still bad, smoke in the atmosphere persistent except when the town closed down for a holiday. Beauty, one would think, was not to be sought in such places.

If so, one would think wrongly. The more beauty is lacking the more intensely is it sought. Leeds may not have offered much scope to the lover of landscape, but Leeds was earnestly musical. The music of the choir in Leeds Parish Church was a model for the whole country; their fame had been achieved under the guidance of a great musician, Dr Samuel Sebastian Wesley, supported by a great clergyman, Dr Walter Farquhar Hook, and carried out by a willing body of parishioners with financial assistance from the great local industrialists. With this went civic pride in music, fostered by voluntary societies.

In Leeds we have a weekly series of concerts in the Town Hall, under the management of the Town Hall Concerts Society. At these concerts two rival musical societies give, alternately, choral music of the highest order.

This statement is all the more credible because it was made by a Bradford man. T. K. Longbottom had trained a choir in the villages round Bradford, which had won first prize at a choral competition held in the Crystal Palace in 1860.

On our return after the competition, we were complimented by an invitation to sing for the Concerts Society and thus to stand in the place of the best choral singers in Yorkshire. I accepted the offer. . . . The audience was an assembly of critics [1] who every week listen to the best choral singers. The West Riding Choir acquitted itself well. Some of the best musicians in the district showed us great praise. . . .

In such a town about that time was born Frank Kidson, with no silver spoon in his mouth, but with an innate fondness for beautiful things. He helped his brother in his antique-dealer's business, discovering much to interest him in old china, pottery, and pictures. He became a landscape painter, staying on his sketching tours with the countrymen in their cottages on the Yorkshire moors. He knew the variations in their dialects, listened to them sing their old songs, and noted them down. He collected songs in Goathland, Flamborough, Redcar, York, Knaresborough, Leeds, and Liverpool—the last being a good place for children's singing-games. In Leeds he made friends with street singers whom other musicians disdained, and got from them many old tunes unknown in the concert world. His niece, who kept house for him (he never married), has described how he went to work. 'I recall him bringing in a man who was playing the whistle in the street,' she wrote,[2] 'and saying to him:

'You play very well, what is your trade?'
The man said: 'I have been a sailor'. He bared his wrist and said to me: 'You see, Miss', showing many tattoo marks.
At last Uncle got from him *The Isles of France*.
The man said: 'I've seen tears running from my Captain's eyes when we sang that song'.
Then he gave the shanty, *Goodbye, fare thee well*, and the tune of *The Gentle Damsel*.

This was song-collection from the mouths of the common people.

---

[1] Mr Longbottom does not mean professional critics.
[2] Cf. *Journal of the English Folk Dance and Song Society*, Vol. V, No. 3 (December 1948).

Kidson did it in addition to acquiring knowledge from every other source available to him. He formed a private library of old music, rare song-books, broadsides, books on art, archaeology, and antiquities. He found the editor of the *Leeds Mercury* willing to accept articles on *Old Songs with Airs* as early as 1886, and in 1891 his friend Taphouse of Oxford—an enthusiastic antiquary—published a small collection of *Traditional Tunes*, unharmonized and unembellished. Truth to what was really being sung guided their choice. This was a spirit which had rarely shown itself since Playford's age: Malchair and John Broadwood are the two names most to be honoured in the intervening period, but their work did not reach a wide public. Most people believed that the English had no folk-song. The very word 'folk-song' only came into use somewhere in the latter half of the nineteenth century, and nobody seems to know how.[1] In Devon the Rev. Sabine Baring-Gould was collecting songs, some of which were published as *Songs of the West* in 1889. In 1893 appeared Lucy Broadwood's collection of *English County Songs* with pianoforte accompaniments by herself and J. A. Fuller-Maitland.

Frank Kidson's researches led to the publication of two volumes in the nineties, edited by his niece, Ethel, and harmonized by Alfred Moffat, entitled *English Peasant Songs*, and *Songs of the North Countrie*. The titles of these are revealing, for such Olde Englyshry as 'countrie' was the businessmen's idea of how to sell the books. The other title was even worse. 'Please do not think I had anything to do with its title,' wrote Ethel Kidson.[1] 'I did not want the word "peasant"; it is not English, and all country people would be offended if you called them peasants; but the publishers wanted it, so I had to give way.' (The word is still used as a term of abuse to countrymen by some ignorant townsmen.) The publishers, living in a literary world, were out of touch with rural opinion; a townsman can only understand the countryman by appreciating his mode of life. There is no need to be sentimental about it: the countryman's mode of life was his education—his way of accumulating skill and understanding. When in 1843 the Government appointed a commission to investigate 'Conditions of Employment of Women and Children in Agriculture' they expected to get at the truth. One of

[1] See, however, Margaret Dean Smith, *A Guide to English Folk Song Collections*, 1954.
[2] *Journal of the English Folk Dance and Song Society*, Vol. V, No. 3, pp. 129–30.

the commissioners, Mr Vaughan, reporting on what he found in Kent, Surrey, and Sussex, had this to say:

Now the employment in agriculture, i.e. the special education of the agriculturist, is of a purely practical and material kind, and furnishes a discipline the most opposite to the formal education of the school. Here he lives in a world entirely material and sensible, acts upon it by material means, and receives from his conversation with it an education of the muscles and senses, and to a certain degree of the understanding and imagination, but in the most unconnected and least intellectual form. There is nothing in the practical occupation of the youth to give new animation to the knowledge he may have acquired, or even to sustain it in the shape in which it may have been imparted, or to keep it in exercise as a mere practical instrument for the purpose of life. The employment of the artisan is different; he is engaged in scenes of commerce, and opportunities occur hourly for the use and application of what he has learned. Education, spreading from the town to the country, has transferred its subjects from the mechanic to the agriculturist, but it has not met with practical interest so congenial to its character. The employment of the agriculturist does not in the same way invite the application of the knowledge that has been imparted. It gives, therefore, no new interest to the instruction while it is going forward, and it often overlays it instead of expanding it when it is over.[1]

If this be true, we can well understand the disinclination of the countryman to 'march with the times'. The times he knew did not march; they moved with the same slow roll the seasons had always known. What had served his forbears was still to a large extent good enough for him.

The agricultural labourer spends his life amongst the works of nature, possesses much manual skill, a quick insight, a faithful and exact memory (as all must know who have been in the habit of hearing him examined), an observation by no means naturally inert, yet his knowledge has hardly any form or shape; and of the laws of the natural, and vegetable, and mineral world, which he daily sees and handles, he is ignorant. Superstition (the result here, at least, of ignorance) still lurks among the labouring classes in these counties. The belief in charms for the healing of bodily hurts is not uncommon; faith in the same means of fertilizing the ground and trees is said to exist; that in witchcraft has hardly expired.[2]

[1] *Reports of the Commissioners on the Employment of Women and Children in Agriculture*, 1843, p. 157.
[2] Ibid., pp. 158–9.

Mr Vaughan, indeed, did not restrict his findings to the labourers, for in a footnote he added:

I was informed credibly of a very substantial farmer in the north-east of Kent, who, within a few years, used to arrange scythes in a particular order around his stables, to secure the horses from witchcraft.[1]

Those who think of folk-songs as so much beautiful moonshine may like to turn to this official report, but they should come back later to the findings of folk-song collectors. There is no discrepancy. If you would seek discrepancies, look to the educated poets, to Wordsworth, who invested in railway stock, yet wrote:

> Is there no nook of English ground secure
> From rash assaults?

Or if you would have moonshine, look to Ebenezer Elliott, the Corn-Law Rhymer, who certainly moved with the times:

> The metal god that yet shall chase
> The tyrant idols of remotest lands,
> Preach science in the desert, and efface
> The barren curse from every pathless place.

Utilitarian thinkers saw only progress in the use of machinery, while right under their eyes other results could hardly be avoided.

> Up and down the City Road,
> In and out the Eagle,
> That's the way the money goes;
> Pop goes the weasel.

The verb 'to pop', meaning to pawn, has survived, but what the weasel is in this context I do not know.[2] There is no sham in the song, vulgar though it may be. The Eagle in the City Road, London, was a music-hall, a centre for inebriation and popular song. Like so many satirical poems originally intended for adults, it now remains to us as a children's song. Anyway, it did no harm. (Children's songs are indeed generally the relic of songs made by adults, except

[1] *Reports of the Commissioners on the Employment of Women and Children in Agriculture*, 1843, p. 159.

[2] Various claims have been made: (*a*) a flat-iron, (*b*) a saddler's tool, (*c*) a watch (Cockney rhyming slang Weasel = Bezel—the ring by which a watch-glass is held). All are equally incredible to me.

It now seems to be established that 'to pop the weasel' means 'to lose one's temper'.

perhaps in the case of some singing games.) Comparisons are not always odious, as may be seen by putting these versions of the *Wassail Song* side by side. The first two were collected in Lancashire by Anne Gilchrist, and the third by Frank Kidson in Leeds.

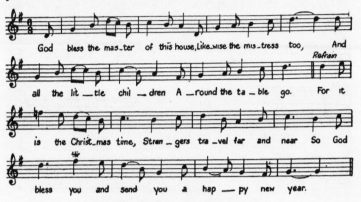

2. We are but little children
   That beg from door to door;
   We are the neighbours' children
   That you have seen before.

* Sometimes sung sharp—sometimes natural.

In the first song the flattened seventh note of the scale should be observed. It is a feature which the Rev. John Broadwood found in Sussex, and which he insisted was correct despite his musical adviser's recommendation to alter it. The third version, which follows, is in the aeolian mode; it is related to the first of our examples, and also to the tune of *God rest ye merry, Gentlemen*.

The singers of these songs were not unlettered; their education would be such as was provided in board schools, or voluntary schools, for school attendance had been compulsory since 1876. We must, in fact, take care not to attempt too strict a classification of folk-singers. We were all at some time singers of children's traditional songs. Some of us are given educations which take us right away from vulgar influences, but anyone brought up in an elementary school would have two cultures—the one taught and the other inherited with local customs—and these could not be completely separated. Dialect is a friendly speech between equals, which cannot be correctly assumed by strangers; trade names and customs may be outmoded, but tend to persist until some strong hand removes them, not infrequently causing resentment. The weaving, pottery, and mining industries are full of the most surprising survivals—even so basic a procedure as counting the results of the work done—and these are industries where large-scale capitalism is the rule. As for trades like thatching, Cotswold masonry, saddlery, printing, they are little cultural environments which only the initiates understand, but which do not separate them from anything they may do outside their working hours.

Nevertheless, we should be very obtuse if we tried to avoid the implications of contrasting ideas on our way of life. We know how literature needs sometimes to bring the thoughts of common people into books intended to be read by educated people. We know how some writers, like Rudyard Kipling, have in the process produced poetry which, though vital and well-constructed, has yet been condemned for its vulgarity.

> Gentlemen rankers out on the spree,
> Damned from here to Eternity,
> God ha' mercy on such as we.

The gentleman ranker was a social catastrophe in late Victorian or Edwardian times, though not perhaps so great a catastrophe as the man who took the tragedy out of that poem to bowdlerize it for American kindergarten.

> Gentlemen songsters on the spree,
> Doomed from here to eternity.

'Eternity' seems very out of place in this context. Kipling in fact worked on material true to life, but gave it a direction which belonged to a national belief we now know to have been temporary. We may illustrate this with a soldiers' song which he used in *Soldiers Three*. The version we print, however, comes from Sussex.

It's of a ge-nel-man sol-dier, in a sen-try he did stand, He
fell in love with a fair maid, and bold-ly took her hand; He
kind-ly did sa-lute her, he kiss'd her in a joke, He
drill'd her in-to a sen-try box, wrapt up in a sol-dier's cloak.

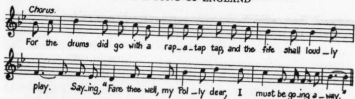

For the drums did go with a rap-a-tap tap, and the fife shall loud-ly play. Say-ing, "Fare thee well, my Pol-ly dear, I must be go-ing a-way."

2. It's of a genelman soldier, then won't you marry me?
   'Oh, marry you, my dear Polly, such things can never be;
   For married I am already and children I have three—
   Two wives are allowed in the army, but one's too many for me.'

Frank Kidson had a ballad-sheet containing the words of this song, and he told Anne Gilchrist that a 'gentleman soldier' meant one of the yeomanry—i.e. cavalry militia. Kipling evidently thought of the term as meaning 'gentleman ranker', i.e. a man of good family enlisted in the ranks after some personal disgrace. He has the lines

> I bid you take care of the brat, says he,
> For it comes of a noble race.

Which is right, Kipling or Kidson? On the internal evidence of the song Kipling, for drums and fifes belong not to the cavalry but to the infantry. Kipling may have got the tune in India, but it may be from Ireland, for a dance version was printed in Levey's *Dance Music of Ireland* about 1870.

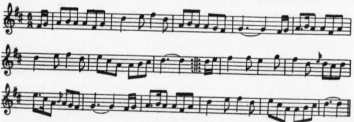

In its dance and song forms the composition is in good taste, yet when Kipling takes these things in hand he is liable to mar them, not because of faulty technique, but by infusing jingoistic sentiments into the result. The word 'jingo' came in a music-hall song, and had vulgar associations which were later applied to political theories. British colonial administrators had during the nineteenth century turned a policy of unadulterated mercantilism into a conception of responsibility—of trusteeship. Such men as David Livingstone and General Gordon could not at that time have come from any race but the British. Their ideas originated in Edmund Burke, who claimed that societies grow in their own traditions and needs, and that to force on them rules of law they cannot understand upsets the stability governed by their moral code. The men who understood how to apply this theory to colonial peoples, however, were few, and not in parliament. In 1872 Disraeli turned the Conservative party towards an imperialist policy; in 1875 he 'changed the sign of the Queen's Inn to the Empress Hotel Ltd' by the passing of the Royal Titles Act which made Victoria Empress of India; by 1878 we were scrambling with others for parts of Africa. Then it was that the word 'jingoism' came into use.[1] Yet some eminent musicians failed to see the sham of it, and in 1889 it was even mistaken for English folk-song.

Any of you who have heard a chant of sailors heaving up anchor would perhaps be surprised if you knew that such a thing as this is folk-music in its simplest form. In some countries this process of development of folk-music is in greater activity than others. . . . Even in England it is not totally extinct, although it is not rapidly produced. Still, songs occasion- ally appear which, although of lowly and even vulgar origin, possess a certain English stamp, and may, after the refining processes of time have done their work, be included in some collection of national music a century or two hence. I should probably horrify you by instancing the notorious tune of 'We don't want to fight' as just such a song; it contains some vulgar phrases and illustrates what to some may be objectionable sentiments, but in spite of that it has a true British ring about it. It would not be the first folk-song which has begun by being the organ of a political party, and ended by meeting with a general acceptance quite independent of its associations.[2]

To understand the full import of this it should be recognized that in 1889 music was generally conceived as being either morally good or bad, at least in educational circles. Music had been taught for

[1] The song dates from 1874, and was applied to Disraeli's policy by the Liberals in 1878.
[2] *Music in Elementary Schools. A Lecture delivered to the Managers of the London Board Schools in 1889*, by C. V. Stanford. Reprinted in *Studies and Memories*, 1908.

years as a mollifying influence, to induce sweet sentiments and by its association with good words turn men's thoughts to noble aims. It must have taken courage to question this theory; Stanford did not do it in 1889, but Lucy Broadwood and J. A. Fuller-Maitland did four years later, when they issued *English County Songs*. 'It is perhaps natural, after all,' they wrote in their preface, 'that young people brought up on the Tonic Sol-fa System, with all that it involves in the way of fatuous part-songs and non-alcoholic revelries, should turn up their noses at the long-winded ballads or the roystering ale-house songs beloved of their grandparents.' So much for Mr Curwen and his followers; but his opposites, the music-hall song vendors, were soon to have their shock. It came from Stanford's colleague, Sir C. Hubert H. Parry, at the first annual meeting of the Folk Song Society on 2nd February 1899.

The modern popular song reminds me of the outer circumference of our terribly overgrown towns, where the jerry-builder holds sway, and where one sees all around the tawdriness of sham jewellery and shoddy clothes, the dregs of stale fish, and pawnshops, set off by the flaming gin-palaces at the corners of the streets. All these things suggest to one's mind the boundless realms of sham. It is for the people who live in these unhealthy regions, people who have the most false ideals, who are always scrambling for subsistence, who think that the commonest rowdyism is the highest expression of human emotion; for them popular music is made, and it is made, with a commercial object, of snippets of slang.

What remedy was there for such a state of evil? It was to be found in true folk-song, which in Parry's view was associated with a state of society which had passed.

It grew in the heart of the people before they devoted themselves so assiduously to the making of quick returns; and it grew there because it pleased them to make it, and because what they made pleased them; and that is the only way good music is ever made. . . . Even to the sophisticated it is a hopeful sign that a society like ours should be founded to save something primitive and genuine from extinction . . . to comfort ourselves by the hope that at bottom our puzzling friend Democracy has permanent qualities . . . which may yet bring it out of the slough which the scramble after false ideals, the strife between the heads that organize and the workmen who execute, and the sordid vulgarity of our great city-populations, seem in our pessimistic moments to indicate as its inevitable destiny.

While he said it the errand-boys whistled in the street:

> We don't want to fight, but by jingo if we do,
> We've got the ships, we've got the men,
> We've got the money, too,

and the Government was preparing to teach the Boers a lesson. This was the climax of jingoism, the South African War; by the time it was over many were ashamed, and many more relieved. The vulgar sentiments of the music-halls had somehow become associated with national life. The period was short; by the election of 1906, when Joseph Chamberlain's party was defeated, the jingoistic spirit was out of favour among responsible people. In music Elgar was made a scapegoat from about that time onwards, and a young composer began to be heard whose notion of patriotism was rooted deep in folk-song. His name is Ralph Vaughan Williams. Bluster has no part in his conception of nationalism.

If this outline of events has given the impression that the Folk Song Society was politically inspired, it has failed in its object. The Folk Song Society was a voluntary society of amateurs in the real sense, who came together solely for 'the collection and preservation of Folk Songs, Ballads, and Tunes, and the publication of such of these as may be advisable'. The society did not incorporate the word 'English' in its title advisedly, for they had no intention to be merely English. This reflects no slur on their patriotism, for by understanding the nature of our own song in relation to that of other countries they hoped to get a better grasp of what the Englishman stood for. The Folk Song Society is not mentioned in histories —even social histories—yet its influence has grown continually for half a century while artistic and literary movements in vogue at the beginning of the twentieth century—and named in history—have all had their day. Chesterton, Belloc, Shaw, Arnold Bennett, Kipling, Galsworthy, are thought of as men of their period, but the work of Vaughan Williams has grown in strength during the time of their decline, and our whole attitude towards music—melody, the modes, integrity of purpose, and truth in transcription and interpretation—has been transformed.

Yet of the original members of the Folk Song Society only three names are likely to appear even in histories of music. Sir Alexander Mackenzie, Principal of the Royal Academy of Music, J. A. Fuller-Maitland, music critic of *The Times*, and Mrs Lawrence (afterwards

Lady) Gomme, the collector of children's songs. Two figureheads were acquired soon afterwards, named Parry and Stanford, but the actual work was done by the enthusiasts immediately drawn on to the committee of management—Frank Kidson, Lucy Broadwood, and W. Barclay Squire in 1898. Cecil Sharp and Ralph Vaughan Williams were elected to the committee in 1904; the next year saw the entry of Percy Grainger, Roger Quilter, Frederick Keel, and Anne G. Gilchrist. Time was short. The songs in which they were interested were vanishing from the memory; in most cases they had to be taken down from the singing of elderly people. Every year someone died with a store of priceless songs left unrecorded.

The songs were taken down from the lips of the singers—unlettered singers many of them, but all the more trustworthy for that reason. It was a sad fact that those who could read assimilated ideas from books and then began to disdain what writers had thought too vulgar to print. The opinion held by compilers of books on ballads and national songs had been that where these differed from academic theory the songs had been subjected to corruption by the low minds of the uneducated; but the members of the Folk Song Society reversed this attitude, claiming rightly that the unlettered singers sang the old tunes as they had been taught them orally, and transmitted them faithfully. Proof of this was in the structure of the tunes they sang, many of which were cast in scale-forms which cultivated musicians had altered centuries ago.

Something of scales and modes we have already noted; another problem set by the folk-singers was of rhythm. For centuries musicians had been accustomed to regular barlines, within which the rhythm was confined. This had its value in dance music, where the step followed a prearranged pattern, and instrumental forms of music are mainly derived from dance music; song, however, need not follow the same rules, and much of it—plainsong, for example —was opposed to the tyranny of the barline. The unlettered singer of folk-songs had never succumbed to this tyranny, so his songs presented difficulties of barring to the transcriber. The difficulties could easily be overcome by 'correcting' the barring, i.e. making it conform to an academic preconception of what it ought to be, but that was not the new way. Here is one of Miss Gilchrist's transcriptions, written down from the singing of Mr J. Collinson, a Westmorland blacksmith.[1]

[1] For words to this song—*The Thresherman*—see page 187.

It's down in yon val_leys, in yon val_leys of late, There lived a poor thre_sher_man whose fa_mi_ly it was great. He'd a wife and se_ven chil_dren, and most of them were small, And he'd no_thing but hard la_bour for to main_tain them all.

Collinson had learnt this song from an old quarryman at Hutton Roof, an isolated spot, and had sung the song at the Westmorland Competitive Festival of 1906. These festivals were the work of Mary Wakefield, who got the idea from the famous nineteenth-century choirmaster Henry Leslie, at whose concerts Miss Wakefield had sung. Leslie retired to Oswestry in Shropshire, where he came to know the Welsh passion for competitive singing in their eisteddfodeu. He consulted John Curwen, who had tried the idea in 1860 at the Crystal Palace,[1] and after Leslie's Oswestry model Mary Wakefield built her Westmorland Festival.

Not only were competitive festivals exciting local events, but they were a boon to musical educationists, since by the introduction of any music on the syllabus of a competitive festival numerous competitors would be required to learn it. This produced as pretty a conspiracy as can be imagined, the object of which was to direct the musical taste of the amateur. Composers wrote music for competitive festivals, and their influence (log-rolling apart) was the best; but there was, besides, the policy of the Board of Education, with an army of teachers required to carry it out. Now the educational policy of the British Government had grown out of the necessity of making slum-dwellers into useful citizens. The findings of Dr Hullah in 1841 were still unchallenged. (Even his rivals accepted the basic theory of the social value of learning to sing.)

[1] At which festival Longbottom's Yorkshire choir, mentioned earlier, gained first place.

One of the chief means of diffusing through the people national sentiments is afforded by songs which embody and express the hopes of industry and the comforts and contentment of household life; and which preserve for the peasant the traditions of his country's triumphs, and inspire him with confidence in her greatness and strength.[1]

Plenty of genuine folk-songs did this. We may recall *The Bonny Bunch of Roses*, or *The Royal Oak*.

> 'Pull down your colours, you English dogs!
> Pull down your colours, do not refuse.
> Oh, pull down your colours, you English dogs,
> Or else your precious life shall lose!'

> Our captain being a valiant man,
> And a well-bespoken young man were he:
> 'Oh, it never shall be said that we died like dogs,
> But we will fight them most manfully!'

Certainly they had pride in their countrymen.

> If anyone then should enquire
> Or want to know of our captain's name,
> Oh, Captain Wellfounder, our chief commander,
> But the *Royal Oak* is our ship by name.[2]

But did the Board of Education recommend such songs?

Look at the grammar. Were not the inhabitants of our slums sufficiently rude already? The national songs advocated by education officials included those of Arne, Boyce, and Dibdin, but not many which by any stretch of imagination could be described as folk-songs. Nevertheless the committee of the Folk Song Society felt that they had gained some ground, and expressed their approval of the inclusion of folk-song as recommended in the *Suggestions* of 1905. Fortunately for posterity discipline within the society was lax, and Cecil Sharp disapproved of what the schools were doing.

---

[1] *Report to the Privy Council's Committee on Education*, 1841.
[2] For the whole of the song, and tune, see page 144.

There was much correspondence on the nature of English folk-song carried on in the press. It did little good. There was need for a full exposition of the subject. In 1907 appeared Cecil Sharp's book *English Folk-Song—Some Conclusions*, with this statement in the Preface.

The main thesis of this book is the evolutionary origin of the folk-song. Now this is not a question of merely an academic interest, but one upon which many practical considerations depend. The claims, for example, made by those who advocate the re-introduction of folk-songs into our national life, all hinge upon this question of origin. They rest upon the assumption that folk-music is generically distinct from ordinary music; that the former is not the composition of the individual and, as such, limited in outlook and appeal, but a communal and racial product, the expression, in musical idiom, of aims and ideals that are primarily national in character. Once establish the fact that the folk-song has not been made by the one but evolved by the many, and its national character and its fitness to serve a national purpose follow as a natural consequence. Musicians would then no longer place 'Tom Bowling' and 'The Seeds of Love' in the same category, but perceive that they typify, respectively, two distinct species of music, that differ not in degree but in kind. The educationist, too, would be alert to the danger of confounding folk-songs with art-song, and realize that, although both may serve his purpose, he must, nevertheless, be careful to assign to each a separate niche in the ideal educational scheme.[1]

The songs he pleaded for were those which had entered into the bloodstream of the nation. They had come in with Celts, Danes, Saxons, Normans, pagan and Christian rituals, and a host of individual balladeers. Their part in our history had been an honest one, but lowly, and somehow [2] they had fallen into contempt among the educated classes and survived only among the unlettered. Sharp based his theory of origin on Parry's theory contained in *The Evolution of the Art of Music* (1893) which was in turn an application of the theory of evolution as expounded by Herbert Spencer. Sharp postulated three principles necessary to create a true folk-song: [3] (*a*) Continuity—which is the stream of song flowing through national life; (*b*) Variation—which is the influence of individual minds on the structure of the song, and (*c*) Selection—which is the

---

[1] Cecil Sharp, *English Folk-Song—Some Conclusions*, 1907, p. x.
[2] Sharp was not an historian. He suggests reasons, but does not prove them.
[3] Op. cit., Chapter III.

reaction of society to the variations, accepting or rejecting according to the dictates of popular taste.

Cecil Sharp's book was a convincing exposition of the advanced thought of the times. It stopped the playful antics of the Board of Education, and shook some organ-lofts far more vigorously than their 32-ft. diapasons had ever done, but it was nevertheless theory. Folk-song has become the cultural influence it now is not on account of evolutionary theory but on its own artistic merits. When Vaughan Williams first heard *Bushes and Briars* sung in East Anglia something in the tune tugged at his being and the course of his life-work was altered. It was not in Cecil Sharp but in this tune:

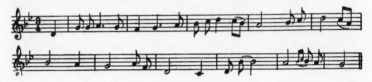

Vaughan Williams knew, as did all of them, that when once the tune had been written down something different would begin to happen. The notes set down would be crystallized—the process of evolution from that point would cease. Nevertheless, in the form set down—and it was a beautiful one—the song was saved for posterity. Another kind of development was hardly preventable from this point: it would be treated as art-music, set for many voices, used in an instrumental work, or in some other way not contemplated by the unlettered singers whose property it once had been. This would not mean that the song would be better, but that it would flow, as Sharp had said, into another stream.[1] When Percy Grainger heard a man named Joseph Taylor sing *Brigg Fair* at a Lincolnshire festival, he recorded it on a phonograph and played the record to his friend Frederick Delius, who made of it an orchestral rhapsody very different from folk-song, but it was a contribution to the larger stock of English music. The time would come when England—a land at that time singularly lacking in orchestras—would demand great instrumental music. That time has come. Even in the Edwardian period there was a demand for great music, though our resources were more limited. Every town—even those which had taken on the evil appearance of industrialism—had its choir. Sir Hubert

---

[1] Vaughan Williams's views are expressed in his book *National Music*, 1935.

Parry knew this in 1899 when he spoke at the first annual meeting of the Folk Song Society. His detractors make much of his dependence on the then modern theory of evolution, but how many of them have seen it in true perspective? He stood in a tradition, he made a variation on it, and society has used its privilege of selection upon that variation. His detractors have but added another variation. The proof of it? Turn back to Parry's speech in 1899 and read it again, with all your little smattering of post-Parry psychology.

I think I may premise that this society is engaged upon a wholesome and seasonal enterprise. For, in these days of high pressure and commercialism, and that little smattering of science and heredity which impels people to think it is hopeless to contend against their bad impulses, because they are bound to inherit the bad qualities of countless shoals of ancestors, the tendency is to become cynical; and the best remedy is to revive a belief in one's fellow-creatures. And nothing has such a curious way of doing this as folk-music.

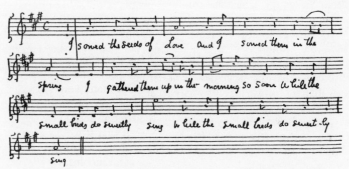

Facsimile of the first folk-song noted down by Cecil Sharp.

XII. Conclusion

Happy have we met,
Merry have we been,
Happy may we part
And merry meet again.

OLD TOAST

IT IS ONE of the minor diversions of popular psychology that, according to Freud, none of us can become a man until he has killed his father. Like the sons in the English Sword-dance who have to kill their father the fool, we may do it with regret, but done it must be. So will a philosopher kill the reputation of his forerunners in fame, setting up today a theory to discredit that of evolution, which in its time had discredited the story of the Creation found in the Bible. In an age when the common people were being offered the cultural fruits of a commercial age—an age of material progress— Parry lashed out at the vulgarity of the times; fifty years earlier the advanced thinkers were condemning the songs of the common people as crude, long-winded, lugubrious. It is well known among musicians that the novelties of yesterday are the clichés of today, and that the originality of today, if it catches on with the public, will be the vulgarity of the twenty-first century. One would think, since scholars know this so well, that they would avoid being carried on the bob of this eternal pendulum, if only in the cause of clear thinking, but no—they are impelled with the same urge which moves all mankind.

We may not draw from traditional lore to say 'we told you so', for that would be rude, but in an age of intellectual iconoclasm we might draw attention to the full import of the mummers' play and the sword-dance. The sacrificed fool came to life again, if not entirely of his own volition, with the help of a quack doctor.

See! Sir, comes this noble doctor,
I travel much at home,
I carry good pills
To cure all ills,
Past remedy and time to come.

But in this version of the play, which comes from Kempsford in Gloucestershire and is clearly related both to the traditional mummers' play and the ballad of *Robin Hood and the Tanner*, the quack is astute enough to make a certain reservation.

I can cure this man or any other man if he's not quite dead. If you were to bring me an old woman seven years dead, seven years laid in her grave, if she can rise up and crack one of these golden pills

> In the bond I'll be bound
> Of fifty pound
> Her life to quickly save.

Now that is just what the founders of the Folk Song Society did. The songs were not quite dead, but had been condemned by whole generations as fit to die. Cecil Sharp thought that the snap in tradition had come in the eighteen-forties: he found it useless to try to get the type of song he sought from people under sixty years of age. His book is still a valuable document, and is the best outline yet of the Topsyan theory that folk-songs were not born of any one composer but 'jes' growed'. This theory had come originally from the Grimm brothers, and, like so many German theories, had been expounded with a profound vagueness. Of course it was attacked, and still is; no scholar who approaches a subject through literary channels will easily admit that there was no first author: he shuns the Grimm ghost. Field workers in folk-song recovery often agree with Sharp, however; and even if they will not commit themselves on the subject of origin, they generally agree that the development of folk-song is a communal process; but there is a modern wave of opinion which claims that folk-singers are not creative at all, but are extremely conservative, and therefore only preservers of the songs.

The singers whom Cecil Sharp and the pioneers of the Folk Song Society approached certainly were conservative. They were sought out for that very reason. Elderly people often object to the ways of the young, who disturb the quiet life which the aged wish to enjoy, and propound ideas which the old think or know from experience to be wrong. A more important factor, however, is the way elderly people can remember. The scenes of childhood become very vivid to the aged, and songs which they had known in their youth (and perhaps ceased to care for in middle life) seem especially attractive in age. In this way the songs were recalled, noted down, taught to children in the schools, and by these children taught to their parents —the very generation which had previously neglected them. The songs came back into circulation.

But it would be wrong to suggest that somewhere about 1840 the common people stopped making songs. We have only to go among them to discover songs which, like certain types of food, are relished by the working class. A Tyneside football crowd will sing this:

I went to Blaydon Races, 'twas on the ninth o' June,
Eighteen hundred and sixty-two on a summer's afternoon;
I took the bus fra Balmbra's and she was heavy laden;
Away we went along Collingwood Street that's on the road to
    Blaydon. *

Everyone knows the chorus:

The song is not an escape from life but an exultation.

We flew past Armstrong's factory and up to the *Robin Adair*.
Just gannin doon to the railway bridge the bus-wheel flew off there.
The lasses lost their petticoats off an' the veils that hide their faces;
I got two black eyes an' a broken nose in gan to Blaydon Races.

Some went to the dispensary, some to Dr Gibbs, some to the infirmary to mend their broken ribs, but the hero went on:

They called on me to sing a song, I sang them *Paddy Fagan*,
I danced a jig an' swung my twig that day we went to Blaydon.

* Words by George Ridley, a crippled pub comedian.

The song is uncompromisingly nineteenth century, and therefore not folk-song as the revivalists defined that term. Nevertheless it is good sturdy stuff. And is the behaviour of the nineteenth-century roughs much different from that of the Berkshire lads who for centuries had hit each other on the head with backswords just for fun? As for the horses, were they any worse off than in the eighteenth century? Here is a verse from *Rob o' the Capper*, the words Scottish but the tune probably Irish.

> He'd a lang knotted whip that he managed discreetly
> On the rump o' his Neddy tae mak him gang sweetly,
> But if he rebelled I pity his napper,
> Balaam was a flea-bite to Rob o' the Capper.

We know quite well that the same point of view will be held by successive generations of people; it appears from their songs, their stories, and their behaviour, though it often happens that practical applications of their ideas have to wait on favourable circumstances, while the songs can give expression to them at any time. This fondness for the well-tried song-theme has its repercussions among songwriters, who find it most profitable to give the public what it wants. The results are often lamentable; we all know that the circulation of newspapers increases as the reading-matter they contain becomes more sensational; so it has always been with ballads meant to please the crowd. The ballads of crime and punishment plumb the lowest depths of degradation; sex does not draw a line at incest, nor political feeling at the grossest injustice. In our inquiry we have glanced at the vulgarity of the Elizabethan jigs, but these were decent in comparison with the ballads of Thomas Deloney, who lived at the same time. Not only did he write ballads, but novels of low life like *Jack o' Newbury*. John Gay's *The Beggar's Opera* descends pretty low at times, as when Filch is likened to a knighterrant for saving the lives of ladies in distress. The ladies being imprisoned and likely to be sentenced to be hanged, he—for a consideration—got them with child, which enabled them when they came up for trial to 'plead their bellies'. By law a woman could not be hanged until after her child was born.

If we look again into the reports of commissioners on the employment of women and children in agriculture in 1843 we shall see that everyone did not take to the songs of rural labourers as the Rev.

John Broadwood did. In Dorset a clergyman mentioned that at fairs they would find 'a good many itinerant singers and sellers of ballads, many of which are of the most obscene character'. No doubt they were printed in the towns,[1] but they were equally popular in the country. Their character would be the same as those described by Henry Mayhew in 1851.

Mayhew, like the folk-song collectors of today, went for his information to the common people, copying down what they said as truly as he could, but he operated in London, and half a century before the folk-song collectors got together. In his book *London Labour and the London Poor*, published in 1851, may be seen pictures of various kinds of street entertainer, including the seller of ballads. Of the 'patterers' or retailers of cheap literature he has a long description, which includes this statement:

'Next to murders, fires are "tidy browns",' I was told by a patterer experienced both in murders and fires. The burning of the old Houses of Parliament was very popular among street-sellers, and for the reason which ensures popularity to a commercial people; it was a source of profit, and was certainly made the most of. It was the work of incendiaries—of ministers, to get rid of perplexing papers—of government officers, with troublesome accounts to balance—of a sporting lord, for a heavy wager—of a conspiracy of builders and of 'a unsuspected party'. The older 'hands' with whom I conversed on the subject, all agreed in stating that they 'did well' on the fire.

Sometimes a patterer would have a ballad-singer to attract a crowd and enable him to sell his wares. Low as the literature was, the patter was lower. Purchasers often found on reading the literature that it was nothing like so lurid as the advertisers had proclaimed. From this cesspit of art some of the retailers never emerged. (Indeed, their successors with the 'glossies' and pulp novels are still with us.) But a century ago there was money in Improvement with a capital 'I'. Men calling themselves ballad-singers had taken to higher things. Mayhew tells of an old ballad-singer who from the age of thirteen had been a child of the streets, dependent on his own resources. This is how he became a professional musician.

I went to live in church-lane, St Giles, at a threepenny house; and

---

[1] But not only in the big wicked cities. Small market towns like Highworth in Wiltshire provided some interesting examples.

having a tidy voice of my own, I was there taught to go out ballad-singing, and I have stuck to the business ever since. I was going on fifteen when I first took to it. The first thing I did was to lead at glee-singing. I took the air, and two others—old 'hands'—did the second and the bass. We used to sing *The Red Cross Knight*; *Hail, Smiling Morn*; and harmonize *The Wolf* and other popular songs. Excepting when we needed money, we rarely went out till the evening. Then our pitches were quiet streets and squares, where we saw, by the light of the window, some party was going on.

The singer stated that the three of them would earn nine or ten shillings a night. It was a superior occupation for street-singers.

Wedding-parties was very good, in general quite a harvest. Public-houses we did little at, and then it was always with the parlour company; the tap-room people have no taste for glee-singing.

We can compare this with the description of the superior saloon given in Disraeli's *Sybil*,[1] and with the efforts of educational and moral reformers from the forties onward. Mayhew's informant told him, however, that glee-singing in the streets, for money, had died out by 1850, being then confined to the provinces. It was certainly continued among amateurs everywhere, at concerts and private parties, until well into the present century. Meanwhile the London ballad-singers followed the new demand.

When any popular song came up, that was our harvest. *Alice Gray*, *The Sea*, *Bridal Ring*, *We met*, *The Tartar Drum* (in which I was well known), *The Banks of the Blue Moselle*, and such-like, not forgetting *The Mistletoe Bough*. These were all great things to the ballad-singers. We looked at the bill of fare for the different concert-rooms, and then went round the neighbourhood where these songs were being sung, because, the airs being well known, you see, it eased the way for us. The best sentimental song I had, which lasted me off and on for two years, was Byron's *Isle of Beauty*. I could get a meal quicker with that than with any other.

So we see that the decline of the ballad was partly due to a commendable desire for the approval of the middle classes. But this was not all. It will be recalled that Dickens thought the comic singer at

[1] Cf. Chapter VIII, p. 177.

Vauxhall Gardens a bore. He sang apparently the folk-song of *The Seven Ages*.[1] Should we consider it a bore? The words might be worse, and the tune is a good one. Look again at that tune, and compare it with *The Mistletoe Bough*. Surely the latter is the more doleful. This is not a matter of class-preference but of musical taste. The folk-song *The Seven Ages* was out of date in the eighteen-thirties, being modal (mixolydian) and to the Victorian mind redolent of antiquity. The up-to-date market was for major and minor keys with luscious harmonies after the fashion of the hymn-writers or the Italian opera. As the century went on these got more and more cloying, like Barnby's *Sweet and Low*, and *White Wings*—those nostalgic dreams of our grandparents, soon to become period pieces! So does the pendulum of taste swing. To keep a modal tune in circulation a century ago it would be modernized, and its original features distorted. So too with the words; *William and Dinah* became Cockneyized as *Villikins and his Dinah*; sometimes, however, the song was not spoilt, but brought up to date with additional verses. A lovely old folk-song is *The Jolly Waggoner*, and very true to life.

> When first I went a-waggoning, a-waggoning did go,
> I filled my parents' hearts with grief; with sorrow and with woe.
> And many are the hardships that I have since gone through.
>
> > Sing wo, my lads, sing wo.
> > Drive on, my lads, I-ho!
> > Who would not lead the stirring life
> > The jolly waggoners do.

Paul Bedford would sing this in character costume in 1835, much as Dickens described the singer at Vauxhall Gardens, and he brought it up to date with the addition of two verses.

> Along the country roads, alas, but waggons few are seen.
> The world is topsy-turvy turned and all things go by steam.
> And all the past is passed away, like to a moving dream.

Was Bedford the singer Dickens saw? Remember Dickens said he 'bears the name of one of the English counties, if we recollect

---

[1] Cf. Chapter VIII, p. 178.

right'. Anyway, old-fashioned he was. Fancy bemoaning the coming of a benefaction like steam!

> The landlords cry 'What shall we do? our business is no more.
> The railway it has ruined us, who badly fared before.
> 'Tis luck and gold to one or two, but ruin for a score.'

And this, mind you, in an Age of Progress!

The unspoilt song continued among the country people; the example quoted was collected by the Rev. Sabine Baring-Gould, who lived in Devon in the nineties.

Now, we have said that the attraction of a song works two ways; it draws the hearer to the singer, and it urges the man who would be popular to imitate the songs the hearers like. In this way it is useful as propaganda. Ballads were not only made to sell, but were also a means of disseminating ideas. We have observed how Pitt made use of Dibdin to stimulate patriotism during the Napoleonic Wars. Similarly, political reformers used songs to inspire their followers. The more desperate the followers the more effective the songs. Always they excused their behaviour by reference to their wrongs. The Luddites [1] went about breaking machinery, but sang

> Brave Ludd was to measures of violence unused
> Till his sufferings became so severe
> That at last to defend his own Interest he rous'd
> And for the great work did prepare . . .
> And foul imposition was the cause
> Which produces these unhappy results.

The Luddites, in a way, show the beginning of the decline of the practicality of the old dreams. They had a Robin Hood mentality; Ned Ludd,[2] their supposed leader, was said to live in Sherwood Forest, waging war on their capitalist oppressors. The Luddites smashed and murdered, but had no constructive policy. They were

---

[1] 1811–16.

[2] Actually the real Ned Ludd was a Leicestershire village half-wit who lived half a century earlier. The rioters in Yorkshire and Nottinghamshire adopted his name to confuse the authorities. (Cf. *State Trials*, Vol. XXXI.)

doomed to failure. In contrast to these we may mark the Chartists (1838–53), who were Radicals inspired in the first place by middle-class leaders. They had a programme—their Charter—by which necessary reforms of government might be achieved. Their working-class leaders had in some cases learnt their power of persuasion in nonconformist classes, and they organized great meetings on the principle of the Methodist camp meetings, where they sang in their thousands, not ballads—but political hymns.

> Britannia's sons! though slaves you be,
> God, your Creator, made you free:
> And life to all, and being gave,
> But never—never made a slave.

> All men are equal in His sight:
> The bond, the free, the black, the white:
> He made them all—them freedom gave:
> He made the man—the man the slave.

Karl Marx saw the breaking of the Chartists, and it is part of his theory that reform movements must fail: only revolution can succeed, and that would come inevitably, having its seeds in the capitalist system. He thought as a German, without sufficient allowance for the crazy way British minds work. Chartism was broken up, but all the six points of the Charter are now law, excepting number four—annual parliaments.[1] Where the Chartists failed dismally was in their policy of land settlement. Excellent as it seemed to put a man in an independent position as a smallholder, it overlooked the fact that farming is a highly skilled occupation, and the weather in the British Isles unreliable. The townsman and the countryman had drifted apart; they did not understand each other. The townsman's attitude towards the land was either sentimental, like

> That fine old English gentleman,
> One of the olden time,

or it was antagonistic—free trade and cheap food from abroad.

[1] Point No. 3—equal electoral districts—may still be disputed, but as far as practicable it has been attempted.

These things were the scourge of the rural areas, yet the plight of the rural worker was made worse by his isolation, lack of scholastic education, and by the conservatism of the society of which he was part. The landlords and the clergy ruled the villages, dispensed knowledge and law, the farmers did the best they could for themselves, the labourers did the work and took what was given to them. They knew it well enough; we have seen it in the folk-song *The Labouring Man*,[1] and in *The Nobleman and the Thresher*.[2] There are folk-songs about poaching, but none in favour of the Game Laws. These songs were the secret thoughts of the Secret People—the people of whom G. K. Chesterton could write:

There are no folk in the whole world so helpless or so wise.
There is hunger in our bellies, there is laughter in our eyes;
You laugh at us and love us, both mugs and eyes are wet:
Only you do not know us. For we have not spoken yet.

A labourer might easily be turned out of his cottage for speaking up for himself. He need not commit a crime to be punished. One of the greatest scandals of English history is the transportation, for seven years, of six farm workers from Tolpuddle in Dorset, because they swore men into membership of a lodge that was desirous of joining a trade union. It was not proved that they had in fact joined this union. They had not started, or even threatened, a strike, or asked for higher wages. This was the way they were treated in 1834. There was no National Agricultural Labourers' Union until 1872, when it burst on the country like a thunderbolt. The organizer was Joseph Arch, a skilled agricultural worker of Methodist upbringing who owned his cottage at Wellesbourne in Warwickshire. Within a year he had enrolled 100,000 members in his union, and 50,000 agricultural workers had joined other unions.

Looking back at this surprising development one is astonished most at the evidence of degradation which was revealed in their complaints. The pleasant rural cottage, which was so much photographed and admired by urban visitors, was often dark, damp, and overcrowded. Arch's own brother-in-law was stopped by a policeman and made to turn out his pockets on his way home from buying

[1] p. 188.   [2] p. 187.

the weekly groceries in Warwick, though the policeman had no
reason to suspect that he had ever poached. Arch's children were
sent back from school on their first attendance, being requested to
bring a letter of recommendation from the clergyman of the parish
before being admitted. Arch sent them back with a note from himself saying that the law allowed the children to be educated, and the
school was there for that purpose; if they were not admitted he
would keep them at home and inform the authorities. They were
admitted. Arch, a Methodist, was appalled at the class-distinction
observed in the parish church at Communion. There were three
groups to approach the altar, separately—the landowners, the
farmers, the labourers. In every way the workers were made to
recognize their inferiority—even in the presence of God. It came
out in the songs his followers sang.

Come lads and listen to my song, a song of honest toil;
'Tis of the English labourer, the tiller of the soil;
I'll tell you how he used to fare, and all the ills be bore,
Till he stood up in his manhood, resolved to bear no more.
    This fine old English labourer,
    One of the present time.

He used to take whatever wage the farmer used to pay,
And work as hard as any horse for eighteen pence a day;
And if he grumbled at the nine and dared to ask for ten,
The angry farmer cursed and swore, and sacked him there and
    then.
    That fine old English labourer,
    One of the present time.

He used to tramp off to his work while townsfolk were abed,
With nothing in his belly but a slice or two of bread;
He dined upon potatoes, and never dreamed of meat,
Except a lump of bacon fat sometimes by way of treat.
    That fine old English labourer,
    One of the present time.

He used to find it hard enough to give his children food,
But sent them to the village school as often as he could;

But though he knew that school was good, they must have bread
    and clothes,
So he had to send them to the fields to scare away the crows.
    That fine old English labourer,
    One of the present time.

He used to walk along the fields and see his landlord's game,
Devour his master's growing crops, and think it was a shame;
But if the keeper found him with a rabbit or a wire,
He got it hot when brought before the parson and the squire.
    That fine old English labourer,
    One of the present time.

But now he's wide awake, and doing all he can,
At last for honest labour's rights he's fighting like a man;
Since squires and landlords will not help, to help himself he'll try,
And if he doesn't get fair wage he'll know the reason why.
    That fine old English labourer,
    One of the present time.

They used to treat him as they liked in the evil days of old;
They thought there was no power on earth to beat the power of
    gold;
They used to threaten what they'd do if ever work was slack,
But now he laughs their threats to scorn with the Union at his back.
    That fine old English labourer,
    One of the present time.

This is a propaganda song. It tells the hearer what he wishes to
believe. It is partly true to the established facts and partly clever
suggestion. The actual economic circumstances were as bad as the
song reveals, but the labourer is credited with a desire for education
of his children when in fact he often saw little need for this. As the
parliamentary report of 1843 had stated, the education of a rural
worker was in the fields, not from books, and the children often
disliked school anyway, so there was a great temptation for a lad to
'make himself useful'. Children who went to school regularly were
usually of the type with a thirst for knowledge, of whom Joseph
Arch had been one. Education depended largely on inclination
before schooling became compulsory in 1876. (William Cobbett
educated himself in the fields, like Hardy's fictional Jude.) Squire

and parson would often help a scholarly lad with the loan of books, and the village genius could get his poems into print. (Hundreds of such poems exist—rarely of any great merit.) As a general policy, however, the agricultural worker was not encouraged to think, and therefore was not fit to vote for parliamentary candidates, though the townsmen had been enfranchized by the Reform Act of 1867. Here was another rural grievance. Why should the town labourer be treated better than the rural labourer?

> There's a man who represents our shire
>   In the Parliament House, they say,
> Returned by the votes of the farmer and squire
>   And others who bear the sway;
> And farmer and squire, when laws are made
>   Are pretty well cared for thus;
> But the County Member, I'm afraid
>   Has but little care for us.
> So we ought to vote, deny it who can,
> 'Tis the right of an honest Englishman.
>
> Whenever a tyrant country beak
>   Has got us beneath his thumb,
> For justice then he ought sure to speak,
>   But the County Member is dumb.
> Whenever the rights of labour need
>   A vote on a certain day,
> The County Member is sure to plead
>   And vote the contrary way.
> So we ought to vote, deny it who can,
> 'Tis the right of an honest Englishman.
>
> We ask for the vote, and we have good cause
>   To make it our firm demand;
> For ages the rich have made the laws
>   And have robbed the poor of their land.
> The Parliament men false weights have made
>   So that justice often fails;
> And to make it worse, 'The Great Unpaid'
>   Must always fiddle the scales.
> So we ought to vote, deny it who can,
> 'Tis the right of an honest Englishman.

The agricultural workers got the vote in 1884, but not through trade union action. This phase indeed was short. Throughout 1872 and 1873 the union made progress, and wages increased from one and six to half a crown a day. This was during a time of prosperity, but the prosperity was short; 1874 saw a drop in food prices; farmers really were in desperate circumstances, and the union was broken; but while the agitation lasted it revealed some dreadful facts, not the least of these being the intensity of hatred shown by the gentry and the clergy towards any men who expected to earn more than ten shillings a week. One bishop recommended that organizers of unions should be ducked in the horseponds, and there was general surprise that meetings of rural workers should be held at all—'meetings positively where men made speeches!'[1]

The Liberal townsmen tried to help in their way. It was they who got the rural workers the vote, but they also stuck to Free Trade and cheap food, so the farmers never had a certain market for their grain. The songs of Joseph Arch's followers are not true folk-songs, but modelled on the townsmen's thoughts and tunes. The material facts may be right, but the ideas, like so many of the time, were imported from the towns.

If we would know the countryman's thoughts, we must turn again to the history of folk-song. Three years after Joseph Arch's union was broken, Alfred Williams was born in South Marston, Wiltshire. He was a poor lad, destined never to be anything but poor in goods, but he was rich in the spirit. You may see his memorials on the top of two hills in that neighbourhood—Liddington Hill and Barbury Hill—on stones which also commemorate Richard Jefferies. Another memorial is on the Town Hall at Swindon, describing him as 'Lyrical Poet, Classical Scholar, Master of English Prose, Who, self-taught, self-inspired, while toiling at the forge, illuminated all around him with

> The light that never was on sea or land,
> The consecration and the Poet's dream.

> *Sunt hic etiam sua praemia laudi,*
> *Sunt lacrimae rerum et mentem mortalia tangunt.*

[1] Cf. G. D. H. Cole and Raymond Postgate, *The Common People*.

"His achievement is an abiding spiritual example to the workmen of this country."—Robert Bridges.' His grave is in the churchyard at South Marston, however, and there is his best memorial, for it is in his own words:

> I will sing my song triumphantly.
> I will finish my race.
> I will work my task.

The only time when Alfred Williams got a living wage was when he worked in the forge at the Great Western Railway works at Swindon. He loathed it. He left of his own accord and wrote a book about it which reveals a detestation of factory life far more intense than any political agitator has described. He was a man of the open fields; he hated the town and its ways; he would rather exist on ten shillings in the country than earn thirty in the town. He wrote about the villages he knew—their inhabitants, their traditions, customs, stories, and songs. Tunes he could not collect, but he wrote down a great many verses. He was never a member of the Folk Song Society, he preferred to work alone; he was an individualist. He is probably the most important of folk-song verse collectors because he not only went to the mouths of the people— he was of the people. He set down what they really sang in the villages named in his book *Round About the Upper Thames*; and what they sang was not confined to Cecil Sharp's definition of folk-song. The men Williams knew sang folk-songs, ballads, catches, and glees. He shows how only the least intelligent of the rustics stuck entirely to true old folk-songs, and how the men in the 'local' sang in competition, for as long as twelve hours at a stretch, without repeating a single song—all from memory. He had a great love of his fellow men, and never ceased to plead the cause of the English yeoman, but he would have disliked Joseph Arch intensely. He was concerned to preserve what was good in the old life—not to improve it.

The collecting of folk-songs had been carried out in most of the counties of England before I began the work here. To tell the truth, it really wanted doing badly. Because no one had attempted to examine the locality methodically for folk-songs it was assumed that none existed. The opinion was current that this was about the dullest part of England. We are an agricultural people here. What had we to do with music and merriment? Far from the large towns and cities, far from ship-bearing rivers and the sea, cut off, as it were, from the heart of the great world, its commerce and civilization, inhabiting a region calmly beautiful, but destitute of very stirring or striking scenery, engaged all their lives upon the soil, how could the hearts and feelings of the people become quickened? It was not to be expected that they should be so, much less that the village folks should discover any surprising and unusual propensity to and aptness for cultured and artistic sports and entertainments. It was not expected, and the natural inference was drawn. It was supposed that the people were stupid and ignorant, thick-headed, unmusical, and unimaginative—mere clowns and clod-hoppers. I hope that we have effectively shattered that illusion. Whatever other counties possess in the matter of folk-songs they can scarcely claim to have more materials than have we of the Upper Thames. And the quality of the songs is good. I believe that versions of most, if not all, the best-known folk-songs were to be obtained in the villages around us, together with many that appear unfamiliar to residents in other quarters. The intensity of the life as it was in the villages is remarkable, and it would be inexplicable if we were to believe all that has been written concerning the 'misery, poverty, and starvation' rife among the agricultural populations a century or three-quarters of a century ago.[1] If that had been literally true I should not be writing now. A proof of its falsity is in the abundance of evidence we have of the gaiety and optimism of the rustics, in the records of life remaining to us, not in books and histories, certainly, but in the aged surviving villagers themselves. One may doubt books, but he may not controvert living witnesses; and the evidence of the music, songs, pastimes, feasts, and games is final and conclusive. Whoever, in the future, pens a history of English rural life, and omits to take full cognizance of these, and the part they played, will have neglected half his subject.[2]

Alfred Williams died in 1930, but if he could return to his village today he would find it very noisy, with jet-propelled aircraft taking off from some of the fields he knew. Apart from this, however, the farms lie undisturbed; only, the farmers have learnt new tricks. An advertisement of a local carnival would almost certainly offer a series of races by farm tractors, with the added enticement—'Bookmakers will be in attendance'. Ploughing matches with tractors have replaced those Williams so vividly described in his book *Round About the Upper Thames*, and he might have found it hard to understand a farm worker taking as much pride in machinery as

[1] Written in 1922.
[2] Alfred Williams, *Folksongs of the Upper Thames*, 1923, pp. 25–6.

once he took in horses. He certainly takes more interest in sulphates than he ever took in muck. Williams would find elderly men, however, as firmly in favour of horse-ploughs as once they were of the neglected folk-songs. Such behaviour is part of the way of life.

Yet it is not all. The old folk-singers Williams knew were only partly right. For centuries men had wanted to sing in harmony. They learnt rounds, catches, glees, and during the nineteenth century developed a passion for choir-singing in which men and women joined. When Sir Hubert Parry spoke of the vulgarity of commercial music he meant the music-hall ditty, but he could have said some equally scathing things about popular choir-music. One of the things which Parry's pupil Ralph Vaughan Williams has done, has been to adapt good folk-songs for the use of trained choirs, and by so doing improve the standards of taste among their audiences. Modern British music is of our time, yet the best of it is grown from roots deep in our musical history. When we try to follow the lead of those who create new and abstract systems we make some sorry blunders. British music—like British institutions—has to grow, not to be made. We have the knack of creating anew without killing the old. Without having made a study of British institutions, Alfred Williams knew this instinctively. He applied it to his life-work.

We want not to kill the new spirit, nor suppress it, but to chasten and purify it. We want, as it were, new blood in the old veins, not old blood in the new veins. Things dead are dead, the good as well as the bad. But be sure a thing is dead before you heap oblivion's dust upon it. I claim that the spirit which animated the old poetry, and even that which animated the ballads and folk-songs, is not, and cannot be, dead, and that it might, in part at least, be revived to advantage, not in the form, nor in the absolute spirit, but as a basis for future work.[1]

It happens, however, that Williams, like many others, miscalculated the effect of the blood-transfusion he advocated. Not all poets provided blood of the right group for the patient. Modern poetry presents problems of transmission which the educationists are only now learning how to tackle. To a lesser degree the same is true of music. Modern music and poetry have made enemies, and their advocates are mistrusted; for let the truth be known, some of us, in our zeal for tolerance, and a desire to give the unknown a fair hearing, have championed some pretty bad stuff in our time.

[1] Alfred Williams, *Folksongs of the Upper Thames*, 1923, pp. 10–11.

Moreover, there is a theory very rife among musicians, that music is its own justification. This is true enough but should not be extended to a claim that music has no relation to life. This theory is typical of our time, but it is—as we have seen in folk-song— unhistorical.

We shall do well to trace a common theme through, from an early nineteenth-century beginning, in order to understand how a system of songs may grow by variations from an almost forgotten original.

In the midst of the Romantic revival in Germany, when ghostly themes were popular, and corpses in literature inevitably produced a superstitious shudder, there appeared this song. *

> There once were three students came over the Rhine,
> And entered an inn for a flagon of wine,
> And entered an inn for a flagon of wine.

Cutting out the repetitions the poem will run.

> 'O landlady, keep you good vintages, pray,
> And where is your pretty young daughter today?'

> 'My vintages all are as good as can be,
> My daughter is lost now forever to me.'
> The students craved leave to behold the fair dead,
> And stood in her presence, whose spirit had fled.

> The first raised the veil that was drawn o'er her face,
> And gazed on the form wrapped in death's cold embrace.
> 'Ah me! if on earth thou wert fated to stay,
> Fair maid, I would love thee henceforth from today.'

> The next o'er her face drew the veil once again,
> And murmured these words in a sorrowful vein.
> 'Oh, take from my heart this sad tribute of tears,
> Fair maid, I have loved thee most fondly for years.'

> The third, thereupon, drew the veil from her brow,
> And kissing her cried: 'Oh, how beautiful, thou!
> I loved thee, yea, always; I love thee today,
> And still shall I love thee for ever and aye.'

* *Es zogen drei Burschem wohl über den Rhein.*
Uhland (18th cent.)

The style is an imitation of an imitation: a copy of the literary style which grew from admiration of romantic balladry. In the year 1815, however, when the Prussians were feeling pleased with themselves for having got to Waterloo in time to chase the French, the following song came into use.

> Three Prussian officers crossed the Rhine,
>   Skibboo, skibboo;
> Three Prussian officers crossed the Rhine,
>   Skibboo, skibboo,
> Three Prussian officers crossed the Rhine,
> They were on the lookout for women and wine,
>   Skibboo, skibboo,
>   Skibumpity-bump, skibboo, skibboo.

But now something has happened to the song. It deals not with a fashionable literary theme but with a common fact of soldier life; moreover, it is capable of addition by improvisation. While the first couplet is being repeated the singer has time to think up a rhyme for the sixth line, and that is the extent of original thought required to carry the verse. Cutting out the repetitions to save space, we arrive at the following.

> They came unto a wayside inn,
> And nearly battered the doorway in.

> 'O landlord, have you any good wine,
> Fit for a soldier of the line.'

> 'O landlord, have you a daughter fair,
> With dark blue eyes and golden hair.'

> 'Oh yes, I have a daughter fair,
> Skibboo, skibboo.
> Oh yes I have a daughter fair,
> Skibboo, skibboo,
> But my daughter fair she's far too young
> To be taken out by a son of a gun,'
>   Skibboo, skibboo,
>   Skibumpity-bump, skibboo, skibboo.

'Mais non, mon père, I'm not so young,
I've often been kissed by the padre's son.'

It's a hell of a song that we've just sung,
  Skibboo, skibboo;
It's a hell of a song that we've just sung,
  Skibboo, skibboo;
It's a hell of a song that we've just sung,
And the fellow that wrote it ought to be hung,
  Skibboo, skibboo,
Skibumpity-bump, skibboo, skibboo.

The tune is widespread. It is well known in America, in the minor
key, with the words 'When Johnny comes marching home again,
hurrah, hurrah!' and as a by-blow of a railroad song under the title
of *The Runaway Train*. Whether the tune got to America from a
German or an Irish source I do not know—it could be from either.
In England it was used for a music-hall song to the words 'A little
bit off the top.' The reader may think of other variations of this
tune. (The most recent is a colourful Western version called *The
Ghost Herd in the Sky* which depends on its orchestration for the
right effect.) Let us return to the army, however. *Three Prussian
Officers Crossed the Rhine* was sung without losing favour until 1916,
when it developed a rival on the other side of the barbed wire. One
version of it is known to everybody.

Mademoiselle from Armenteers,
Parlez-vous.[1]

The nearest relation to the German song, however, was known only
in the army.

'O Madam, have you any good wine?
  Parlez-vous;
O Madam, have you any good wine?
  Parlez-vous.
O Madam, have you any good wine,
Fit for a soldier of the line?
  Inky-pinky, parlez-vous.'

[1] Sung to a version of the tune in the major mode.

'O yes, I have some very good wine,
Fit for a soldier of the line.'

'O Madam, have you a daughter fair,
With bonny blue eyes and golden hair?'

'O yes, I have a daughter fair
With bonny blue eyes and golden hair.'

Then up the stairs and into bed,
Parlez-vous.

By the time you have repeated the line ending with 'bed' three times you ought to have discovered a word to rhyme with it. If not, sing it with a company of others and someone will help you out. This is the argument for the communal origin of folk-song. From the evidence we have now produced it may equally be contended, however, that folk-songs are not produced by the folk, but are either parodies or corruptions of songs produced by someone with poetic ability. Certainly parody has a great deal to do with it; the common man is no great thinker; he is not such a fool as to invent a tune when he knows one already which will fit the words he has in mind; anyway the tune must be infectious, which means that it will be compounded of clichés. The clichés of today are the originalities of the Victorians, and we all know what *they* were. Parry's accusation of vulgarity will stand so long as we regard popular nineteenth-century art as ugly; if ever it becomes quaint (as some of it must, in time) our children will laugh at us for our lack of discernment. Meanwhile, what of the songs which are being produced?

Of these we may pick on such as are not able to command a wide market anyway, but are keenly felt by those to whom they belong. Great disasters must be recorded, as this of 1934:[1]

You've heard of the Gresford disaster,
    The terrible price that was paid;
Two hundred and forty-two [2] colliers were lost,
    And three men of a rescue brigade.

[1] A. L. Lloyd, *Come, All Ye Bold Miners*, 1953. 'Taken down by W. MacColl from the singing of a young miner named Ford.'
[2] Actually 265 miners lost their lives, including the three rescue workers.

It occurred in the month of September,
  At three in the morning, that pit
Was racked by a violent explosion,
  In the Dennis where gas lay so thick.

The gas in the Dennis deep section
  Was packed there like snow in a drift,
And many a man had to leave the coal-face
  Before he had worked out his shift.

A fortnight before the explosion,
  To the shotfirer, Tomlinson cried:
'If you fire that shot we'll all be blown to hell,'
  And no-one can say that he lied.

The fireman's reports they are missing,
  The records of forty-two days;
The colliery manager had them destroyed
  To cover his criminal ways.

Down there in the dark they are lying,
  They died for nine shillings a day;
They have worked out their shift and now they must lie
  In the darkness until Judgment Day.

The Lord Mayor of London's collecting,
  To help both our children and wives;
The owners have sent some white lilies
  To pay for the poor colliers' lives.

Farewell, our dear wives and our children,
  Farewell, our old comrades as well;
Don't send your sons down the dark dreary pit;
  They'll be damned like the sinners in hell.

The style owes something to a comedian, Stanley Holloway, whose monologues on *The Lion and Albert* and *Sam, Pick up thy Musket* were popular in the nineteen-thirties. The ballad, nevertheless, is sincere. One may contend that these are not songs of the peasantry but industrial songs. So they are. If Alfred Williams could return today he would find much in the songs of our time of which he would disapprove, but he would find also a certain change for the better. Men are not ashamed of the old songs as they were when Williams cycled about the villages having to coax songs from the lips of elderly people. Tell a man today that you are interested in old customs and old songs and he is friendly. He may not know any old songs, but he does not condemn them. Compilers of sound radio and television programmes find that bona-fide folk-songs are in demand; the sale of gramophone records, especially of American singers, is increasing rapidly, and in America itself folk-song seems likely soon to challenge the status of jazz. It is true, as we have already observed, that the impetus now comes largely from the U.S.A., though the work of folk-song reclamation has never been allowed to drop in Britain, while Ireland, Scotland, and the Border Country have kept their traditions alive without any help from specialists. Where difficulty arises about publication of many common songs is in their obscenity. In the old days one just bowdlerized, but people are getting too knowledgeable for that nowadays. All who have served in the armed forces know songs that they cannot repeat in public. It is said to be possible to buy secretly some gramophone records of songs known in the Royal Air Force during the last war which would be subject to legal action if put on the open market; but this is an old problem; the obscene are always among us.

We need not for this reason condemn everything. Men behave today much as they have always behaved. The tune of *Yankee Doodle* was stolen from the enemy in the American War of Independence, and *Lili Marlene* similarly became common property in the Second World War. It could not stop at that. Soon the inevitable variation arrived.

> We beat them on the Desert down at Alamein,
> They thought they'd taken Alex, we pushed them
>   back again;
> Egypt and Libya, Tunis too,
> We knocked the spunk right out of you,
> And pushed you in the sea,
> And pushed you in the sea.

Then good old Alexander sailed across the sea,
And landed all his troops on the shores of Sicily;
Then once again we chased the foe,
And poor old Jerry had to go
Across to Italy,
Across to Italy.

Hot on his heels we landed on the toe,
We landed at Salerno and then at Anzio,
After Cassino Rome looked fine,
And now we've reached the Gothic Line,
En route for Germany,
En route for Germany.

Soon it will be over, Europe will be free,
And all the Nazi leaders will dangle from a tree;
Send us to Berlin, we won't complain,
We'll fight the butchers there again,
And finish them off for ever,
To get back home again.

This is just as much an historical document as *Boney's Lamentation*. The Britisher did not hate Napoleon personally, though he feared him; he hated the followers of Hitler, however, because he knew them and their hideous doctrine. It matters not that the old school of folk-song experts would contend that this is the sort of song which soldiers never sing. If they did not do so once, they do so now. The military historian would probably note it as an indication of morale. What was true of the men in the armed forces was true also of the women: they had their *esprit-de-corps*, and a truly communal song, too, whatever its musical merit may be.

It wasn't the WAAFS who won the war,
    Parlez-vous.
It wasn't the WAAFS who won the war,
    Parlez-vous.
It wasn't the WAAFS who won the war,
The A.T.S. were there before,
    Inky-pinky parlez-vous.

It isn't the NAAFI who do all the work,
Parlez-vous.
It isn't the NAAFI who do all the work,
Parlez-vous.
It isn't the NAAFI who do all the work,
The A.T.S. they never shirk,
Inky-pinky parlez-vous.

It isn't the WRENS who get the men,
Parlez-vous.
It isn't the WRENS who get the men,
Parlez-vous.
It isn't the WRENS who get the men,
The A.T.S. are there again,
Inky-pinky parlez-vous.

The A.T.S. are doing fine,
Parlez-vous.
The A.T.S. are doing fine,
Parlez-vous.
The A.T.S. are doing fine,
Kissing the boys behind the line,
Inky-pinky parlez-vous.

They say they've mechanized the war,
Parlez-vous.
They say they've mechanized the war,
Parlez-vous.
They say they've mechanized the war,
Then what the heck are we marching for?
Inky-pinky parlez-vous.

It is not easy to end a book on a subject which is still in an interesting process of development. (For I believe this to be the case
despite all the evidence that the modern songs I have quoted are not
to be compared with many of the old.) If our taste inclines us to
great art—to the symphony and opera—these are now to hand, and
we can judge them by high standards of criticism. If we have
sympathy with ordinary folk, however, the same standards simply
do not apply to what is going on around us; nevertheless I believe

that in a modern folk-song we have the answer. Though we may not think things what they might be, yet we have to love them.

> O when I was single I wore a black shawl;
> Now I am married I've nothing at all.
> Still I love him,
> I'll forgive him,
> I'll go with him wherever he goes.

The tune is one which has already been condemned by folk-song collectors as corrupt—*Villikins and his Dinah*—on to which a Victorian waltz tune has been grafted. It is not modal, it is not high art, but it works. The common mind may be unfortunately conditioned but it is resilient; circumstances may divert us, philosophers mislead us, but like the traveller lost in the wood we must go on, and having done so, find in time that we have again arrived at our original base. We may still be lost, but we can make another start.

A SHORT BIBLIOGRAPHY

'ARBEAU, Thoinot,' *Orchesography*, 1588, trans. C. W. Beaumont, 1925.

ARCH, Joseph, *The Life of Joseph Arch*, 1898.

BASKERVILL, C. R., *The Elizabethan Jig*, University of Chicago Press, 1929.

BROADWOOD, Lucy, and FULLER-MAITLAND, J. A., *English County Songs*, 1893.

CHAMBERS, Sir Edmund K., *The English Folk-play*, Clarendon Press, 1933.

DIBDIN, Charles, *Musical Tour*, 1788.

DICKENS, Charles, *Sketches by Boz*.

DISRAELI, Benjamin, *Sybil*.

FRAZER, Sir James, *The Golden Bough* (abridged edition, 1923).

FREUD, Sigmund, *Totem and Taboo*, Penguin Books.

HAMMOND, J. L. and Barbara, *The Village Labourer*, 1911.

HARDY, Thomas, *Under the Greenwood Tree*.

HAWKINS, Sir John, *History of Music*, 1776.

HOOKE, S. H., *The Labyrinth*, S.P.C.K., 1935.

HUGHES, Thomas, *Tom Brown's Schooldays*; *The Scouring of the White Horse*.

KENNEDY, Douglas K., *England's Dances*, Bell, 1949.

LLOYD, A. L., *The Singing Englishmen*, Workers' Music Association; *Come, All Ye Bold Miners*, Lawrence & Wishart, 1953.

MAYHEW, Henry, *London Labour and the London Poor*, 1852.

NETTEL, R., *The Englishman Makes Music*, Dobson, 1952.

PERUGINI, Mark Edward, *The Omnibus Box*, Jarrold, 1933.

SACHS, Curt, *Music in the Ancient World—East and West*, Norton (U.S.A.), 1943.

SHARP, Cecil, *English Folk Song—Some Conclusions*, 1907.

SHEPPARD, Sara, *Charles Auchester*.

STRANGWAYS, A. H. Fox, and KARPELES, Maud, *The Life of Cecil Sharp*, Oxford University Press, 1933.

TATE, W. E., *The Parish Chest*, Cambridge University Press, 1946.

WEARMOUTH, Robert F., *Methodism and the Common People of the Eighteenth Century*, Epworth Press; *Some Working-class Movements of the Nineteenth Century*, Epworth Press, 1948.

WILLIAMS, Alfred, *Folk-songs of the Upper Thames*, Duckworth, 1923; *Round About the Upper Thames*, 1922.

WILLIAMS, Iolo, *English Folk Song and Dance*, Longmans, 1935.

Folk Song Journal, 1889–1931.

Journal of the English Folk Dance and Song Society, 1932–52.

INDEX

N.B. Proper names are given with surname first, e.g. Addison, Joseph, but songs as printed in text, e.g. *John Barleycorn*. Songs without composer's name are traditional.

275